T his
wide
evitable s
relations
In this li
'non-capi
author see
ance', cho
countries,
marginali
threaten t

The au
(the advar
that is no
relative to
body of
patterns c
participati
and betwe
in which s
lives by p
he conclu
intervene
coupling c

realm in order to open up spaces of hope that offer alternatives to, and different paths of, development.

This powerfully developed analysis of modern capitalism is bound to command widespread intellectual attention and controversy within the social sciences, as well as drawing attention to changes in economic activity at the grassroots of industrial societies.

About the Author

COLIN C. WILLIAMS is Professor of Work Organization and Director of the Collective of Alternative Organization Studies (CAOS) in the University of Leicester Management Centre (ULMC). He has published widely on alternative economic practices and the informal sector. His recent books, all co-authored, include *Alternative Economic Spaces* (Sage, 2003); *Poverty and the Third Way* (Routledge, 2003); *Bridges into Work? An Evaluation of Local Exchange and Trading Schemes (LETS)* (Policy Press, 2001); and *Revitalising Deprived Urban Neighbourhoods: An Assisted Self-Help Approach* (Ashgate, 2001).

A Commodified World?

Mapping the Limits of Capitalism

COLIN C. WILLIAMS

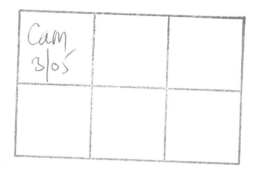

ZED BOOKS
London & New York

A Commodified World? was first published in 2005 by
Zed Books Ltd, 7 Cynthia Street, London N1 9JF, UK,
and Room 400, 175 Fifth Avenue, New York, NY 10010, USA

www.zedbooks.co.uk

Designed and typeset in Monotype Baskerville by Illuminati, Grosmont
Cover designed by Andrew Corbett
Printed and bound by Biddles Ltd,
www.biddles.co.uk

Distributed in the USA exclusively by Palgrave Macmillan, a division of
St Martin's Press, LLC, 175 Fifth Avenue, New York, NY 10010

A catalogue record for this book is available from the British Library
Library of Congress Cataloging-in-Publication Data available

ISBN 1 84277 354 2 (Hb)
ISBN 1 84277 355 0 (Pb)

Contents

PART II   The Uneven Contours of Commodification

Tables and Figures

Acknowledgements

This book argues that it is necessary to recognize and value work beyond profit-motivated monetary transactions so as to open up alternative possible futures for work. It would be an act of gross ineptitude, therefore, if I did not display gratitude to all those people who have freely given their time, intellectual capacities and efforts without charge so as to help me write this book.

On the one hand, there is Jan, who through her ongoing and considerable unpaid work has liberated the space in my life to enable me to write this book. Despite being in full-time employment herself, she has continuously taken on far more than her fair share of the housework and childcare. I do not begin to know how to thank her.

On the other hand, there are many people who over the years have played a significant part in helping me formulate and develop ideas on the nature of work, ranging from friends, relatives and neighbours to referees of journal articles, conference participants and even people whom I have met on buses and trains who have given me a privileged insight into their lives and feelings. All these people have freely engaged in conversation and provided material help without seeking financial reward and it is precisely their actions that this book is about. Contrary to the belief that every nook and cranny of human existence have been penetrated by profit-motivated monetized transactions, the way in which so many have freely offered advice, information and time to me over the years is a clear rebuke of any such notion. Among the people I need to thank in this regard are Theresa Aldridge, Angus Cameron, Graham Haughton, Roger Lee, Andrew Leyshon, Ed

Mayo, Claire Mercer, Chris Paddock, Peter Roberts, John Round, Richard Smith, Richard White and many more. Without them, this book could not have been written.

I would also like to display my deep appreciation to all of my new colleagues at the University of Leicester Management Centre (ULMC). In what can only be described as one of the most exciting experiments taking place in management studies today, a group of heterodox critical scholars have come together who have a common interest in studying how the contemporary world has come to be organized as it is, and how it might be reimagined. The result is that ULMC has shown a clear commitment and desire to become the major worldwide location for scholarly, creative and iconoclastic thought that challenges common assumptions about the means and ends of organizing in particular, and rethinking management, business and organization more generally. In the short time that it has been my privilege to be part of ULMC and work with such stimulating colleagues, I have gained renewed hope that it is still possible for universities to remain breeding grounds of radical and critical thought even in these troubled times. For reigniting that flame in my life, which was flickering out more than they will ever know, I owe them all 'big time'. I sincerely hope that it will be possible for many of them to become enduring friends as time unfolds.

Finally, the fact that this book was written during a period of study leave from the University of Leicester needs to be formally acknowledged. For that, and that alone, I am grateful to my employer.

I

Introduction

E very society must produce, distribute and allocate the goods and services that people need to live. As such, all societies have an economy of one type or another. Economies, however, can be organized in a multitude of different ways. To depict the configuration of economies, most analyses differentiate three modes of producing and delivering goods and services, namely the 'market', the 'state' and the 'community' (Boswell, 1990; Giddens, 1998; Gough, 2000; Polanyi, 1944; Powell, 1990; Putterman, 1990; Thompson et al., 1991). Analysed in these terms, the widespread consensus is that most nations are witnessing a common trajectory so far as the nature and direction of their economies are concerned. A view predominates that the market is becoming more powerful, expansive, hegemonic and totalizing as it penetrates deeper into each and every corner of economic life and stretches its tentacles ever wider across the globe to colonize those areas previously left untouched by its powerful force.

Indeed, for many academic commentators, politicians and journalists, this has taken on the semblance of an indisputable and irrefutable fact. Even among the swelling ranks of those opposed to the encroachment of the market into every crevice of life, a certain fatalistic despondence prevails, for it is widely accepted that this is a natural and inevitable process about which little can be done. The notion of an unstoppable transition towards a commodified world is so widely held and felt that it is difficult today to consider any other future. As Amin et al. (2002b: 60) put it, 'the pervasive reach of exchange-value society makes it ever more difficult to imagine and legitimate non-market forms of organization and provision.' Like the vast majority of commentators, for them the future is already cast in stone and it is one in which what is variously referred to as a process 'commercialization', 'marketization' or 'commodification' is taking place.

In this book, however, this widely held fatalistic acceptance that there is a natural and inevitable ongoing penetration of the market is put under the spotlight. Here, I wish to subject to critical scrutiny what is surely one of the last remaining meta-narratives of our times, namely the notion that goods and services are increasingly produced for monetized exchange by capitalist firms for the purpose of profit, rather than by the state or community. Instead of treating this as an irrefutable fact, the starting point of this book is the recognition that acceptance of this 'commodification thesis' has so far been based on the flimsiest of evidence. As will be shown, in nearly all cases where this inexorable shift towards a commodified world is extolled, little evidence of any kind is offered to show that this is the case. Indeed, where commentators warrant it necessary to give some sort of justification for this apparently 'common sense' fact, all that is often deemed necessary are fuzzy and simple statements such as how subsistence economies are increasingly rare or that commodified 'ways of viewing' are penetrating into ever more spheres of our lives.

It is thus seemingly the case that the ability to view each aspect of daily life in commodified terms (e.g. 'the marriage market') has led commentators to believe unswervingly that every facet of life *is* now commodified. The common-sense understanding seems to be that the colonization of daily life by the market is so ubiquitous and obvious that no corroboration is required. For many of these adherents to the commodification thesis, it would seem foolish to raise questions about its validity. After all, it is widely accepted. Yet it is precisely this that I wish to do in this book. No other idea in the social sciences is accepted without detailed corroboration and there is no reason for this meta-narrative to be exempt.

Perhaps it is indeed the case that the commodification of economic life is so ubiquitous and obvious to all that no evidence is required. Perhaps, however, it is not. As I wish to uncover throughout this book, once one starts to move beyond simply accepting commodification as an irrefutable and indisputable fact, and begins to scratch the surface by exploring whether this is indeed the trajectory of economic development, this grand narrative no longer seems to have such solid foundations. If this commodification thesis was but an 'academic' theorization in the most derogatory sense of the word (i.e. of little or no importance), then perhaps the way in which so many commentators seem blindly to accept it would not even matter. But it takes only a moment's reflection to realize that the commodification thesis is much more than simply an academic theory about the trajectory of economic development.

To illustrate this, let me take a few examples. Consider, for instance, how the world is conventionally divided up into a first, a second and a third world. The first world, composed of the supposedly 'advanced' economies of the West, is so defined because it has undergone the transformation from non-market to market modes of production to the greatest extent. Based on the view that commodification is a natural and inevitable trajectory of economic development that all nations will and must follow, these first world nations are thus placed at the front of the queue in this linear and unidimensional vision of 'economic development' while those nations in the second and third worlds are positioned behind them in the queue due to their slower progression towards the hegemony of the market. Indeed, so dominant is this depiction of a universal trajectory of economic development towards commodification that the countries comprising the second world of central and eastern Europe are now commonly referred to as 'transition' economies because they are seen to be undergoing a transformation from a state-oriented economic system to one in which the market is becoming more hegemonic. The way in which economies that are more grounded in 'community' or 'subsistence' are labelled 'backward' compared with economic systems that are market-orientated, meanwhile, is nowhere better seen than in those countries aggregated together under the banner of the third world. Labelled 'developing', 'undeveloped' or 'underdeveloped' countries precisely due to their slowness in moving towards commodification, these name-tags denote that there is only one possible trajectory available to them and a singular 'route to progress', and it is towards a commodified world.

The commodification thesis, nevertheless, does not only lead to a hierarchical ordering of countries according to the extent to which they are commodified. This economic discourse also serves to shape thinking about what action is required by supranational institutions, national governments, economic development agencies and individuals themselves in the name of progress. Take, for example, Western governments. Grounded in this grand narrative about the trajectory of economic development that views the market as the increasingly dominant sector of their societies, governments of Western nations have tended to concentrate on developing this sector and view the state and community sectors as, at best, playing a supporting role and, at worst, deleterious to development and something to be commodified so as to allow this trajectory of economic development to be implemented. It is similarly the case in the ex-socialist bloc of central and eastern Europe where the whole thrust of economic policy has been focused upon how a market system can be implemented so as to facilitate the 'transition' to a market economy. In the third world, it is again the pursuit of commodification that sets the economic policy agenda. One has only to consider the structural adjustment programmes applied to these countries to realize that a strong normative view exists that progress lies in encouraging a successful transformation towards an economic system where the market becomes an increasingly dominant mode of producing and delivering goods and services. Throughout the world, therefore, the process of commodification whereby the market replaces the state and community sectors is not only a theory that believes itself to be describing the trajectory of economic development but also a thesis that is shaping the actions taken in the name of economic development.

The commodification thesis, in other words, is not just an abstraction that is seeking to reflect reality but also an economic discourse that is being used to shape the material world. As Carrier (1998: 8) puts it, there is a 'conscious attempt to make the real world conform to the virtual image, justified by the claim that the failure of the real to conform to the idea is not merely a consequence of imperfections, but is a failure that itself has undesirable consequences'. In this virtualism, economic thought and practice thus shape each other in an ongoing recursive and reflexive loop 'driven by ideas and idealism [and] the desire to make the world conform to the image' (Carrier, 1998: 5). This is nowhere more finely shown than in the seminal work of Escobar (1995), who displays how so-called third world economies became viewed as a problem due to their lack of 'development' (i.e. commodification) and then charts the ways in which a whole range of institutions and practices were constructed to make them conform more to the desired image of a marketized society at whatever cost.

The outcome of such a commodification discourse, therefore, and whether it is the first, second or third world that is under the spotlight, is that the future is closed. There is only one future so far as the story of economic development is concerned and it is one in which economies pursue a linear and unidimensional development path towards a commodified world. Imagine just for a moment, however, that it became apparent that economies were not becoming ever more commodified and that the market was actually receding in many quarters as a mode of producing and delivering goods and services. Rather than the future being cast in a straitjacket of the ever wider and deeper encroachment of the market, the future would suddenly become much more open and full of endless new possibilities. For those who believe in the grand narrative of a commodifying world, this probably comes across as nothing more than idealized and romantic dreaming by some anti-capitalist propagandist. What I wish to show in this book, however, is that this is far from a romantic daydream. Once one starts to unpack the commodification thesis and analyse the validity of this linear and unidimensional development path, it becomes quickly apparent that there is a need for some large question marks over the metanarrative of commodification and that it is perhaps those who assume the ubiquity of commodification who are living in a dream world rather than facing the stark reality of economic life today.

As this book will reveal, even in the heartlands of commodification – the advanced 'market' economies – survey after survey uncovers that non-market work is not some minor remnant left over from precapitalist formations and rapidly dwindling as a mode of producing and delivering goods and services. A cursory glance at the recent time-use surveys conducted by Western governments instantly informs even the most ardent believer in a commodified world that unpaid domestic work takes up a sizeable proportion of the total time that people spend working in the advanced economies. When this evidence is coupled with the recognition that there is widespread engagement and rapid growth in volunteering throughout the advanced economies, it starts to become obvious that the commodified sphere is far from hegemonic. Large swathes of economic life continue to take place outside of the commodified realm on a scale that can hardly be described as minor or marginal, and may even be growing.

By charting the shallowness of commodification in the advanced economies and its uneven contours, the intent of this book is to open up the future to possibilities other than an ongoing commodification of work. In its enacting of an alternative reading of the current mode of economic organization and the direction of economic development to that found in the commodification thesis, this book seeks to tell a rather different story to the oft-told tale in which there is an inexorable and unstoppable march towards a commodified world. By documenting the current mode of economic organization in the advanced economies and the direction of change, my aim is to open up the future of work to one in which it is wholly feasible, valid and necessary to reimagine a future of work beyond a commodified world.

In this book, to put it starkly, the intention is to evaluate critically the thesis of an unstoppable march towards a commodified world. To do this, answers are sought to a number of questions. How deeply has the logic of the market penetrated life in the advanced economies? Is the trend towards ever more commodified economies? Are there spaces of non-commodified work? If so, what form do they take? And how can one explain their existence? Are they mere leftovers of precapitalist formations, the by-product of post-Fordist economic restructuring and/or 'spaces of resistance' to the logic of commodification? And what implications does this have for the policy options that might be pursued? This book sets out to answer these questions.

Argument of the Book

To commence this process, Part I evaluates critically the widely accepted notion that late capitalism involves an inevitable and natural shift towards ever more commodified economic relations under the market-driven search for corporate profit. In this linear view of the trajectory of economic development, 'non-capitalist' activities are assumed to be disappearing. To contest the idea that we live in an increasingly commodified world in order to open up alternative futures, Part I thus interrogates the extent, pace and depth of the penetration of commodification so far as working life is concerned. In order to achieve this, Chapter 2 sets out the commodification thesis and displays how such a thesis is widely held, albeit often implicitly, in social enquiry. This will reveal that although profit-motivated monetized exchange is almost universally seen to be colonizing ever more spheres of working life, there is a very disturbing lack of corroboration of this commodification thesis. Given the paucity of evidence for this accepted canon of wisdom, it is here argued to be necessary to put the commodification thesis under the spotlight. To do this, Chapters 3–5 thus analyse the extent to which various forms of non-commodified work persist in the advanced economies. Given that the commodity economy is based on profit-motivated monetized exchange, analysed first is the persistence of non-exchanged (or subsistence) work, in Chapter 3; second, the prevalence of non-monetized exchange, in Chapter 4; and, third, the existence of not-for-profit monetized exchange, in Chapter 5. This will reveal that for all of the talk of a hegemonic, enveloping, dynamic, pervasive and totalizing commodified realm, there exists in the heartlands of commodification – the advanced 'market' economies – a non-commodified sphere that is not only as large as the commodified sphere but also growing relative to it.

To start to understand why this is the case, Part II of the book charts the uneven contours of commodification along with the reasons for the persistence of work outside the commodity economy. Analysing the socio-economic disparities in Chapter 6, the uneven geographies of commodification in Chapter 7 and the gender disparities in Chapter 8, it will be shown that despite some populations in advanced economies attempting to seize greater control over their lives by pursuing non-commodified practices of resistance, others surplus to the requirements of capitalism are finding themselves cast adrift from the commodified world and offloaded into the non-commodified sphere. Chapter 9, meanwhile, examining the transition economies of central and eastern Europe and the third world, finds that even if some might wish to see non-commodified work in these regions of the world as resistance practices, the stark reality is that reliance on such work is more often the result of severe economic pressures that deeply constrain the achievement of a commodified world and consign the poor and marginalized to a life outside it.

What, therefore, are the various policy options and their implications? In Part III, three alternative policy approaches to the non-commodified realm are considered, namely commodification, doing nothing or harnessing this sphere so as to pursue a post-capitalist society. In Chapter 10, the first option of further commodifying work is considered. Its argument is that, at least in the advanced economies, there appears to be surfacing a commodified/non-commodified balance beyond the limits of which populations do not seek to pass and capitalism seems incapable of transcending. There exist 'blockages' that capitalism cannot overcome. Drawing upon examples from across the advanced economies of the existence of blocked exchanges, work–life balance debates, changing attitudes towards commodified work and the emergence of resistance practices, this chapter calls into question both the feasibility and the desirability of further commodification.

Chapter 11 considers the implications of doing nothing with regard to the balance between the commodified and decommodified spheres, if an ongoing process of commodification does not appear achievable. Pointing to the ways in which those cast adrift from the commodified realm throughout the advanced economies are also the least able to eke out an existence in the non-commodified sphere, the argument of this chapter is that a strategy of 'doing nothing' is not an option. Such a non-decision will serve merely to leave those marginalized from the commodified realm bereft of the means of survival.

Chapter 12 thus considers the option of cultivating economic pluralism. Here, the implications of working with the grain, so far as the current mode of economic organization and direction of change are concerned, are explored. Reviewing previous rationales for such an approach found in third-way thought, non-market social-democratic thought, radical ecology and post-development theory, this chapter argues that governments and communities, rather than actively pursuing a more commodified world or doing nothing about the situation, should instead seek to intervene in what is happening by deliberately fostering economic plurality so as to provide people with diverse means of meeting their needs and desires rather than relying solely on the commodity economy.

In order to show how this might occur, Chapter 13 then considers an issue that has so far received little attention, namely how to cultivate work beyond the commodity economy. Here, and in order to show the ways in which such work might be facilitated, a number of both bottom-up and top-down initiatives are outlined that directly tackle the barriers confronting those who wish to engage in non-commodified work but cannot do so. In so doing, it sets out a preliminary tool-kit for cultivating economic plurality so as to provide those excluded from the commodified and non-commodified spheres with new means of livelihood to enhance their coping capabilities.

The overarching message of this book, therefore, is that it is time to unshackle our imaginations so far as the future of work is concerned from their imprisonment in a view of a commodified world and, in doing so, to open up the future to new possibilities. In the concluding chapter, in consequence, the threads of the preceding chapters are pulled together to show how once one transcends the idea of an expansive, pervasive and all-encompassing capitalism, new spaces of hope are opened up that offer alternatives to commodified work relations and different development paths to those currently seen as inevitable.

PART I

The Penetration of Commodification:
A Critical Evaluation

2

The Commodification Thesis

The notion that we live in a 'capitalist' society organized around the systematic pursuit of profit in the marketplace is something commonly assumed by business leaders, journalists and academic commentators of all political hues. In this chapter, therefore, I wish first of all to unpack what is meant by such a mode of economic organization and, following this, to highlight the very disturbing lack of evidence provided in support of this thesis, so as to set the scene for the next three chapters, which evaluate critically the degree to which commodification has penetrated working life in the advanced economies.

In this opening chapter of Part I, therefore, I show that the widely held consensus is that one particular mode of producing and delivering goods and services is in the ascendant. Conventionally, that is, three different means of supplying goods and services are discerned, namely the 'market', the 'state' and the 'community' (Boswell, 1990; Giddens, 1998; Gough, 2000; Polanyi, 1944; Powell, 1990; Putterman 1990; Thompson et al., 1991), although different name-tags are sometimes used, with Polanyi (1944) referring to 'market exchange', 'redistribution' and 'reciprocity', and Giddens (1998) discussing 'private', 'public' and 'civil society'. Despite the different names, however, the near universal perception is that of these three modes of delivering goods and services, it is the market that is expanding while the other two spheres are contracting (e.g. Lee, 1999, 2000a; Polanyi, 1944; Scott, 2001; Smith, 2000; Watts, 1999). Variously referred to as a process of 'commercialization', 'marketization' or 'commodification', the hegemonic depiction is of a world in which 'goods and services ... are [increasingly] produced by capitalist firms for a profit under conditions of market exchange' (Scott, 2001: 12).

Throughout the book, I refer to this widely held view as 'the commodification thesis'. In this opening chapter of Part I, therefore, the intention is first of all to outline the tenets of this commodification thesis along with its variants, and then to reveal that despite, or perhaps precisely due to, the dominance of this discourse and its overwhelming influence on how we think about the future, it is somewhat disturbing to find that hardly any evidence is ever brought to the fore to provide corroboration that commodification is in fact taking place. Identifying the paucity of evidence in support of the idea that ever more of daily life is mediated through the market, this chapter concludes that it is necessary to subject this canon of wisdom that so limits our view of possible futures to greater critical scrutiny than has so far been the case. In so doing, the scene is set for the rest of Part I, which evaluates critically the validity of the commodification thesis.

An Implacable Economic Logic?

The term 'commodification thesis' is used as shorthand for the process by which goods and services are increasingly produced and delivered by capitalist firms for monetized exchange for the purpose of profit. Commodified work, therefore, is composed first of goods and services produced for exchange; second of monetized exchange; and finally of monetized exchange for the purpose of profit. If any of these constituent components are missing, then the economic practice cannot be described as commodified.

Given that the non-commodified sphere is by definition composed of economic practices that do not possess one or more of these characteristics, this sphere can be divided here into three distinctive types of work. First, the non-commodified sphere is composed of all non-exchanged or 'subsistence' work. Often referred to as 'self-provisioning', 'self-servicing', 'housework' or 'domestic work', this is unpaid work undertaken by a household member either for themselves or for some other member of the household. A second type of non-commodified work is where goods and services are exchanged but no money changes hands. This non-monetized exchange, which is sometimes referred to as unpaid community work and voluntary work, as well as mutual aid or community self-help, is unpaid work undertaken by a household member for members of households other than their own. The third and final form of non-commodified work is where monetized transactions take place but the profit-motive is absent. This covers a whole range of economic activities, as will be shown, but particularly those taking place in the public sector as well as what is variously referred to as the 'not-for-profit sector', 'third sector', 'social economy' or 'social enterprises'.

According to the commodification thesis, profit-motivated monetized exchanges are expanding and non-commodified economic practices are contracting. Although of course few, if any, analysts would assert that the process of commodification is complete, there is a near universal belief that economies are shifting towards a situation in which the commodified realm is steadily colonizing these other spheres. From populist writers such as Rifkin (2000: 3), who argues that 'The marketplace is a pervasive force in our lives', through political economists such as Ciscel and Heath (2001: 401), who argue that capitalism is transforming 'every human interaction into a transient market exchange', to anthropologists such as Gudeman (2001: 144), who asserts how 'markets are subsuming greater portions of everyday life', and Carruthers and Babb (2000: 4), who believe that there has been 'the near-complete penetration of market relations into our modern economic lives', and geographers like Watts (1999: 312), who states that although 'commodification is not complete ... the reality of capitalism is that ever more of social life is mediated through and by the market', the process of commodification is widely accepted. As Gough (2000: 17) puts it in the context of the changes in central and eastern Europe,

> Following decolonisation and the collapse of state socialism at the end of the 1980s, few areas of the world remain to resist the logic of capitalist markets and economic enterprises. This in turn is imposing the needs of capital in more and more areas of life and is weakening the resources of states and citizens to fight back.

For adherents to the commodification thesis, therefore, contemporary economies are characterized by the increasing dominance of one mode of exchange that is replacing all others. In this view of an increasingly hegemonic capitalism, the market becomes *the* economic institution rather than one form of provisioning among others. Instead of producing use values directly in relation to their needs, people – whether as capitalists, or as workers whose labour has been bought and subsumed by capitalists – produce goods and services that can be sold in the market. While these goods and services must have use value for other people otherwise they could not be sold, the producers regard them solely in terms of their exchange value. As Sayer (1997: 23) puts it,

> The commodity may be valued by the user for its intrinsic use value, but to the seller it is unequivocally a means to an end, to the achievement of the external goal of making a profit, and if it is unlikely to make a profit it will not be offered for sale.

In contemporary thought, few ever raise an eyebrow when this type of economic logic is mentioned. After all, such a process of commodification is widely accepted. Capitalism, it is commonly believed, is extending its reach ever more widely and deeply into economic life. The widespread view is that profit-motivated monetized exchange is slowly and steadily replacing non-commodified economic practices.

How, for example, can the focus upon formal employment in general, and employment in the private sector in particular, when studying work otherwise be explained if it is not based on the assumption that the formal and commodified sphere is growing and the informal and non-commodified sphere diminishing? For example, why is it that most studies of regional economic development and policy focus upon the private commodified sphere in particular and formal employment more generally? Inward investment, for example, concentrates largely on attracting private enterprise rather than on fostering public service, not-for-profit enterprises or forms of non-monetized or non-exchanged work. The only conclusion that can be reached is that it is widely believed that this commodified realm is not only the expanding sphere but also the lead sector upon which all of the other spheres of economic practice are dependent.

Indeed, this is perhaps precisely why one witnesses changing fashions in inward investment in terms of the type of enterprise that it seeks to attract. Over the past few decades, the demise of manufacturing employment throughout the advanced economies has led inward investment to expand the spheres in which it is interested to, first of all, producer services and more recently a whole range of consumer services including industries involved in sports, culture, retailing, tourism and even education (see Williams, 1997). In all cases, however, it is private-sector enterprises that remain the focus of attention. This is without doubt due to the widespread and steadfast belief that it is the commodified realm that is growing and is the lead sector upon which all other activities are dependent, and that one needs to identify the subsectors within this commodified realm that are expanding fastest. It is thus little surprise that the non-commodified sphere receives relatively little attention.

Wherever one looks, there is very little questioning of the commodification thesis. The view that the commodified realm is expanding and the non-commodified realm shrinking has become something of an irrefutable fact. However, although few question whether a process of commodification is taking place, there does exist some discussion and debate on its pace, extent and unevenness.

Take, for example, the extent of commodification. For some, the process is rather more complete and the commodity economy more hegemonic than for others. Comeliau (2000: 45), for example, talks of 'its almost *exclusive* use to solve the great majority of economic and social problems', while Thrift (2000: 96) asserts that 'What is certain is that the process of commodification has reached into every nook and cranny of modern life.' For others, however, there is still seen to be a greater distance to travel before the total commodification of working life is achieved (e.g. Gough, 2000; Lee, 1999; Watts, 1999). As Watts (1999: 312) puts it,

> The process by which everything becomes a commodity – and therefore everything comes to acquire a price and a monetary form (commoditization/commodification) – is not complete, even in our own

societies where transactions still occur outside of the marketplace. But the reality of capitalism is that ever more of social life is mediated through and by the market.

Among all such commentators, therefore, there is no question that a process of commodification is taking place. The only debate is over the extent to which it has colonized the non-commodified realm and the distance that needs to be travelled before this process is complete. To assess this, and as can be seen above, commentators give little more than some broad-brush qualitative judgement. None attempts to measure, even in the crudest terms, the extent of its penetration (we will return to this later).

It is similarly the case when both its pace and unevenness are considered. For most analysts, the issue of the pace of commodification is seldom considered in any explicit manner. If it is, then the remark most often made is that it is speeding up. On the issue of the unevenness of its penetration, however, judgements are at least a little more considered, even if they are again only broad-brush qualitative measures rather than evaluations that use indicators of some type or another. As Harvey (2000: 68) posits with regard to what he considers a highly uneven process,

> if there is any real qualitative trend it is towards the reassertion of early nineteenth-century capitalist values coupled with a twenty-first century penchant for pulling everyone (and everything that can be exchanged) into the orbit of capital while rendering large segments of the world's population permanently redundant in relation to the basic dynamics of capital accumulation.

Indeed, this is the consensus. The widespread view is that, even if the market is reaching ever outward to pull in more spheres of life and colonize areas previously untouched by its hand, this is a highly uneven process. This is clearly seen in discussions and comparisons of the first, second and third worlds. In nearly all analyses, the stark differentials between the penetration of the commodity economy in the first world compared with the second and third worlds are continually drawn so as to highlight the unevenness of commodification. Few, however, doubt that a near universal process of commodification is taking place across all of these regions.

Neither is there much difference between right- and left-wing political discourses on the issue of commodification. There is concurrence on the right and the left of the political spectrum that the overarching process is one of commodification, even if the reasons for asserting this and the normative views on its consequences vary considerably. As such, besides discussions on the pace, extent and unevenness of the process of commodification, there are also contrasting normative positions about, first, whether it is to be celebrated or not, and, second and often inextricably interrelated, whether it is a 'natural' and 'organic' or a 'socially constructed' process.

On the issue of whether this turn towards the market is to be celebrated or not, two starkly different positions exist. For neoliberals, the process of commodification is generally seen in a positive light as resulting in liberation, freedom and progress from the irrational constraints of tradition and collective bonds, creating a social order from the market-coordinated actions of free and rational individuals. This advocacy of commodification is often inextricably tied to a view of market-oriented behaviour as the natural basis for all social life. In this view, portrayed in Thatcherism, a cultural and political revolution is required to remove from social life anything that might reduce the centrality of market models as the basis of social order.

As Block (2002) has pointed out, this celebratory view of capitalism in neoliberal thought has taken on board many of the tenets of what originally was a critical Marxian discourse. On the one hand, the very term 'capitalism' that until the late 1960s was not used in polite company has now been adopted by these neoliberal thinkers in a much more positive sense to convey the type of society that is being sought. On the other hand, the core Marxist idea that the economic organization of society sets the basic frame for the larger society, which was previously considered objectionable and rejected as 'vulgar materialism', is now widely accepted by these neoliberals. The result is that today capitalism is now the name that the business press uses to describe both Western and global economies, and the idea that the structure of the economy determines the basic frame of the larger society has been transformed from 'vulgar materialism' to common sense.

Even more importantly, the fundamentally Marxian claim that capitalism as an economic system is global, unified and coherent has been embraced by Margaret Thatcher, Ronald Reagan and other apostles of neoliberal ideology in order to encourage the same common strategy of privatization, deregulation and public-sector retrenchment if countries are to prosper in an increasingly global capitalist economy.

For many on the left of the political spectrum, meanwhile, there is again an acceptance that commodification is taking place but it is seen more negatively. For them, the reason for wishing to extol the increasing penetration of the market is to show how one needs to be wary of this development due to its eroding of communal life and the deleterious consequences for social values that might stand above the merely economic measure of price (e.g. Comeliau, 2002; Slater and Tonkiss, 2001). As Comeliau (2002: 45) for example states,

> wherever market rationality acquires dominance, it transforms *social relations in their entirety*. Resting as it does upon private appropriation and competition, it entails individualist rivalry far more than mutual support as the basis for relations among the members of a society. It thus has a destructive impact upon the 'social fabric' itself.

Such wariness about the deleterious consequences of market penetration is by no means recent. Indeed, Beveridge (1948: 322), widely recognized as the founder of the modern welfare state, was extremely concerned about the advent of what he called the 'business motive'. For him, there was a need to make and keep 'something other than the pursuit of gain as the dominant force in society. The business motive ... is ... in continual or repeated conflict with the Philanthropic Motive, and has too often been successful.' He concludes that 'the business motive is a good servant but a bad master, and a society which gives itself up to the dominance of the business motive is a bad society.' This negative view of commodification thus views the implementation of an implacable logic of quantification and formal rationality as producing inequality, social disorder, loss of substantive values and a destruction of both the individual and social relations.

Related to this debate on whether commodification should be celebrated or treated with wariness is a debate on whether it is a 'natural' and 'organic' or a 'socially created' process. For neo-liberals, the process of commodification is usually seen as a natural or organic process, whilst for those critical of the consequences of such a process it is more commonly viewed as socially constructed. Before analysing these contrasting positions, however, it is necessary to reiterate that there is a shared 'buying into' the meta-narrative of commodification by both bodies of thought. Not only those who view it as a natural phenomenon but also those who see it as socially constructed believe that the trajectory of economic history is a linear and uni-dimensional path towards ever more commodified economies. As Slater and Tonkiss (2001: 3–4) assert, 'recent political and economic orthodoxies treat markets as self-evident, permanent and incontestable'.

In the 'natural' or 'organic' view of capitalism, such a trajectory of economic development is portrayed as an inevitable, colonizing, all-powerful and all-conquering system, even a supernatural force that is unstoppable. Indeed, this 'natural force' is even sometimes assigned with human characteristics and emotions. In the business press, for example, markets are often described as buoyant, calm, depressed, expectant, hesitant, nervous and sensitive. Sometimes the pound sterling, euro or US dollar has a good day, at other times it is ailing or sinking fast. Markets seem, therefore, often to take on human attributes beyond the control of mere mortals. They become superhuman figures. This is more than simply an attempt to make them more comprehensible to the public by financial jour-nalists. It is a way of imbuing them with the force of nature, even a reflection of divine will. The result of such imagery is that 'there is no alternative' but to obey the logic of this all-powerful force. Read in this manner, capitalism is often constructed as existing outside of society or even above it. Reflecting the view of many economists and formal anthropologists, the perception is that the economy is a separate, differentiated sphere in modern society, with economic transactions defined no longer by the social or kinship obligations of those transacting but by rational calculations of individual gain. It is sometimes further argued that the traditional situation is reversed: instead of economic life being submerged in social relations, these relations become an epiphenomenon of the market; there is an economization of culture.

For those adopting a more critical view of the advent of capitalism, however, this 'un-embedded' and organic view of the system is rejected. For them, the view is that this is a socially constructed system and that although there is a momentum towards an ever more commodified world, this does not mean that it cannot be stopped. Following Polanyi (1944: 140), it has been widely recognized that 'the road to the free market was opened and kept open by an enormous increase in continuous, centrally organized, and controlled interventionism' and, as such, that commodification is a created system rather than an organic one. As Faraclas (2001: 67) puts it,

> Corporate globalization is presented to us as inevitable ... discussed in the media as if it were a natural phenomenon. But can the most massive transfer of wealth in the history of humanity from the poor to the rich sponsored by the World Bank/International Monetary Fund ... and enforced by the World Trade Organization ... under the agenda of corporate globalization be considered natural?

One way in which this view of commodification as a created system has started to come to the fore, albeit implicitly, is in the literature on the 'varieties of capitalism' (e.g. Albert, 1993; Berger and Dore, 1996; Coates, 2002a, 2002b, 2002c; Crouch and Streek, 1997; Hollingsworth and Bayer, 1997; Orru et al., 1997; Whitley, 2002). Here, the argument is that different varieties of industrial capitalism have developed in Anglo-Saxon countries, Continental Europe and East Asia and that this shows that there is no one single variety with one uniform logic but a multiplicity of strains that reflect the different social systems in which they are created. The key problem with this varieties-of-capitalism literature, however, is that it has been largely silent on the critical issue of capitalism as a natural system (Block, 2002). Although it is implicit in this body of literature that there is no single unified system that operates like a force of nature, it is not dealt with explicitly. Until such time as there is an effort to unpack and discuss this issue more directly, therefore, the view is likely to persist that capitalism is some natural or organic system beyond the control of the societies in which it exists.

Nevertheless, even if the future literature manages to escape from the view of capitalism as an organic system and to understand how it is a created system, it is likely that this will still be insufficient to raise any questions concerning the validity of the commodification thesis. Until now, many who view the development of the market as created rather than organic have failed to question whether capitalism is reaching wider and penetrating deeper. For them, a commodification of economic life is still seen to be taking place. Although, in principle, social constructionists need not argue this since they recognize that commodification is not inevitable, in practice few have questioned it. To transcend the commodification thesis, in consequence, it is necessary to investigate much more directly whether there is evidence to support this meta-narrative of the trajectory of economic development.

Where is the Evidence
to Support the Commodification Thesis?

Given the overwhelming dominance of this belief that a commodification of the advanced economies is taking place, one might think that there would be mountains of evidence to support such a stance. Yet one of the most worrying and disturbing findings once one starts to research musings on this subject is that hardly any evidence is ever brought to the fore by its adherents either to show that a process of commodification is taking place or even to display the extent, pace or unevenness of its penetration. For example, the above-stated pronouncements by Rifkin (2000: 3) that 'The marketplace is a pervasive force in our lives', Ciscel and Heath (2001: 401) that capitalism is transforming 'every human interaction into a transient market exchange', and Gudeman (2001: 144) that 'markets are subsuming greater portions of everyday life' are offered to the reader with no supporting data of any kind. Similarly, the assertion by Carruthers and Babb (2000: 4), mentioned earlier, that there has been 'the near-complete penetration of market relations into our modern economic lives' is justified by nothing more than the statement that 'markets enter our lives today in many ways "too numerous to be mentioned"' and the spurious notion that the spread of commodified *ways of viewing* particular spheres of life signal how commodification has permeated ever deeper into daily life. Watts (1999: 312), in the same vein, supports his above-stated belief that although 'commodification is not complete ... the reality of capitalism is that ever more of social life is mediated through and by the market' merely by avowing that subsistence economies are increasingly rare.

The thin evidence offered by these authors is by no means exceptional. Few, if any, commentators attempt to move beyond what Martin and Sunley (2001: 152) in another context term 'vague theory and thin empirics'. As a widely accepted canon of wisdom, the process of commodification is hardly ever subjected to critical investigation. If this was some minor process, it might be unimportant. However, commodification is seemingly the principal rationale underpinning the approach adopted for restructuring both 'transition' economies and the 'third world'. It is also the main concept underpinning the focus upon the market in policies planning economic development in the advanced economies. It is thus crucial that this key issue is interrogated. Unless this occurs, then one will not know whether the current focus of economic policy upon the market realm is built upon firm foundations or not.

Perhaps the process of commodification is so obvious to all concerned that there is little need to provide evidence. Perhaps, however, it is not. No other idea in the social sciences is accepted without detailed corroboration. Indeed, the advent of postmodern discourses has put under the spotlight a whole range of grand narratives and deconstructed their totalizing discourses so as to reveal their flimsy bases. There are no grounds for exempting the commodification thesis from a similar process of inquiry. The only reason to do so would be if one believed that it is an irrefutable fact. However, then one should not of course mind the interrogation conducted here, for it must surely prove that case. Indeed, given the paucity of evidence so far provided, such corroboration should be welcomed by anybody who adheres to this thesis.

Before setting out on the journey to seek out evidence of whether the commodification thesis can be corroborated or not, it is perhaps first worthwhile briefly exploring why there has so seldom been any attempt to seek out data to validate it. One principal reason is that the commodification thesis is a meta-narrative that is seldom challenged. Given this, adherents are rarely, if ever, called upon to justify it. Indeed, with such challenges few and far between, the mode of inquiry adopted by adherents to the commodification thesis tends to lead to a self-fulfilment of their view of the world. For those who adhere to the commodification thesis, that is, their focus of inquiry is nearly always the market sphere. The result is that they find, and even create, what they seek. By focusing upon commodified work practices, they have accumulated a body of work that can do nothing else than reinforce the picture that commodified work is now the dominant mode of economic organization. Ignoring non-commodified economic practices as of minor and diminishing importance, their lack of emphasis on documenting such practices reinforces the image that this work is unimportant. Casting one's eyes along the bookshelves of our academic libraries in search of information on the economy, it is as though there is only one form of work that is now of any importance, namely commodified work.

For Carrier (1997) this is because 'the Market Idea' has had a central role in organizing the modern West's conceptual and normative universe. For him, such a view of the hegemony of the market is central to Western cosmology and constrains action and thinking about the future. It is encapsulated in the view of the so-called advanced economies as 'market economies/societies', implying a primacy of one mode of exchange – based on profit-motivated market transactions – that, as indicated above, has been far from corroborated. Indeed, such a view, as Kovel (2002: ix–x) points out, is very recent:

> for generations ..., a consensus existed that capitalism was embattled and that its survival was an open question. For the last twenty years or so, however, with the rise of neoliberalism and the collapse of the soviets, the system has acquired an aura of inevitability and even immortality. It is quite remarkable to see how the intellectual classes go along, sheeplike, with these absurd conclusions, disregarding the well-established lessons that nothing lasts for ever, that all empires fall, and that a twenty-year ascendancy is scarcely a blink in the flux of time.

What Kovel (2002) fails to recognize, however, is that it is far from certain that such an ascendancy of the market to a hegemonic position has even taken place. To refer to the economies of Western nations as being 'market economies/societies' assumes that one mode of exchange is now dominant. Yet there is a question of whether this is the case. As Slater and Tonkiss (2001: 199) put it, 'no society is entirely ordered by a single mode of exchange'. Or, as Comeliau (2002: 68) states more explicitly, 'No modern organization of the economy is based purely on the market. Always the market is combined with various types of collective intervention – by public bodies, associations and so on.' Even the briefest of glances at the advanced economies allows one to recognize that this is the case. There persists a large amount of non-exchanged work in the form of what is variously called 'domestic work' or 'housework', non-monetized exchange in the form of volunteering continues to take place, and not-for-profit monetized exchange in either the public sector or not-for-profit sector is far from eradicated. So-called 'market economies', in consequence, are a long way from being purely embedded in market-like profit-motivated exchange relations. Other modes of producing and delivering goods and services continue to persist. The interesting issue is whether these other modes of producing and delivering goods and services are declining as the market supposedly colonizes ever more realms of economic life. For adherents to the commodification thesis, of course, such an erosion of these other spheres is an irrefutable fact.

Indeed, one common argument used by adherents to the commodification thesis to support their belief in a more hegemonic commodified realm is that the emergence of commodified 'ways of viewing' each and every aspect of daily life signifies how commodification is reaching into each and every crevice of life in the advanced economies. To take just one example, recent years have seen the advent of discussions of a 'marriage market' whereby people seek out and take decisions on partners much like in any other profit-orientated investment. Yet just because a sphere of human life has been read in a commodified manner does not mean that this sphere is now commodified. Just because one can read marriage and partnership in such a commodified way does not now mean that everybody marries or chooses partners for profit-motivated purposes. The advent of a commodified way of viewing each and every aspect of life does not signify the deeper and wider penetration of commodification itself.

Just because interpretations of any such aspect of social behaviour can be read through the lens of commodification does not mean that this behaviour is now conducted under the social relations of profit-motivated monetized exchange. And just because the language of the commodity economy is now colonizing more and more areas of human existence, reaching far into inviolable sanctuaries, such that we now talk of emotional investments and of the returns on our relationships, does not mean that all human relationships are viewed in a commodified manner. Making such and such a friendship might pay dividends, be profitless, rewarding, cost us dear; we may shop around for new friendships, be in the market for a new relationship, have the assets of our youth, intellect or energy so that we can make capital out of them; there may be pay-offs, bonuses to be had and meagre returns from friendships and we may all have our price, but this language of commodification does not mean that commodification is omnipresent.

One of the most worrying aspects of the logic of adherents to the commodification thesis, therefore, is that they use the idea that commodified 'ways of viewing' are becoming increasingly dominant to support their assertion that commodification must be occurring. There is a widespread perception that what Bourdieu (2003) calls 'the tyranny of the market' is enveloping all of human existence. Wolff (1989), for example, argues that the logic of the market has increasingly penetrated our most intimate social relations of family and community. While areas of solidarity, altruism and affection do persist in American life, according to Wolff, he greatly worries that the boundaries between civil society and the market have been progressively weakened and that 'in a way unprecedented in the American experience the market has become attractive not only in the economic sphere, but in the moral and social spheres as well' (Wolff, 1989: 76). Yet he is confusing the advent of a way of viewing with the process of commodification itself.

Despite this imagining of an increasingly commodified society from the incursion of commodified 'ways of viewing', commentators must know deep down that this is not the case. They live in society as much as anybody else and must know the social mores that prevail. In contemporary Western societies, that is, the application of profit-price terms to all social transactions is widely understood to be unacceptable and inappropriate. We all know, for example, that even if one acts in a market-like manner in commercial transactions, the same does not apply to exchanges between friends and kin where reciprocity, altruism and charity should and must prevail. To act otherwise would be inappropriate and unacceptable. Different forms of exchange relations are appropriate and valid in different social situations. Doing a favour for kin, friends or neighbours is very different to selling a service to a client, and disputes over whether something is a favour or a service depend on whether the relationship is friendship or commerce. Just because an altruistic favour can be read as market-like and profit-motivated does not make it so.

Even in the so-called advanced economies, therefore, there persist both blockages to commodification and modes of producing and delivering goods and services that are not commodified. Yet the 'market idea' or 'commodification thesis' masks from view this plurality of economic practices that is still a core characteristic of the advanced economies. Even if there are still very few commentators who seem willing to question whether more of economic life is becoming commodified, therefore, recent years have seen a number of analysts recognize that if working life is to be more fully understood, one cannot solely study the commodified world. As Bourdieu (2001: 280–81) states,

> It is in fact impossible to account for the structure and functioning of the social world unless one reintroduces capital in all its forms and not solely in the one form recognized by economic theory. Economic theory has allowed to be foisted upon it a definition of the economy of practices which is the historical invention of capitalism; and by reducing the universe of exchanges to mercantile exchange, which is objectively and subjectively oriented toward the maximization of profit, ... it has implicitly defined the other forms of exchange as noneconomic, and therefore disinterested. In particular, it defines as disinterested those forms of exchange which ensure the transubstantiation whereby the most material types of capital – those which are economic in the restricted sense – can present themselves in the immaterial form of cultural capital or social capital and vice versa.

For Bourdieu (2001: 281), in consequence, 'the constitution of a science of mercantile relationships... is not even a science of the field of economic production, [and] has prevented the constitution of a general science of the economy of practices, which would treat mercantile exchange as a particular case of exchange in all its forms' or what Davis (1992) refers to as a 'repertoire' of exchange practices.

What is now necessary, it appears, is to move beyond this recognition that other economic practices persist in 'market economies' and to consider the degree to which the commodified realm can be seen to have penetrated wider and deeper over time. So far, although the plurality of economic practices that characterize the advanced economies have started to be recognized, few have deemed it worthy to consider whether such non-commodified economic practices are growing or depleting relative to the commodified realm. The consensus, embedded in the commodification thesis, is that the commodity economy is increasingly totalizing, hegemonic, all-encompassing and universal, despite the distinct lack of evidence to corroborate this meta-narrative.

Conclusions

In this chapter, the commodification thesis has been introduced. Defined as the belief that goods and services are increasingly produced and delivered by capitalist firms for a profit under conditions of market exchange, this is today a meta-narrative with which few disagree, as has been shown. There is widespread agreement among business leaders, politicians, journalists and academic commentators of all political hues that there is a linear and uni-dimensional trajectory of economic development towards a commodified world. Although this process is seen in different manners, with some viewing such a trajectory in a positive light and others with greater wariness, and some viewing it as natural and organic trajectory and others as socially constructed, this chapter has revealed that until now there has been little, if any, attempt to evaluate critically this meta-narrative of commodification.

One of the most disconcerting and worrying findings of this chapter, moreover, is that hardly any evidence is ever brought to the fore to provide corroboration that commodification is in fact taking place. Identifying this paucity of evidence to support the idea that ever more of daily life is mediated through the market, this chapter has thus argued that it is necessary to subject this canon of wisdom that so limits our view of possible futures to greater critical scrutiny than has so far been the case. Although it has been recognized by many authors that the advanced economies remain characterized by a plurality of economic practices rather than the dominance of one mode of exchange, there has so far been little attempt to evaluate whether these non-commodified modes of producing and delivering goods and services are declining or growing relative to the commodified realm. Instead, it is simply assumed that they are in demise. In the rest of Part I of this book, therefore, and given the lack of evidence so far marshalled together to test the commodification thesis, an evaluation is undertaken of the size of the various non-commodified modes of producing and delivering goods and services and whether they are growing or declining relative to the commodified sphere.

3

Subsistence Work

There is a widely held view that goods and services are increasingly produced and delivered for monetized exchange by profit-seeking capitalist firms. The first constituent component of this commodification thesis that needs to be evaluated critically, therefore, is the suggestion that in the advanced economies, goods and services are increasingly produced for the purpose of exchange. According to those who believe that we are now living in an ever more commodified world, it is often asserted there are few remaining vestiges of non-exchanged (or subsistence) work in the advanced economies and those that do persist are little more than mere leftovers of precapitalist economic practices and rapidly dwindling (e.g. Watts, 1999). Even if many others would not perhaps go that far, a widespread belief is that the realm of non-exchanged work is steadily declining as the commodified realm slowly and surely penetrates ever more deeply and widely. In this chapter, in consequence, this view of non-exchanged work as a dwindling sphere of activity is evaluated critically. To do this, a number of questions are posed. What is the conceptualization of subsistence work in the commodification thesis? How can one assess whether such work persists? And what is the extent of such work and how is its magnitude changing over time?

In order to answer these questions, the first section of this chapter outlines how non-exchanged work is conceptualized in the commodification thesis. This will show how it is viewed as a marginal vestige of precapitalist formations that is rapidly dwindling and only of very limited importance in our rapidly commodifying world. To evaluate critically this view of non-exchanged work, the second section of this chapter outlines the various methods that can be and have been used to assess the extent of such work in the advanced economies. With an understanding of these methods in hand, the third section then documents their findings so far as the magnitude of such work is concerned, followed by an assessment of its changing size in contemporary advanced economies. This will reveal that, contrary to the tenets of the commodification thesis that declare the disappearance of subsistence work, the populations of the advanced economies now spend the same amount of time engaged in non-exchanged work as they do in paid formal employment. Moreover, the amount of time spent in subsistence work over the past forty years will be shown to have grown relative to the time spent in formal employment. If there is any trend to be discerned, therefore, it is not the demise of subsistence work but its resurgence in the advanced economies.

Before commencing, however, it is necessary first of all to define what is meant here by subsistence work. In this respect, there are many possible definitions that could be drawn upon. For Bennholdt-Thomsen (2001: 224), for instance, 'subsistence refers to the manner in which people produce their own lives and re-produce them day by day, as well as to how and to what degree they hold these processes in their own hands in terms of material, substance and society.' Here, a slightly more operational definition is adopted and one that defines such work directly in relation to the tenets of the commodification thesis. Throughout this chapter, subsistence work refers to all non-exchanged work undertaken on an unpaid basis by household members for themselves or for some other member of their household that might otherwise be undertaken using commodified labour. As such, subsistence work refers here to what is commonly known as 'housework', 'domestic work', 'do-it-yourself activity' or what might alternatively be called 'self-provisioning'.

Indeed, this definition of subsistence work adheres very closely to many previous definitions of unpaid household work. Take, for example, the definition adopted by Reid (1934: 11), who defines household production as consisting of

> those unpaid activities which are carried on, by and for the members, which activities might be replaced by market goods, or paid services,

if circumstances such as income, market conditions, and personal inclinations permit the service being delegated to someone outside the household group.

Akin to the definition adopted here, she defines this economic practice as unpaid work conducted by and for household members and then applies a 'third person' approach so as to distinguish it from leisure. That is, if the activity could be replaced by commodified labour, then this is seen as unpaid household work rather than leisure. As will become apparent later in the book, this issue of whether it 'could' be replaced by commodified labour and why it is currently not is very important in understanding the shallow and uneven penetration of commodification in the advanced economies. For the moment, however, this is left aside; it will be returned to in Part II where the uneven contours of the commodity economy are analysed. Here, it is first necessary to understand how subsistence work is viewed in the commodification thesis, along with how to measure it and its changing size relative to the commodity economy, so as to evaluate whether there is clear evidence of a process of commodification in the advanced economies.

Subsistence Work in the Commodification Thesis

Has subsistence work more or less disappeared in the advanced economies? Reading the literature cited in the last chapter on how the advanced economies are witnessing a process of commodification, it might certainly be believed that this is the case. There is an overwhelming perception in this literature that subsistence economies have been replaced by commodified practices. Indeed, so obvious is this to such commentators that few of them ever pause long enough on this issue to question whether this is the case. Instead, their eagerness to display how we are now living in a commodified world results in them adopting a particular discourse in relation to non-exchanged work that allows them quickly to dismiss its existence and to get on with the task of showing the ways in which the advanced economies are becoming more and more commodified.

In the commodification thesis, that is, subsistence work is caricatured as some 'peasant' or 'backward' form of production that has been replaced in 'advanced' economies by commodified forms of production in which goods and services are now delivered through monetary transactions by capitalist firms. By interpreting such non-exchanged work as a precapitalist mode of production undertaken by households as their means of survival, such work is quickly dismissed. Few, if any, individuals or households are seen as being dependent on subsistence production in the advanced economies and, as such, the subsistence economy is read as some minor vestige that now persists in only a few minor crevices of the advanced economies. There may be the odd example of either peasant households where subsistence living is practised or of 'alternative' types, such as 'downshifters', who attempt to engage in more simplistic living (Jacob, 2003), but on the whole such a mode of production is viewed as a minority practice and of little or no importance to understanding contemporary commodified societies.

Here, in consequence, and reflecting much modern thought, there is seen to have been a major historical shift from household production for domestic consumption to a situation in which household members work for employers in exchange for wages. They are therefore said to secure the livelihood of themselves and their co-dependents by selling their labour as a commodity within the labour market rather than producing goods that satisfy their own immediate needs. This development is itself part of a broader separation or dispossession of people from the means of production. Unable to produce their own goods for immediate consumption, modern workers (or their 'breadwinners') must sell their labour on labour markets in exchange for cash to purchase goods on consumer markets. The view is that in the early stages of industrial capitalism, goods which had been made in the home or by local craftsmen for barter and only occasionally for market exchange were gradually replaced by goods production en masse in factories. Goods production, ranging from items of furniture, cloth and later clothes, utensils, soap, and countless other homemade items, was shifted out of the home into the factory where they could be made cheaper and in greater volume. This led to the separation of the home and production. Those who had previously made these goods for their own use began 'for the first time, to use their new factory wages to purchase factory-made items in the marketplace' (Rifkin, 2000: 81).

Indeed, there are now numerous texts in economic and social history that have traced this process of commodification. Analysing the data in the US Census Bureau for the period 1889 to 1892, for example, Smuts (1971: 11–13) reveals that at this time more than half of the families surveyed were still baking their own bread. While men's clothes were generally store-bought, the clothes of women and children were still tailored and stitched at home, first by hand, then by the Singer sewing machine. Similarly, Braverman (1971) notes that as late as 1900 in North America, much of production was still centred in the home, even in dense urban areas. Families living in the highly industrial regions, like the coal and steel communities of Pennsylvania, continued to produce most of their 'food at home and more than half of all families raised their own poultry, livestock, and vegetables, and purchased only potatoes at the market' (Braverman 1971: 273–4). The tale, however, is that this overlap between a subsistence economy and industrial capitalism did not last long. The pace of commodification soon led to these households becoming more dependent on commodified goods and services in order to meet their needs and wants. The result, according to adherents to the commodification thesis, is that subsistence households have all but disappeared as the commodity economy has stretched out to envelop household life. The outcome is that economy and household, despite having the same Greek root – *oikos*, meaning 'managing the household' – have become separated.

However, this commodification discourse that subsistence work has all but disappeared is highly contestable. A key problem with this reading is that people and households cannot and should not be classified according to their reliance on one principal form of work to get by. It is much more an understanding of how households combine different modes of production that is important if the nature of work in the advanced economies is to be more fully understood. Of course, if one examines how many people today rely solely or primarily on subsistence production in order to survive, then there is little doubt that the Western economies have probably witnessed the death of the subsistence economy. As Jacob (2003) displays, even those who have sought to go 'back-to-the-land' in the USA and return to a subsistence economy have found that pursuing a single mode of production is difficult, if not impossible, to achieve. The mistake of these 'back-to-the-landers', however, as with the commodification theorists, is that they view subsistence production as a separate 'economy' rather than as one of many forms of work that can be used by households in their coping practices.

Once one reconceptualizes subsistence work as part of a plurality of economic practices used by households in contemporary advanced economies, then a very different reading of such work emerges. Commodification theorists may be correct when they state that the subsistence 'economy' (i.e. people and households relying on this as their principal mode of production) hardly exists in advanced economies. However, this is not correct so far as subsistence 'work' is concerned. Moreover, even if goods production has moved out of the household, it is very doubtful that this is also the case with service production. Households still engage in a tremendous range of self-servicing activity, from routine housework, cleaning windows, cooking, gardening, child- and elder-care through to car maintenance as well as home maintenance and improvement activity. The move of goods production into the marketplace, therefore, seems to have been only partially followed by the shift of service provision into this sphere (Williams and Windebank, 2001h).

This different reading of the prevalence of subsistence work in the advanced economies is by no means novel. Indeed, throughout the last century, and particularly from the 1970s onwards, a current of literature has been bubbling under the surface of mainstream social science that has sought to highlight how non-exchanged production persists even if it remains hidden from view (e.g. Delphy, 1984; Oakley, 1974; Williams and Windebank, 2003a). Perhaps it is the fact that such labour remains largely women's responsibility that results in it not being recognized by commodification advocates. But exist it does and in large quantities. Just because it is apparently not recognized or valued by exponents of the commodification thesis, and even sometimes seen as somehow inferior to the mainstream commodity economy, is no reason to ignore it. Bennholdt-Thomsen and Mies (1999: 11) refer to this process by which such work is swept out of sight as 'housewifization'. As they state, 'women's work under capitalism is universally made invisible and can for that reason be exploited limitlessly'. For them, this concept of the invisibility of women's work 'applies not only to "housewives" in the narrow sense in the industrial countries but also to the work of the women who do home work, to farm labourers, peasants, small traders, and factory workers', and it also applies increasingly to 'men of the North' (Bennholdt-Thomsen and Mies, 1999: 11–13). For Bennholdt-Thomsen (2001: 224), therefore,

> Anyone who thinks a subsistence orientation should be banished 'to the stone age' or 'to the Middle Ages' or to the Third World, because in our developed society we have allegedly outgrown both self-provision and worries about subsistence, has failed to recognize that subsistence does not disappear, but rather changes through history and takes different forms in different contexts. At the start of the twenty-first century, subsistence looks different from the way it did twenty centuries ago or even fifty years ago. Subsistence in the city takes on forms that are different from those it adopts in the country. Subsistence displays different characteristics in households with children than it does in childless households. But no matter when, where, or who practices it, subsistence means providing for oneself.

Viewed in this manner, all of the hyperbole by advocates of the commodification thesis that subsistence work is of only marginal relevance in advanced economies seems narrow at best, and derogatory at worst. Subsistence work is ubiquitous. Households everywhere continue to provide many goods and services for themselves on an unpaid basis. Everyday, members of households cook meals, clean, tidy, mow, iron, repair and maintain goods and engage in service provision. The interesting questions, of course, are whether the extent of such work is relatively minor compared with the commodity economy, and whether it is diminishing over time. To lay the foundations for answering these questions, in consequence, the next section reviews the methods that can be and have been used to measure the extent of such work.

Measuring Subsistence Work

Throughout the past century, but particularly from the 1970s onwards, a vast social science literature has called for recognition and valuing of subsistence work. Indeed, although commentators do so for a multiplicity of reasons, for the sake of simplification four main streams of thought can be identified. First, there are the non-market radical social democrats with their anti-capitalist agenda who see the harnessing of subsistence work as a means of developing alternative modes of production beyond the commodity economy (e.g. Beck, 2000; Gorz, 1999). Second, there are radical ecologists (e.g. Dauncey, 1988; Douthwaite, 1996; Lipietz, 1995) who see in such work the seeds of a different, more ecologically sustainable, future. Third, there are post-development theorists, or postmodern deconstructivists, who by pointing to the persistence of such work seek to enact and imagine alternatives to capitalism (e.g. Community Economies Collective, 2001; Escobar, 1995; Gibson-Graham, 1996). Fourth and finally, there is a literature written from the perspective of feminism that sees such work as one of the principal sources of women's continuing oppression (see Beneria, 1999; Delphy, 1984; Gregory and Windebank, 2000; McDowell, 1991). Of all of these interrelated literatures, it is without doubt the latter that has been most successful in encouraging a wider recognition of the existence of such work.

Calls for unpaid household work to be recognized and valued have been made throughout the past century. A pioneer of this approach was Margaret Reid, who in her 1934 book *Economics of Household Production* expressed concern about the exclusion of unpaid domestic work from national income accounts and designed a method to estimate the value of such work (Reid, 1934). This demand for unpaid domestic work to be recognized became more intense from the late 1960s onwards when the international women's movement engaged in a campaign for unpaid subsistence work to be measured (see Beneria, 1999; Chadeau and Fouquet, 1981; James, 1994; Luxton, 1997). Indeed, this campaign has met with considerable success.

Of potential long-term significance is a recommendation, made in 1993 by the United Nations after a review of the United Nations

System of National Accounts (UNSNA), that 'satellite national accounts' be developed that incorporate the value of unpaid work. This was the culmination of changes that had been recommended by various commentators (e.g. Boulding, 1968) since World War II, when the UNSNA was set up. Such a recommendation became an obligation for signatories to the Final Act of the 1995 UN Fourth World Conference on Women in Beijing (United Nations, 1995: Section 209: f, g). Those nations signing this Act agreed to develop these 'satellite' national accounts as an adjunct to the standard national accounts. For the purpose of this chapter, the results of these 'satellite' national accounts would have proven very useful in providing a measure of the amount of subsistence work in numerous nations. The problem, however, is that they are only now starting to come on stream in many nations. Consequently, earlier studies conducted before this obligation was passed have had to be used here in order to assess the magnitude of such work and how it is changing. There is little doubt, however, that in a few years time a much greater wealth of data will become available than is currently the case.

How, therefore, can one measure the level of subsistence work in an economy? In theory, a wide variety of analytical methods are available. One could measure the volume or the value of either the inputs or the outputs of such non-exchanged work (Goldschmidt-Clermont, 1982, 1993, 1998, 2000; Gregory and Windebank, 2000; Luxton, 1997; OECD, 1997, 2002). In practice, however, the standard approach has been to measure the volume and value of the inputs. This is achieved by measuring how people use their time in the form of time-budget studies (e.g. Gershuny, 2000; Murgatroyd and Neuburger, 1997; Roy, 1991). These analyse whether people perceive their activity as work or leisure and then measure the time spent in various forms of activity. To do this, participants complete diaries chronicling the number of minutes they spend on various activities over the course of a day. From this, the time spent in paid work, non-monetized exchange and non-exchanged work is calculated (see Gershuny and Jones, 1987; Gershuny et al., 1994; Juster and Stafford, 1991).

Conventionally, these time-budget studies have been used to investigate issues such as the changing work–leisure balance (e.g.

Gershuny, 2000), the existence of social capital (e.g. Ruston, 2003), and gender divisions of labour, especially regarding domestic work (e.g. Dumontier and Pan Ke Shon, 1999; Gershuny, 2000; Murgatroyd and Neuberger, 1997; Robinson and Godbey, 1997; Roy, 1991). However, they can also be used to estimate the total amount of subsistence work that is taking place relative to the volume of paid work in society and how this is changing over time.

Before considering the magnitude of subsistence work relative to paid work, however, it is important to state that time-budget studies are not the only method available, even if it is the dominant methodology currently employed. There have also been studies that examine the forms of work used to undertake a range of everyday tasks. These studies of 'household work practices' derive in a Western world context from the seminal study conducted by Pahl (1984) on the Isle of Sheppey, where he analysed the sources of labour used to conduct forty-two everyday household tasks.

The advantage of these studies is that they can directly assess the extent to which non-exchanged work, non-monetized exchange, not-for-profit monetized exchange and commodified labour are used to conduct a whole array of everyday tasks (see Wallace, 2002). Indeed, since the original study by Pahl (1984), such studies have been repeated in a range of locality types in the advanced economies. For example, there have been studies of lower- and higher-income neighbourhoods in urban and rural England (Williams and Windebank, 2001a–g, 2003a, 2003b), a deprived council estate in Belfast (Leonard, 1994) and urban and rural localities in Belgium (Kesteloot and Meert, 1999) and the Netherlands (e.g. Renooy, 1990). Although there is some suggestion that, by focusing upon how domestic services are delivered, these studies underemphasize the degree to which commodification has penetrated the advanced economies since they focus upon a sphere in which the permeation of the commodity economy is probably relatively weak (i.e. household services), their value is that they document how in everyday life there persist a plurality of economic practices and act as an important counterweight to the majority of studies of economic life, which solely analyse commodified work and fail even to recognize the existence of work beyond employment.

The Magnitude of Subsistence Work

To measure the amount of subsistence work, the results both of these time-budget studies conducted throughout the advanced economies and of the household work practices method are reported here. Starting with time-budget studies, the overwhelming finding of these surveys is that a large amount of time is still spent engaged in subsistence work in the advanced economies. Take, for example, the results of the UK time-use survey conducted in 2000 in response to the above UN commitment to provide 'satellite' accounts. This identifies that while the average time spent on formal employment and study is 3 hours and 25 minutes, an additional 3 hours and 6 minutes is spent engaged in subsistence work, 4 minutes on formal volunteering and 8 minutes on giving informal help to others (see Ruston, 2003). In total, therefore, non-commodified work occupies 3 hours and 18 minutes of people's work schedules, while formal employment and study occupy only a few minutes more. This means that of total working time, some 49 per cent of time is spent on unpaid work, the bulk of which is spent engaged in subsistence work (i.e. some 94 per cent of the total time spent on unpaid work is spent engaged in subsistence work).

Indeed, this finding is not unique to the UK. The common finding throughout the advanced economies is that so far as work schedules are concerned, subsistence work occupies roughly the same amount of time as paid work (see Table 3.1). The tentacles of commodification, therefore, do not appear to have extended as far as many previously imagined. The sphere of subsistence work, so long considered the residual and diminishing 'other', is the same size as the paid sphere, measured in terms of the volume of time spent on it. Economic life, in consequence, appears to be far from totally commodified. There is a relatively shallow penetration of everyday work schedules by monetized activity.

This finding, however, is not perhaps as unexpected as it might at first appear. When Polanyi (1944) portrayed 'the great transformation' from a non-market to a market society, he went to great lengths to point out that this was merely a shift in the balance of economic activity from the non-market to the market sphere. He

Table 3.1   Subsistence work as a percentage of total work time, 1960–present

Country	1960–73	1974–84	1985–present	Trend
Canada	56.9	55.4	54.2	Monetization
Denmark	41.4	–	43.3	Demonetization
France[a]	52.0	55.5	57.5	Demonetization
Netherlands	–	55.9	57.9	Demonetization
Norway	57.1	55.4	-	Monetization
UK	52.1	49.7	53.9	Demonetization
USA[b]	56.9	57.6	58.4	Demonetization
Finland	–	51.8	54.5	Demonetization
20 countries	43.4	42.7	44.7	Demonetization

Sources: *a* Chadeau and Fouquet, 1981; Roy, 1991; Dumontier and Pan Ke Shon, 1999; *b* Robinson and Godbey, 1997. Other countries derived from Gershuny, 2000: Tables 7.6, 7.12, 7.16.

never meant to imply that it was total. Even if some have since viewed this transformation as rather more complete than Polanyi ever wished to portray (e.g. Thrift, 2000; Harvey, 1989), the above data display that Polanyi was quite correct not to exaggerate the reach of the market.

In many of these time-use surveys, the next step taken is to try to measure the value of the large amount of time spent engaged in subsistence work. To put a monetary value on this time, three techniques have been adopted: opportunity costs, housekeeper wage costs, and occupational wage costs. In each, monetary values from the market sector are used to impute values to unpaid domestic labour or its products (Luxton, 1997). The opportunity–costs model calculates the income the worker would have earned if s/he had been in the paid labour force instead of undertaking subsistence work. The housekeeper wage-costs approach calculates how much a worker in paid employment doing similar work is paid. The occupational wage-costs approach measures the price of household inputs by calculating market equivalents for the costs of raw materials, production and labour and comparing it with market prices for each product and/or service. An extensive literature assessing the various approaches exists, and methods have become increasingly sophisticated (e.g. Ironmonger, 2000, 2002; Luxton, 1997; OECD, 1997, 2002).

However, the issue with all of these valuation methods is that they impute subsistence work with market values. They do not, for example, instead attempt to measure the use value created by market production. One consequence is that although more time is spent on subsistence work than paid work, when evaluated in monetary terms it is often deemed to be worth less. In Britain, the survey conducted by the Office of National Statistics (ONS) in 1995 finds that using the various methods, subsistence work was worth anywhere between 56 and 122 per cent of GDP (Murgatroyd and Neuburger, 1997). Meanwhile, unpaid work in France was worth only one half of GNP in 1975 according to the opportunity-cost and replacement methods (which on the whole use women's wage rates as a basis of calculation) and two-thirds of GNP on the final method, which uses wage rates current for men as well as women (Chadeau and Fouquet, 1981).

Far from being some minor vestige of precapitalism, nevertheless, these time-budget studies clearly display that people living in so-called advanced 'market' economies spend around half of their working time engaged in subsistence work. The extensiveness of this subsistence sphere in contemporary advanced economies is further reinforced when the results of the household work practices approach is analysed. These commonly find that some three-quarters of household tasks are undertaken on a subsistence basis, displaying the relatively shallow penetration of commodification into the domestic sphere. For example, Williams and Windebank (2003a) in their study of higher- and lower-income localities in urban and rural England identify that overall some 71 per cent of the tasks that they analysed were last conducted on a subsistence basis. Similar findings are repeated in the majority of other surveys of household work practices, such as those in the Netherlands (Renooy, 1990) and Belgium (Kesteloot and Meert, 1999).

Reinforcing the results of time-budget studies, therefore, the studies of household work practices again find that subsistence work is far from some marginal leftover in late capitalist society.

It is alive and well and not only occupies nearly half of total working time but is also the most common practice employed by households in order to get everyday tasks completed.

The Changing Size of the Subsistence Sphere

According to the commodification thesis, the story of economic development is one in which the subsistence sphere has declined in size as the commodified realm has taken hold and its reach has extended ever further into every aspect of daily life. It is unfortunately the case that studies of household work practices cannot be used to evaluate this. Until now, no such studies have been conducted on the same population at different moments in time so as to provide a longitudinal picture of the direction of change. Here, therefore, time-budget studies must be relied upon in order to understand the changes taking place.

Examining the time-use surveys conducted throughout the advanced economies, Table 3.1 tells a quite remarkable story. It reveals that over the past forty years, by no means all countries have witnessed a shift of work from the unpaid to the paid sphere. Indeed, in many nations quite the opposite has occurred. In countries such as Denmark, Finland, France, the UK and the USA, subsistence work has occupied an increasing proportion of people's total working time. However, this is not due to an absolute growth in the time spent on such work. The total number of hours spent on subsistence activity has declined. Nevertheless, the time spent in paid work has decreased faster than the time spent in subsistence work (e.g. Gershuny, 2000; Robinson and Godbey, 1997). The result is that work schedules do not reflect an increasing amount of time being spent in the commodified sphere but quite the opposite. Relatively more time is now spent working on a subsistence basis than forty years ago.

One interpretation of these shifts in time use is that over the past four decades a so far unidentified second 'great transformation' has begun to occur in some Western nations whereby there has been a shift towards the subsistence sphere and away from the monetized realm. An alternative interpretation, looking wider than solely these shifting work practices, is that the growing time spent on non-work activities, such as recreation and leisure, coupled with the ongoing commodification of such consumption (see Gershuny, 2000), displays the advent of a market-based consumer culture. However these data are interpreted, the important point here is that working life is not becoming more monetized, as propounded by exponents of the commodification thesis.

These time-budget studies, therefore, reveal how the commodity economy has not only failed to colonize working life fully (cf. Harvey, 1989; Thrift, 2000) but is very far from even approaching such a situation. Indeed, these time-budget data might even be exaggerating the extent to which the advanced economies have become commodified. This is because they overestimate the time spent in paid work and underestimate the time spent in subsistence work. They exaggerate the time spent in paid work because respondents add up the total time that they spend in activity related to the employment place as time spent in paid work. However, much of this time may include meal and coffee breaks, associated travel as well as socializing. Time-budget studies underestimate the time spent in non-commodified work, meanwhile, in three ways. First, they measure only time commitment to concrete activity, excluding the time and effort involved in planning and managing one's own and others' activities. This might occur when watching television, lying in bed or undertaking some leisure pursuit, or indeed when engaged in employment (Haicault, 1984). The result is that this unpaid work might be missed by time-budget studies and classified as sleep or leisure for instance. Second, the emotional and affective activity involved in much subsistence work is either ignored completely, or is portrayed as leisure and socializing (Chabaud-Richter and Fougeyrollas-Schwebel, 1985). Third and finally, they fail to differentiate between profit-motivated and not-for-profit monetary exchange. This is important when it comes to assessing commodification. If that paid work that is non-profit motivated is shifted out of the paid sphere to the decommodified realm, then the extent of commodification will be lower than suggested when all paid work is treated as commodified activity.

However, even though time-budget methods may well be underestimating the volume of non-commodified work relative to commodified activity, the profound finding is that subsistence work still occupies about half of people's total work time and can be valued as equivalent to between 65 and 122 per cent of GDP in the UK, depending on the valuation technique used, and similar estimates are reached about its size elsewhere in the advanced economies. Whether one considers neoliberal advanced economies such as the USA (e.g. Robinson and Godbey, 1997) or more social-democratic 'statist' nations such as France (e.g. Dumontier and Pan Ke Shon, 1999), very similar estimates of the size of subsistence production are arrived at. This is profound because the perception has been that commodified labour has penetrated every nook and cranny of life, while non-commodified work has been seen as a marginal or residual activity. The fact that subsistence work on its own now constitutes around half of the total time that people spend working, and is growing relative to paid work in most advanced economies, means that some serious questions need to be asked about the validity of the commodification thesis.

Conclusions

Contrary to the commodification thesis, which depicts a hegemonic, pervasive, victorious, all-powerful and expansive commodity economy, and thus a weak, primitive, traditional, stagnant, marginal, residual or dwindling non-commodified realm, this chapter has revealed that one constituent component of this non-commodified realm – subsistence (or non-exchanged) work – is not only as large as the realm of paid work measured in terms of the time that the populations of the advanced economies spend engaged in this work, but is also growing. Over the past four decades, a greater proportion of working time has been spent in this non-commodified realm, such that subsistence work is now valued as equivalent in size to the paid sphere. As such, this chapter has cast grave doubts over both the dominant discourse that asserts that we now live in a commodified world and the meta-narrative that a process of commodification is taking place.

Contrary to the nostrums of the commodification thesis, it is certainly not the case that working practices in the advanced economies can be described as commodified, and nor is it the case that the subsistence economy is some leftover of precapitalist production that exists only on the very margins of our commodified world. Indeed, given the size and growth of the subsistence economy, it would not be an exaggeration to say that an anthropologist from another planet parachuting himself/herself into the advanced economies might quickly come to the conclusion that the current mode of economic organization has subsistence practices at its very core, and that if any mode of delivery is on the margins or receding, then it is the commodity economy.

Even if it is perhaps too much to say that the subsistence sphere, rather than the commodity economy, represents the heart of economic practice in the advanced economies, what is certain is that it is not some small realm existing on the peripheries of working life. To view subsistence work in such a manner obfuscates and devalues the tremendous amount of subsistence activity in the advanced economies. As Byrne et al. (1998: 3–4) state, 'to call a society or economy "capitalist" is an act of categorical violence, one that obliterates from view the economic activity that engages more people for more hours of the day over more years of their lives than any other.' Until now, the idea of an ongoing and nearly complete marketization of the advanced economies has been a core narrative of Western thought, or, as Carrier (1997) puts it, central to Western 'cosmology'. The evidence presented in this chapter, however, starts to raise doubts over its centrality and to show the need to reposition the place of the market.

4

Non-monetized Exchange

The commodification thesis, to repeat, posits that goods and services are produced increasingly for monetized exchange by capitalist firms in order to make a profit. As such, in commodified societies, first, goods and services are exchanged; second, these exchanges are monetized; and third and finally, monetized exchanges are engaged in for the purpose of profit. The last chapter revealed that not all goods and services are produced for exchange. It showed instead that a sizeable proportion of time spent working in advanced economies is used for the purpose of undertaking subsistence work and that the share of total working time spent on this non-exchanged work has been growing over the past forty years.

In this chapter, attention turns to a second aspect of the commodification thesis. This is the notion that in commodified societies, whenever goods and services are exchanged, transactions are monetized. Here, the degree to which this is the case is evaluated critically. For adherents to the commodification thesis such as Harvey (1982: 373), 'Monetary relations have penetrated every nook and cranny of the world and into almost every aspect of social, even private life.' Is it the case, therefore, that in commodified societies, non-monetized exchange has ceased to exist?

To answer this question, first, the view of non-monetized exchange in the commodification thesis is outlined, showing how the belief is that in commodified societies such exchanges are perceived either to have depleted to such an extent that they are little more than a marginal leftover or are read as persisting but unrelated to the 'economic' and are instead a form of 'social' or 'welfare' provision; second, the methods of measuring the amount of non-monetized work are reviewed; third, the extent to which non-monetized work persists in advanced economies is evaluated; and finally, consideration is given to whether this work is growing or declining. This will reveal that, although there is a wealth of evidence that such non-monetized work constitutes a sizeable proportion of all exchanges in advanced economies and is growing, commodification theorists seldom associate such activity with work. Instead, it tends to be seen as embedded in the 'social' rather than the 'economic' and as such is not seen as a form of economic practice. Indeed, and analysing the forms of non-monetized exchange that are recognized and whose development is supported by many governments in the advanced economies, this chapter will show that, on the whole, there is a strong focus upon cultivating those forms of non-monetized exchange that are 'socially orientated' rather than 'economically orientated'. That is, many governments in the advanced economies view non-monetized exchanges as synonymous with voluntary or community participation in groups, which tends to be a socially orientated activity, whilst seldom recognizing the array of one-to-one engagements whose ends are more materially orientated to the delivery of goods and services. In the final section of this chapter, in consequence, the current view of non-monetized exchange in the commodification thesis is evaluated critically, showing how non-monetized exchange needs to be not only recognized but also seen as one of the plurality of economic practices in the advanced economies.

Before commencing, however, it is necessary to define what is meant here by non-monetized exchange. Throughout this chapter, non-monetized exchange refers to unpaid work undertaken by household members for members of households other than their own (e.g. Davis Smith, 1998; Field and Hedges, 1984; Lynn and Davis Smith, 1992). This can occur either through organizations, associations and groups, such as when somebody volunteers to coach football to children, or on a one-to-one basis between in-dividuals, such as when a favour is offered to kin living outside the household, friends or neighbours. In much of the literature, this non-monetized exchange that takes place through groups,

associations or organizations is referred to as 'formal' volunteering
or community engagement whilst one-to-one aid is referred to as
'informal' volunteering or community involvement (e.g. Coulthard
et al., 2002; Davis Smith, 1998; Field and Hedges, 1984; Kershaw
et al., 2000; Krishnamurthy et al., 2001; Lynn and Davis Smith,
1992; Prime et al., 2002). This distinction between the formal and
informal forms of non-monetized exchange, as will be more fully
explicated below, is central to any understanding of the nature of
such work in the advanced economies, and a vital step towards an
approach that seeks to use such activity as a means of providing
material aid.

Non-monetized Exchange
in the Commodification Thesis

In the commodification thesis, goods and services are viewed as
increasingly produced for monetized exchange for the purpose of
making a profit. As such, non-monetized exchange is viewed in
one of two ways. On the one hand, it is simply seen as a minor
work practice left over from precapitalist economic formations that
is rapidly depleting and of little importance. On the other hand,
and where it is recognized as existing in some sizeable proportions
in the advanced economies, such non-monetized activity is seen
as a 'non-economic' or welfare activity and separate from the
'economy' proper. In this section, therefore, these different ways
of viewing the non-monetized sphere in the commodification
thesis are outlined.

The first perspective, that non-monetized exchange has all but
disappeared in commodified societies, remains popular despite
all of the evidence, shown below, that people still participate in
voluntary activity, kinship and friendship exchange and community
activities on an unpaid basis. According to adherents to the commodification thesis, the ongoing march of commodification has
already made massive inroads into this non-monetized sphere. As
Rifkin (1990: 30) asserts, 'What we have lived through in the rich
world has been the accelerating passage of non-monetized activity
into the formal economy, its colonization by market transactions.'

Yet is the penetration of the commodity economy so total and complete as this commentator intimates? Those who recognize that this colonization of non-monetized exchange by the market is not as complete as suggested above meanwhile do not go on to question the notion that there is an ongoing incursion of commodification. This is due to the way they conceptualize non-monetized exchange. By recognizing the persistence of non-monetized exchange in the advanced economies but conceptualizing it as a 'non-economic' practice, they ensure that its existence represents no challenge to their view that work is becoming more commodified. The way in which this intellectual conjuring trick is achieved is by drawing an artificial distinction between the 'economic' and 'social/welfare' spheres and then categorizing non-monetized exchange in the latter.

To see how this manoeuvre is performed in practice, let me take the normative view of such activity adopted by the New Labour government in the UK. Since their election in 1997, there has been a renewed emphasis on harnessing non-monetized exchanges, which is often referred to as 'community self-help' or 'volunteering' (e.g. Countryside Agency, 2000; DETR, 1998; DSS, 1998; Home Office, 1999; SEU, 1998, 2000). Cultivating such activity is seen to bolster community spirit (e.g. Gittell and Vidal, 1998; Putnam, 2000), encourage local solutions to be sought to local problems (e.g. Cattell and Evans, 1999; Forrest and Kearns, 1999; Home Office, 1999; Silburn et al., 1999; Wood and Vamplew, 1999), promote local democratic renewal (e.g. SEU, 2000) and deliver support to those in need (e.g. Portes, 1998; Williams and Windebank, 2000a–d). Although some qualify their support for nurturing community involvement with calls for assurances that the development of such engagement will not result in it being used as a substitute for state-provided welfare services (e.g. Eisenschitz, 1997), the widespread consensus is that encouraging such involvement is a worthwhile venture.

However, for New Labour, such activity is not seen to be part of the 'economic' mode of production. Rather, it is seen as a form of welfare provision. New Labour artificially distinguishes between the 'economic' and the 'social' (or 'welfare') and, based upon this, proceeds to advocate the fostering of this 'non-economic' activity as a form of welfare provision. When depicted as an economic activity, however, a very different policy orientation prevails. The widespread belief across the UK government is that the 'informal economy' (as it is called when seen as an economic practice) needs to be eradicated by transforming it into commodified labour (e.g. Grabiner, 1999; Office of the Deputy Prime Minister, 2003).

Measuring Non-monetized Exchange

Even if non-monetized exchange is not recognized as an 'economic' practice or means of livelihood alongside commodified work, there has at least in recent years been recognition that such activity persists in the advanced economies, even if it is seen as a mode of welfare provision rather than an economic practice. Indeed, numerous studies have attempted to measure and value such non-monetized exchange (e.g. Foster, 1997; Gaskin, 1999; Ironmonger, 2002).

Mirroring the study of subsistence work, there is a range of techniques at the disposal of researchers. It is again the case that either the value or the volume of the inputs, processes or outputs can be measured. Some analysts focus upon the output benefits. As Ironmonger (2002) points out, two benefits flow from most non-monetized exchange, namely 'output' benefits and 'process' benefits. The distinction between these two kinds of benefits is illustrated in the example of meal preparation. The positive output benefit is the meal itself, the 'transferable' outputs of the meal preparation that accrue to the people eating the meal. The 'process' benefits of meal preparation, which may be positive or negative, are the pleasure or displeasure the chef obtains from the time spent in meal preparation and cooking. These process benefits are non-transferable to another person. With non-monetized exchange, the transferable benefits are the services provided by others. The non-transferable process benefits are the pleasures obtained by the participants from the time spent giving. So far, as Ironmonger (2002) highlights, methods have not been devised to value process benefits. There is only a subjective method of asking individuals to evaluate the pleasure/displeasure obtained from an activity on a scale of, say, one to five, ranging from very unpleasant to very pleasant. The scaling process does not lead to a monetary valuation of an activity but only allows comparisons between different activities, so that minding grandchildren might be identified as more pleasant than cleaning the toilet.

For this reason, many studies of non-monetized exchange concentrate on the output benefits and several methods have been devised to put a monetary value on these. The Volunteer Investment and Value Audit (VIVA) is one such method that values the resources used to support volunteers (management staff costs, training, recruitment, insurance and administration) in relation to the value of volunteer time. This quantifies the economic investment that organizations make in their volunteers. As many organizers of volunteers would contend, contrary to popular opinion, volunteers are not free of cost. The VIVA states that for every unit of currency invested the return on the volunteers' work is calculated by dividing the value of volunteer time by organizational investments. This method is useful when auditing individual organizations. Gaskin (1999) found that the money spent on volunteers is more than doubled in value and may increase up to eightfold. However, although this method is useful for analysing non-monetized exchange undertaken for organizations, it is not so useful for examining either informal volunteering or one-to-one reciprocal exchanges conducted for and by kin, neighbours and friends.

To estimate the volume and value of all non-monetized exchange, therefore, many have sought to count the specific outputs and to rate these at market prices of comparable goods and services produced and sold in the market. For example, meals provided can be counted and valued at market prices for comparable restaurant and take-away meals. The 'value added' by the unpaid labour is then obtained by deducting the costs of the purchased intermediate inputs of food, energy and other materials and the costs of the household capital used in the meal preparation. The method gives a more accurate reflection of the labour productivity of the technology of the household.

An alternative method involves measuring either the volume or the value of the inputs. This assesses the volume by measuring either participation rates (e.g. Coulthard et al., 2002; Prime et al., 2002) or the time spent engaged in such non-monetized exchange (e.g. Ruston, 2003) and then values this time at a 'comparable' market wage. The wage chosen is the 'opportunity cost' of the time the persons involved in unpaid work could have obtained if they had spent the time in paid work, or the 'specialist wage' costs that would be needed to pay a specialist from the market to do the activity, or the 'generalist' wage that a general housekeeper would be paid to do the unpaid work.

Below, some of the results generated by these diverse techniques are reported so as to provide an indicative measure of the magnitude of non-monetized exchange in the contemporary advanced economies.

Magnitude of Non-monetized Exchange

There are now a multitude of studies of various aspects of non-monetized exchange such as volunteering and unpaid reciprocity (e.g. Berking, 1999; Caplow, 1982; Cheal, 1988; Corrigan, 1989; Dekker and Van den Broek, 1998; Putnam, 2000; Wuthnow, 1992). Many of these studies use a participation-rates approach to show that such work is engaged in extensively in the advanced economies. Wuthnow (1992), for example, points out that in the USA 80 million Americans (45 per cent of the population aged over 18) spend five or more hours each week on voluntary services and charitable activity, which is suggested to add up to well over $150 billion per annum. In the European Union, meanwhile, it has been shown that three out of ten people spend time helping people on a voluntary basis (European Commission, 2001a) and that 6 per cent of citizens provide unpaid informal care to sick or disabled adults and older people in the same household or outside on a daily basis (European Commission, 2000a).

In the UK, similarly, at least four major national surveys have now measured the contemporary extent of participation in such work: the 2000 British Crime Survey (BCS); the 2001 Home Office Citizenship Survey (HOCS); the 2000 General Household Survey (GHS); and the 2001 National Adult Learning Survey (NALS).

For the 2000 BCS, 19,411 people (the main sample), and an additional 3,874 people from minority ethnic communities (the minority ethnic booster sample), were interviewed; of these, 9,659 and 489 respectively answered questions on their voluntary and community activities (Krishnamurthy et al., 2001). The 2001 Home Office Citizenship Survey (HOCS), meanwhile, was the first of what is intended to be a series of surveys to assess social cohesion and civil renewal so as to monitor the Home Office's performance against targets – in the case of the Active Communities agenda, the target of making substantial progress by 2004 towards actively involving 1 million more people in their communities. This survey had a sample of 15,475 people aged 16 and over in England and Wales, a nationally representative sample of 10,015 and a minority ethnic booster of 5,460 (see Prime et al., 2002). The 2000 GHS interviewed 8,221 households, of which 7,857 answered questions on perceptions of their neighbourhood and community involvement (Coulthard et al., 2002). Finally, the 2001 National Adult Learning Survey (NALS) interviewed 6,459 adults in England and Wales on their participation in learning and included questions on the extent to which they were involved in voluntary activities (La Valle and Blake, 2001).

In every case, the survey has collected data on the contours, frequency and/or intensity of participation in both formal and informal non-monetized exchange. All four thus identify the extensiveness of participation. The 2000 BCS survey, for example, finds that while 13 per cent had helped groups or organizations once a month or more, 31 per cent participated once a month or more frequently in helping people directly. The 2001 NALS survey, meanwhile, finds that 17 per cent had engaged in formal volunteering once a month or less, while 24 per cent helped neighbours once a month or more (and 31 per cent and 47 per cent respectively over the last twelve months). Taking the last three years as the benchmark for formal volunteering, meanwhile, the 2002 GHS survey finds that 13 per cent had been involved in local organizations with responsibilities and 8 per cent without responsibilities, while in just the previous six months three-quarters (74 per cent) of respondents had done a favour for a neighbour and a similar proportion (72 per cent) had received a favour from a neighbour.

Measured in terms of participation rates, therefore, such non-monetized work is widespread, although there is a broader culture of engagement in informal than in formal forms of non-monetized exchange. Does this mean, therefore, that the informal kind of engagement constitutes the vast bulk of this sphere? To answer this, data are required on the total number of hours spent by the population in each form of non-monetized work. This information is provided by the 2001 HOCS survey. Akin to the other three surveys, the 2001 HOCS finds that there is wider participation in informal than in formal non-monetized exchange. In the last twelve months, 67 per cent and 39 per cent respectively had engaged in informal and formal non-monetized exchange (and 34 per cent and 26 per cent respectively at least once a month).

Of the 16.5 million people in England and Wales that the 2001 HOCS suggests volunteered formally in the prior twelve months, the mean time spent was found to be 110.5 hours. Extrapolating from this, it can be estimated here that this means that some 1.82 billion hours of formal non-monetized exchange had occurred in the previous twelve months. Of the 28.3 million in England and Wales who had engaged in one-to-one unpaid exchange in the last twelve months, meanwhile, the average number of hours was 66.4 hours. If this is again translated into the total number of hours, then it can be estimated here that some 1.88 billion hours of such exchange were conducted. In total the number of hours spent on each type of unpaid exchange is thus about the same.

Such data on participation rates thus provide a statistical clue as to the proportion of the population engaged in various types of non-monetized exchange. To measure the proportion of exchanges that are monetized, a recent study examined the realm of everyday household services in UK urban areas (Williams and Windebank, 2003a). It found that when external sources of labour were used to undertake these services, 6.8 per cent of such exchanges were not monetized in affluent suburbs, and 15.6 per cent in lower-income neighbourhoods.

Although time-use surveys have been used mostly to assess the amount of subsistence work in the advanced economies, recent years have seen them used also to measure the amount of non-monetized exchange. Examining the volume of the inputs, what is so interesting about these studies is that they identify how this is a small sphere relative to subsistence work, at least when measured in terms of the amount of time spent working in such activity. In the UK, the 2000 Time Use Survey identifies that the UK population spends an average of 12 minutes per day helping others on an unpaid basis compared with 3 hours and 6 minutes on subsistence work (Ruston, 2003). Of the 12 minutes, moreover, some 4 minutes were spent working on an unpaid basis for groups and 8 minutes in informal one-to-one exchanges, suggesting that, at least in terms of the volume of inputs, informal non-monetized work constitutes some two-thirds of this non-monetized sphere.

In consequence, these studies of participation rates in non-monetized exchange, their prevalence in household work practices, and the time spent on such activity portray how such work persists in the advanced economies. For all of the talk of the penetration of monetary relations into everyday life, unpaid exchanges still prevail. What such studies do not provide, however, is a measure of the value of these non-monetized exchanges, or an indication of the overall size or value of unpaid exchange relative to the commodified sphere.

A way forward towards this end is thus to measure the volume of the inputs into unpaid exchange relative to the volume of the inputs into commodified work. Taking the above results from the UK as an example, it has been found that some 3.7 billion hours of volunteering occurred in the previous twelve months. This is the equivalent in hours to the total work of just over 2 million people employed on a full-time basis (i.e. at 35 hours per week). Or, to put it another way, for every 14 hours worked in formal employment in the UK (assuming 27 million people working an average of 35 hours), approximately one hour is spent working on a non-monetized basis. Given that non-monetized exchange constitutes some 7 per cent of the total time that people spend engaged in formal employment in the UK, such work is thus far from some marginal leftover, especially, as will be shown in the next chapter, given that not all paid exchange is commodified work.

Another way of measuring non-monetized exchange relative to the commodity economy is to measure the value of the outputs. To provide a statistical clue of their relative sizes on this measure, evidence from South Australia can be used (see Ironmonger, 2002). This finds that in 1997, unpaid exchange was worth some A\$24–31 billion per annum, depending on the valuation method used. South Australian volunteers are thus estimated to have donated the equivalent of an additional 11.5 per cent of gross state product (GSP) in 2000 to other households, both directly and through organizations and groups. These donations are additional to actual donations of money made directly to other households or through charitable organizations. Alternatively, measuring total volunteer time in relation to the total wages earned by South Australian employees, such activity represents an additional 21.7 per cent of the total value of the wages paid to employees in employment in South Australia in 2000.

Breaking this down into formal and informal unpaid exchange, this study reveals once again that informal is larger than formal non-monetized exchange. In 2000, for instance, Ironmonger (2002) finds, informal volunteering represented some 60 per cent of the total value of the voluntary sector in South Australia, which is roughly equivalent to the UK finding that 66 per cent of the total time spent volunteering is spent in informal volunteering (Ruston, 2003).

In sum, whatever technique is used to measure the amount of non-monetized exchange, the finding is that this non-commodified work is far from being some minor remnant in advanced capitalist societies. It is a significant proportion of the total work that is taking place. The key issue so far as the issue of commodification is concerned, however, is whether this economic practice is growing or diminishing.

Changing Size of the Non-monetized Realm

Although the commodification thesis purports that this economic practice is diminishing, all of the evidence tends to point in the opposite direction. Take, for example, the study of South Australia conducted by Ironmonger (2002). He finds that between 1992 and 2000, the hours per week spent by the average adult on volunteering activity rose from 2.56 to 3.86 hours, composed of a 35

Table 4.1 Hours per week per adult spent engaged in formal and informal volunteering (averaged over all adult population aged 18+), South Australia, 1992–2000

Volunteering	1992	1995	1997	2000	% change 1992–97	% change 1995–2000
Organized	0.62	0.91	1.11	1.40	80	54
Unorganized	1.44	1.58	1.68	2.82	17	15
Travel	0.51	0.55	0.58	0.63	15	14
Total	2.56	3.05	3.37	3.86	32	27

Source: Ironmonger, 2002: Table 2.

per cent increase in the first five-year period (1992–97) and a 30 per cent increase in the second five-year envelope of time (1995–2000). Breaking this down into informal and formal volunteering, moreover, he finds that the growth of formal volunteering has been much faster than the growth of informal volunteering, although informal volunteering still comprises the majority of volunteering in South Australia (see Table 4.1).

In most studies of the changing magnitude of volunteering, the next step in the analysis is to put a market value on such work so as to analyse how its importance is changing over time. Table 4.2 reveals that as a proportion of GSP, non-monetized work is growing. South Australian volunteers donated an additional 7.8 per cent of GSP in 1992 but an extra 11.5 per cent of GSP in 2000 to other households, both directly and through organizations and groups. These donations are additional to actual donations of money made directly to other households or through charitable organizations. Put another way, total volunteer time was equivalent to an additional 14.1 per cent of the total value of the wages paid to employees in employment in South Australian in 1992 and 21.7 per cent in 2000.

Breaking this down according to the type of volunteering, these data reveal, moreover, that one-to-one volunteering remains more valuable than organized volunteering, even if organized

Table 4.2   Total value of volunteer work in South Australia, 1992–2000

Volunteering	1992	1995	1997	2000	% change 1992–97	% change 1995–2000
Organized ($m)	566	948	1,272	1,810	124	91
Unorganised ($m)	1,325	1,650	1,931	2,356	46	43
Travel ($m)	465	575	670	814	44	42
Total value ($m)	2,357	3,174	3,873	4,980	64	57
GSP ($b)	30.3	34.6	37.9	43.3	25	25
Compensation of employees ($b)	14.8	16.9	18.4	20.4	24	20

Source: Ironmonger, 2002: Table 5.

volunteering is growing at a quicker pace. Indeed, by 2000, formal volunteering in South Australia was worth A$1,180 million (40 per cent of the total value of volunteering).

In sum, and contrary to the tenets of the commodification thesis, all of the evidence on non-monetized exchange suggests that this sphere of economic practice is growing in size relative to the commodified realm throughout the advanced economies. As such, it is difficult to accept the view that the commodity economy is penetrating deeper and wider.

Conclusions

At the outset of this chapter, two views of non-monetized exchange in the commodification thesis were outlined. First, there is the view that in commodified societies, non-monetized exchange has all but disappeared; second, there is the view that although non-monetized exchange might persist, it is not viewed as a form of economic practice but rather as an activity that belongs in the sphere of welfare.

Starting with the first view, this chapter has presented an array of surveys that reveal how such activity persists in the advanced economies and is growing in size relative to the commodified sphere. Today, such non-monetized exchange is conducted by a large proportion of the population; it is equal to somewhere around 10–12 per cent of GDP and is growing over time. Contrary to the nostrums of the commodification thesis, therefore, this chapter has revealed that non-monetized exchange is not some insignificant backwater that is dwindling in magnitude as commodification takes hold. When these data are combined with the evidence in the last chapter that subsistence work is also large and growing relative to commodified work, the above findings on non-monetized exchange thus add yet further weight to the call for questions to be raised about the validity of the commodification thesis. Taken together, subsistence work and non-monetized exchange show that non-commodified work is growing rather than depleting relative to the commodity economy in Western nations.

The second view of non-monetized exchange in the commodification thesis, which recognizes how it is growing but does not see this expansion as a challenge to the thesis because such activity is read as a form of welfare provision, is a classic display of how some adherents to the thesis have defined non-commodified work as non-economic practice in order to uphold their view. As Bourdieu (2001) has pointed out, by reducing the universe of exchanges to monetized exchange, which is objectively and subjectively oriented towards the maximization of profit, this view implicitly defines other forms of exchange as non-economic. Yet, as will be seen in Part II, such non-monetized exchange is far from being non-economic. A growing number of studies are revealing how lower-income populations, in particular, use non-monetized exchange, especially of the one-to-one variety, explicitly as an economic practice to improve their material standard of living in the face of their exclusion from access to commodified modes of provision. To denote such non-monetized exchange as non-economic, therefore, is not only a misnomer but also a view of such exchange that reflects the cultures of engagement in such exchange that prevail in affluent rather than poorer populations. This will be returned to in Chapters 6 and 7.

For the moment, it is simply necessary to note that non-monetized exchange is both significant in size and growing in the advanced economies. Combining this with the findings of the last chapter on subsistence work, there is thus strong and mounting evidence that the meta-narrative of a commodifying world appears to be far from the reality. In the next chapter, this finding will be further reinforced when the third and final type of non-commodified work is considered – namely not-for-profit monetized exchange – in order to see if this is growing or declining. It has often been assumed that monetized transactions are conducted for the purpose of what Polanyi (1944) calls 'economic gain'. In the next chapter, then, this third and final assumption of the commodification thesis is put under the spotlight.

5

Not-for-Profit Monetized Exchange

It has been shown in the last two chapters that both non-exchanged work and non-monetized exchange comprise a sizeable proportion of people's work schedules in the advanced economies and that such unpaid work appears to be growing over time relative to paid work. As such, the commodification thesis that views goods and services as increasingly produced for monetized exchange by capitalist firms for the purpose of profit has been brought into question. In this chapter, attention turns to the monetized sphere itself. The assumption in the commodification thesis is that as money has penetrated more areas of life, this has marched hand in hand with the profit motive. Here, this assumption is evaluated critically. Is the monetized sphere everywhere and always composed of transactions conducted for the purpose of economic gain? Or are there realms in which monetary exchanges are conducted for reasons other than profit? If so, are these not-for-profit monetary transactions growing or declining?

To answer these questions and thus evaluate critically the view of monetary exchange in the commodification thesis, this chapter commences by outlining how the monetized sphere is viewed in this thesis. In most analyses of how economies are organized, to repeat, three different modes of delivering goods and services are depicted, namely the market, the state and the community. The assertion in the commodification thesis is that the market is becoming the dominant mode of producing and delivering goods and services and that the other modes are in demise. To evaluate critically whether this is indeed the case, the changing balance between these three sectors is here analysed.

To do this, the changing relationship between the state and the market will first be analysed. This will reveal that although the state is in demise as a direct provider of goods and services, this should not lead one to assume either the demise of the state per se or that commodified modes of delivery are now the principal means of supplying goods and services. As will be shown, although there has been a rolling back of the state as a direct provider of goods and services, it remains a powerful constituent component of late capitalism in its regulatory role and by no means solely contracts out such provision to profit-making capitalist firms. To see this, the chapter then turns its attention to the not-for-profit sector, often referred to as the 'voluntary' sector, 'third sector' or 'social economy', and how this large sphere that is by definition not imbued with the profit motive is capturing a sizeable and growing proportion of all monetary transactions in the advanced economies.

To reinforce further the key point that monetary exchange in the advanced economies is not always profit-motivated, this chapter then turns away from identifying spheres where transactions tend to be not-for-profit orientated to blurring the boundaries between the profit and not-for-profit sectors. Examining two spheres of monetized exchange that are often assumed to epitomize the shift towards profit-oriented monetized exchange in late capitalism, namely 'cash-in-hand' work and formal capitalist firms themselves, it will be shown here that monetized exchange in these spheres is by no means always motivated by profit. In so doing, the intention is to show that the conventional view that economies can be divided into three spheres – the state, market and community – and that it is the market that is coming to dominate life, which is purely motivated by profit, needs to be treated with great caution. This is not only because the three spheres are increasingly interpenetrating each other in complex ways but also because it is by no means certain that monetary exchanges in the market sphere are always, or solely, motivated purely by profit. The overwhelming thrust of this chapter is thus to show how the assumption that the commodified sphere is rising to dominance, and with it the pursuit of profit, is by no means as clear cut as supposed by adherents to the commodification thesis.

Monetized Exchange in the Commodification Thesis

The commodification thesis asserts that over time there has been a shift from unpaid to paid work and that this monetary work is essentially profit-motivated. The last two chapters have already shown how this shift from the unpaid to the paid sphere is by no means certain. This chapter turns its attention to paid work itself and whether this is always profit-motivated. In order to do this, it is first necessary to understand both how analysts look at monetized exchange in the commodification thesis and where they look in order for them to reach their conclusion about the profit-motivated nature of paid work.

On the issue of how analysts look at the paid sphere, it needs to be stated at the outset that the notion that the only type of monetary exchange is that which is profit-motivated runs deep across nearly all economic discourses ranging from neo-classical to Marxist thought. As Jessop (2002) points out, reading monetized exchange as always profit-motivated serves the interests of both neoliberals, whose belief is that this must be met with open arms, and radical theorists, who use this as a call to arms to resist its further encroachment. The result is the perpetuation of a crude view in much economistic discourse of monetized exchange.

Such a narrow view of monetized exchange in economistic discourse is reinforced by a formalist anthropological tradition that sees exchange mechanisms in advanced economies as less 'embedded' than those in pre-industrial societies. In this perspective, the idea is that there has been a separation of the 'economy' from 'culture', resulting in exchanges in Western societies being 'thinner', less loaded with social meaning, and less symbolic than traditional exchanges (see Mauss, 1966). As Crewe and Gregson (1998: 41) incisively point out, however, 'the major defect of such market-based models of exchange is simply that they do not convey the richness and messiness of the exchange experience' in Western economies.

In recent years, in consequence, this profit-motivated view of monetized exchange has started to be contested by a range of commentators. Drawing upon the earlier work of Polanyi (1944), the formalist anthropology approach that assumed price-fixing and profit-motivated markets to be the universal economic mechanism in Western economies has been challenged from a 'substantivist' anthropological position which argues that economic relations are always socially embedded (see Crang, 1996, 1997; Crewe and Gregson, 1998; Davies, 1992; Lee, 2000a; Zelizer, 1994). The result has been the emergence of a stream of literature that has sought to unpack the messy and complex nature of monetary exchange in late capitalist societies by showing the alternative social relations, motives and pricing mechanisms that prevail so as to contest the view that it is always market-like and profit-motivated (e.g. Crang, 1996; Crewe and Gregson, 1998; Lee, 1996, 1997, 2000a, 2000b).

It is not only how one looks at monetary exchanges, however, that influences whether one finds the profit motive. It also depends on where one looks. Until now, the lens of inquiry in the social sciences has been firmly fixed on formal commodified economic spaces when studying 'the economic'. The result is that those studying the commodity economy and seeking the existence of the profit motive have found, or at least believe that they found, what they sought. Recently, nevertheless, the net has started to be cast wider by those questioning conventional economic discourse and the formalist anthropological approach and their related notion of the hegemony of the profit motive in monetary exchange.

The outcome has been a raft of studies investigating what Leyshon et al. (2003) term 'alternative economic spaces' such as the garage sale (Soiffer and Herrmann, 1987), car boot sales (Crewe and Gregson, 1998), nearly new sales and classified advertisements (Clarke, 1998, 2000), second-hand and informal retail channels (Williams and Paddock, 2003), inflation-free local currency experiments such as Local Exchange and Trading Schemes (Lee, 1996; North, 1996, 1999; Williams, 1996a–f; Williams et al., 2001a, 2001b), sweat-equity money projects such as time dollars (e.g. Boyle, 1999; Cahn, 2000; Seyfang and Smith, 2002), gift-giving (Carrier, 1990; Thrift and Olds, 1996) and small horticultural nurseries (Lee, 2000b) to uncover how monetary exchanges are not always and necessarily imbued with the profit motive. For example, Crewe and Gregson (1998), in their study of the car boot sale, highlight how conventions of the marketplace are suspended here and replaced by forms of sourcing, commodity circulation, transaction codes, pricing mechanisms and value quite different from those that typify more profit-motivated market-orientated exchange. Similarly, a burgeoning literature on local currencies has revealed how it is wholly feasible for monetary exchanges to take place under alternative social relations and for motives other than profit (e.g. Cahn, 2000; Offe and Heinze, 1992; Lee, 1996; North, 1999; Williams et al., 2001).

The problem with these studies of alternative economic spaces, of course, is that by studying only small spaces that are viewed as existing on the 'margins' of the mainstream economy they fail to provide any significant challenge to those who view monetary transactions as imbued with the profit motive. Such spaces where the profit motive is absent are simply explained away as minor, trivial or marginal practices existing outside the mainstream commodity economy, and labelled 'peripheral' or even 'superfluous' spaces (see Martin and Sunley, 2001). If the view that there is an inextricable relationship between monetary transactions and the profit motive is to be more forcefully challenged, therefore, it will be necessary to analyse some of the larger spaces of paid work. This is the intention in this chapter. In order to show that monetary exchange is not always imbued with the profit motive, four spheres of activity are analysed here: the public sector, the not-for-profit sector, cash-in-hand work, and mainstream private-sector enterprises.

The State

If goods and services were being increasingly delivered by the state, which by definition is not orientated towards profit, then one would be able to conclude that monetized exchange is by no means becoming increasingly dominated by the profit motive. However, this is not the case. Trends such as privatization and quasi-privatization of the public sphere, the contracting out of goods and services previously provided by the state directly, and various public–private finance initiatives (e.g. Clark and Root, 1999; Kerr, 1998; Tickell, 2001) all suggest that there is a transfer of the mode of delivery of goods and services from the state to the market. As such, these trends intimate that the relationship between monetized exchange and the profit motive is becoming stronger.

However, there are two important points to be made before racing to the seemingly inevitable conclusion that the transfer of production and delivery from the state to the market means that monetary transactions have become more profit-motivated. The first crucial issue, one that is dealt with later in this chapter, is that just because the state is now providing fewer goods and services on a direct basis, this does not necessarily mean that profit-motivated exchange is becoming more dominant. As will be seen later, not all of these goods and services are being provided by the private sector. Many are being transferred to not-for-profit organizations (e.g. Amin et al., 2002a; Birchall, 2001; Lutz, 1999) and this suggests a weaker relationship between the profit motive and monetized exchange. And even when they are provided by the private sector, it is by no means certain that profit is the sole motive in attendance in such businesses. The second issue, and the one dealt with here, is the idea that the transfer of responsibility for directly delivering goods and services from the state to the market means that the state is in decline. As will now be shown, even if the state as a direct provider of goods and services is reducing in importance, this does not mean that the role of the state is being diminished.

As many commentators have shown, the state remains a vital component in the constitution of capitalism (e.g. Jessop, 2002; O'Neill, 1997; Painter, 2003). State power permeates almost all aspects of economic practice; although direct state provision may be in decline, economic practices are affected by the state in deep-seated and enduring ways (Painter, 2003). Contrary to the hyperbole of right-wing politicians in the 1980s and 1990s, the state has not been 'rolled back', if by that is meant that more economic relations are beyond the scope of state power. Indeed, the exercise of state power appears to have become more intense over time, not less. To grasp this, one has only to consider how the state in Western economies seems to implement policies on an ever-widening range of economic issues. New legislation and regulations are added much more quickly than old ones are repealed. Each year, new objects of economic life become subject to surveillance, regulation, intervention and manipulation. The state, market and civil society, therefore, cannot be treated as wholly independent entities. Neither the market, nor civil society, is wholly independent of the state. Indeed, many of the goods and services delivered by both of these spheres are either contracted out from the state sphere or heavily regulated and even controlled by the state. As O'Neill (1997: 291) thus asserts, there is a need to reject

> the politically charged discourse that markets are capable of a separate, private existence beyond the actions of the state's apparatus. Rather, a qualitative view of the state is preferred. In this view, the state is seen to play an indispensable role in the creation, governance and conduct of markets, including at the international scale. Consequently, arguments about the extent of state intervention are seen as being feeble. Because the state is always involved in the operation of markets, the salient debate should be about the nature, purpose and consequences, of the form of state action, rather than about the magnitude of intervention.

Drawing upon the work of scholars such as Polanyi (1944) and Block (1994), O'Neill (1997: 294) thus sets out four tenets concerning the role of the state:

> First, economy is necessarily a combination of three events: markets, state action and state regulation. A corollary of this constitution is that there is an infinite number of ways in which an economy can be organized. Second, although economic efficiency is dependent on markets, markets are state-constrained and state-regulated and thereby incapable of operating in a laissez-faire environment. Third, neither capital nor the state is capable of achieving its goals simultaneously nor independently. Finally, it should be recognized that any coherence that exists about the idea of economy derives essentially from our cultural beliefs, which (in Anglo cultures at least) have led to constructions of economy being overlain with the dichotomy of planned versus market, which, in turn, has had the effect of denying the existence of multiple forms of economy.

These four tenets are important for they show that even if the production and delivery of goods and services have been transferred away from the state to the market, this does not mean either that the state is in demise or that there is now a commodified sphere beyond the reach of the state. More importantly here, the demise of the state as a direct provider of goods and services does not spell the increasing dominance of the profit motive. To argue this is to assume that goods and services provided by the state have been transferred to profit-motivated capitalist firms. This is patently not the case. Many, as will now be shown, are being transferred to either the unpaid sphere (already discussed) or to not-for-profit organizations (e.g. Amin et al., 2002a; Birchall, 2001; Lutz, 1999), and the advent of the latter mode of delivery suggests a weaker (rather than stronger) relationship between the profit motive and monetized exchange.

The Not-for-Profit Sector

The not-for-profit sector is defined here as those organizations that are private (i.e. not part of the apparatus of government), not profit distributing (i.e. do not distribute profits to their managers or owners), self-governing (i.e. fundamentally in control of their own affairs) and voluntary in that membership in them is not legally required and they attract some level of voluntary contribution of time or money (Salamon and Anheier, 1999; Salamon et al., 1999). Using this common definition of the not-for-profit sector, a major international piece of research, the Johns Hopkins Comparative Nonprofit Sector Project, has provided a baseline assessment of its size and nature in twenty-six countries (Austria, Belgium, Finland, France, Germany, Ireland, Italy, the Netherlands, Norway, Spain, Sweden and the UK in Western Europe; the Czech Republic, Hungary, Poland, Romania and Slovakia in central Europe; Argentina, Brazil, Colombia, Mexico and Peru in Latin America; and Australia, Israel, Japan and the United States).

The findings of this cross-national project provide strong evidence that this sector is not some insignificant backwater but is in fact a major 'third prong' in the mixed economies that constitute the Western nations. In the twenty-six countries studied in the first wave of the project, the transactions of non-profit organizations represented 4.6 per cent of GDP on average across these nations, and there were some 31 million full-time equivalent workers (or 6.8 per cent of the non-agricultural workforce), including 19.7 million full-time equivalent paid workers and 11.3 million full-time equivalent volunteer workers. Indeed, if the non-profit sector in the twenty-six nations surveyed were to be a country, its GDP of US$1.2 trillion would make it the sixth largest economy in the world, ahead of the UK, Brazil, Russia, Canada and Spain. The not-for-profit sector, in consequence, is a large sphere of activity that cannot be dismissed as being of only limited or marginal importance, and nor can it be assumed that the transfer of responsibility for delivering goods and services away from the state has resulted in a universal shift to the market rather than the not-for-profit sector.

Indeed, and as the Johns Hopkins Comparative Nonprofit Sector Project reveals, this sector is growing relative to the wider formal economy over time. Examining the changes in non-profit-sector full-time equivalent (FTE) employment in a number of countries relative to overall employment, Table 5.1 reveals that in all eight nations analysed (with the exception of Israel), the pace of job growth in the not-for-profit sector has outstripped total job growth. In the USA, for example, although there was an overall increase in FTE employment of 8 per cent between 1990 and 1995, the growth in FTE employment in the not-for-profit sector was 20 per cent. In the four EU nations considered (France, Germany, the UK and the Netherlands), meanwhile, the 24 per cent growth in overall FTE employment in the not-for-profit sector far outstripped the 3 per cent growth in the economy as a whole, thus accounting for 40 per cent of total employment growth (3.8 million new FTE jobs). In the three other developed countries for which there were employment data (Israel, Japan and the USA), the increase averaged 21 per cent, though this accounted for a somewhat smaller 11 per cent of the 16 million new FTE jobs.

The only conclusion that can be reached is that the not-for-profit sector is a large and growing sphere of activity. Indeed, the inference is that the relationship between monetized exchange and the profit motive might well be growing weaker rather than stronger.

Table 5.1   Changes in non-profit-sector FTE employment, by
country, 1990–95

Country	Non-profit sector 1990–95 change		Total economy[a] 1990–95 change	
	Net	as % of 1990 level	Net	as % of 1990 level
France	157,202	20	−329,000	−2
Germany	422,906	42	2,163,875	8
Hungary	12,200	37	−25,641	−1
Israel	19,182	15	395,237	33
Japan	450,652	27	7,525,680	14
Netherlands	41,623	7	240,000	5
UK[b]	119,068	28	−202,058	−1
USA	1,360,893	20	8,080,793	8
EU total/average 4 countries	740,800	24	1,872,817	3
Other total/average 4 countries	1,842,927	25	15,976,069	14
Total/average	2,583,727	24	17,848,886	8

a Total non-agricultural employment.   *b* Excluding sport and recreation, unions and parts
of education.

Source: Johns Hopkins Comparative Nonprofit Sector Project (www.jhu.edu/~cnp/compdata.
html).

It is also the case, as Table 5.2 reveals, that those countries
where a relatively greater proportion of total working time is spent
engaged in unpaid work are also the countries with a relatively
greater proportion of the workforce employed in not-for-profit
organizations. If this is more widely applicable, then it suggests that
the cross-national variations in the degree to which profit-motivated
monetized exchange has penetrated are somewhat greater than
indicated earlier by the time-budget studies. The two countries in
which the penetration of paid work is shallowest (the USA and
the Netherlands) are also the countries with the largest non-profit
sector. The intimation is that the cross-national variations in the

Table 5.2 Relationship between the prevalence of unpaid work and the non-profit sector: a cross-national comparison

Country	Unpaid work as % of total working time	Non-profit sector as % of total employment
USA	58.4	18.7
Netherlands	57.9	11.9
France	57.5	9.6
Finland	54.5	6.3
UK	53.9	10.6

Sources: Gershuny, 2001; Johns Hopkins Comparative Nonprofit Sector Project (www.jhu. edu/~cnp/compdata.html).

penetration of commodification are more marked and polarized than suggested by the time-budget studies discussed in the last chapter.

However, it is not only the size and growth of the not-for-profit sector that display how the monetized sphere is not always imbued with the motive of profit. As will now be shown, even when economic spaces of monetized exchange are investigated, usually assumed to be heavily imbued with the profit motive, the tenuous nature of this relationship also unfolds. To show this, the motives underpinning monetary transactions in the realm of cash-in-hand work followed by private-sector enterprise are unpacked in order to display that even in those spheres of monetized exchange often viewed as epitomizing profit-motivated behaviour, there seem to be grave doubts that monetary transactions are conducted for purely profit-motivated reasons.

Monetized Exchange in the 'Cash-in-Hand' Economy

Cash-in-hand work, or what is variously called 'informal employment', the 'underground sector', the 'hidden economy' or 'paid informal work', involves the paid production and sale of goods and services that are unregistered by, or hidden from, the state for tax, social security and/or labour law purposes but that are legal in all other respects (European Commission, 1998; Feige, 1990; Portes, 1994; Thomas, 1992; Williams and Windebank, 1998). This is a large sphere of economic activity that is widely accepted to have grown rapidly throughout the advanced economies over the past few decades. The European Commission (1998), for example, estimate that its overall size has expanded from 5 per cent of GDP in the 1970s in the European Union to between 7 and 16 per cent of GDP during the 1990s.

Until now, this type of work has mostly been viewed in market-oriented profit-motivated terms (e.g. Castells and Portes, 1989; Leonard, 1998a, 1998b; Sassen, 1989, 1997). Few have seen cash-in-hand work as anything other than conducted under market-like relations akin to employment for the purpose of profit. Conventionally, for example, the view in the marginality thesis has been that cash-in-hand work is a low-paid form of peripheral employment conducted by marginalized areas and groups for unadulterated economic reasons (e.g. Blair and Endres, 1994; Button, 1984; Castells and Portes, 1989; Elkin and McLaren, 1991; Gutmann, 1978; Matthews, 1983; Rosanvallon, 1980). Indeed, most contemporary analyses remain grounded in such beliefs (e.g. Kesteloot and Meert, 1999; Portes, 1994).

However, a recent study by Williams and Windebank (2001a) of 400 households in higher- and lower-income UK urban neighbourhoods reveals that although the relationship between cash-in-hand work and the profit motive is strong in higher-income neighbourhoods, such work is often conducted for rationales beyond the profit motive in lower-income areas. In only half (50.9 per cent) of the cases where cash-in-hand work was conducted in lower-income neighbourhoods did suppliers do it principally for the money, whilst in affluent suburbs this figure was 90 per cent. Instead, rationales of sociability and redistribution prevailed among both suppliers and purchasers. Therefore, although the profit motive has deeply penetrated monetary relations in affluent suburbs, it has not in lower-income areas. This finding displays the dangers of commentators constructing generalizations from narrow experiential knowledge bases. The theory that profit-motivated monetary relations are penetrating every nook and cranny of social life (e.g. Harvey,

1989; Sayer, 1997), although applicable in the limited context of some affluent populations, is far from the reality elsewhere.

One of the major reasons for this absence of a profit motive in suppliers' and consumers' rationales for cash-in-hand work is because such work is conducted by and for kin, friends and neighbours. As such, it is perhaps of little surprise that the pricing mechanism used to determine value is not wholly grounded in the motive of economic gain. Instead, a fluidity of prices and pricing arrangements is identified depending on the socio-economic context and social relationship between the seller and purchaser. These norms concerning price arrangements are complex and often implicit, as Zelizer (1994) has previously found when discussing how money is earmarked for different purposes.

A key determinant of the price, for instance, is the closeness of the social relations, such as whether the seller and/or buyer are close kin or a more distant friend and/or neighbour. Prices diverge from market norms to a much greater degree when close social relations such as kin are involved than when more distant social relations are the transacting partners, such as a friend of a friend. As social relations between the supplier and customer become more distant in a social sense, therefore, the more there is convergence to market norms, as Leonard (1994) has previously shown on a West Belfast council estate. Another key determinant of price is the socio-economic context, especially the status of the recipient of the cash-in-hand work relative to the seller, and vice versa. This socio-economic context, moreover, combines with the social relationship aspect to produce complex pricing structures. For instance, if the recipient is unemployed and the seller an employed craft person, as well as kin, then the price tends to diverge markedly from the market norm. The more distant the social relations, moreover, the greater is the likelihood of convergence to the market norm.

In sum, the conventional market price is the point of reference, or measuring rod, for quantifying what will be charged. It is the fixed point used to provide the basis for the more fluid and transient modes of determining value. In contrast to Offer's (1997: 453) reading of reciprocity, therefore, this study does not find any evidence that in 'the long term … the exchange value will approximate not to the use value (expressed by the demand curve) but to the market value'. Rather, different pricing mechanisms are identified embedded in socio-economic norms, relations and contexts that continuously override any convergence towards market norms.

As such, despite the popular view that cash-in-hand work is conducted for unadulterated economic reasons, those few studies undertaken of the motives of suppliers and customers reveal that such a market-orientated reading is inappropriate, at least in UK lower-income urban neighbourhoods (Williams and Windebank, 2001a, 2001c, 2001e, 2001f). In these neighbourhoods it appears that monetary relations are being penetrated by alternative logics that lie outside the profit motive and are humanizing the money system by harnessing it to pursue redistribution and sociality at the micro-level. As such, it highlights the demonstrable construction and practice of social relations of production and consumption based on monetary exchange beyond the profit motive.

Therefore one cannot read off from any apparent deepening of the realms of monetary exchange that there is an encroachment of market relations. Money, it seems, is not the disembedding force that is sometimes propounded (e.g. Sayer, 1997). Instead, recent studies of cash-in-hand work reveal that monetary relations can transcend the profit motive and even an encroachment of non-market rationales into monetary relations. This raises the fascinating notion that participants in some contexts sidestep the norms of market relations when engaging in monetary exchanges in a distinctive and possibly suggestive world of production and consumption. They conduct monetary exchanges where price-driven market relations are largely absent and, in so doing, display that the relationship between monetary exchange and market relations is not hermetically sealed. The consequence is that new possibilities for transforming social relations of exchange are being opened up within the existing money system.

The inference, therefore, is that the 'market' economy in general, and monetary relations in particular, might not be as 'pure' in profit-motive terms as sometimes supposed by those who have read Polanyi's (1944) 'great transformation' through the lens of political economy (e.g. Harvey, 1982). This study of cash-in-hand work in UK lower-income urban neighbourhoods shows that the maps of the 'modern' economy are far more complex. At least in these urban areas of the UK, there exists a large alternative economic space within contemporary capitalism constituting some 7–16 per cent of GDP (European Commission, 1998) where monetary exchange is sometimes embedded in alternative social relations, motivations and pricing mechanisms. Indeed, this notion that monetary transactions are not so pure in profit-motivated terms as previously thought is further reinforced when the realm of monetary transactions in private-sector businesses is put under the spotlight.

Monetized Exchange in the Private Sector

It might be assumed that whenever the private sector partakes in monetary transactions, the motive of profit is always to the fore. In a bid to deconstruct this belief so as to deprive capitalism of its solid coherent identity, I here report numerous studies which have recently shown that private-sector enterprises are not all, and always, driven by a common imperative of profit.

The work of Schoenberger (1997), for example, on the social embeddedness of firms traces the effects of culture, tradition and affinity upon enterprise behaviour, and shows the ways in which personal values and relationships within management undermine many of the assumed corporate goals of efficiency and profit maximization. O'Neill and Gibson-Graham (1999), similarly, explore the role of competing discourses of management in shaping the fluid entity that is unproblematically represented as 'the capitalist firm'. Examining an Australian minerals and steel multinational, they produce a disruptive reading that emphasizes the decentred and disorganized actions taken in response to multiple logics circulating within and without the corporation. Their analysis represents the enterprise as an unpredictable and potentially open site, rather than as a set of practices unified by a predictable logic of profit maximization or capital accumulation. No longer tethered to a preordained economic logic, the enterprise becomes recognisable as an ordinary social institution; one that often fails to enact its will or realize its goals, or even fails to come to a coherent conception of what these might be.

Lee (2000b), in a study of the horticultural firms specializing in the production and sale of ornamental hardy nursery stock in the southeast of England, finds that this apparently commercial sector is composed of spaces of production *within* the market but resistant to, and subversive of, capitalist norms. For him, they are spaces of non-capitalist production operating within an apparently hegemonic capitalism. He finds that many of the producers are not so much oriented towards profit or exchange-value but rather do it 'for love'.

A similar finding is uncovered by an examination of the specialist sectors of both model railway and canary retailing (see Burns et al., 2004). In both of these sectors they identify that those engaged in selling these commodities had directly come into this industry because it was their hobby, and from this interest they had then established businesses buying and selling these 'commodities'. The vast majority of micro-businesses identified that were involved in this industry, however, were not driven by profit. For them, it was a way of becoming more 'central' to those sharing their interest and a way of covering the expenses involved in their hobby. Indeed, they shared their knowledge of the industry freely with 'customers' and often engaged in exchanges for reasons that had little or nothing to do with profit.

Moving away from studies of specific market sectors and towards rationales for firms taking particular actions, there are now numerous studies of the charitable contributions that capitalist firms make to the arts and cultural industries (e.g. Morel, 2003). These reveal that the motives underpinning these donations have in most cases little or nothing to do with profit or economic gain but, rather, reflect the desire of the directors or owners to display their taste and refinement. Here, therefore, one has actions taken by firms that are seldom, if ever, related to economic gain either directly or indirectly.

If the commercial sphere of monetized exchange, so dominantly perceived as the embodiment of the profit motive, is not always tethered to the motive of profit and profit alone, then the possibilities increase for uncovering either the absence of this motive or the existence of other motives in additional formal occupations, sectors and exchanges (see, for example, Zafirovski, 1999). However, this field of inquiry is in its infancy. There have so far been relatively few direct and explicit attempts to uncover the degree to which various occupations and sectors are dominated by the profit motive. Such research is desperately required, for it will reveal the absence of the profit motive or the existence of additional motives in the very heart of what is supposed to be the commodity economy.

Conclusions

This chapter has revealed that when goods and services are produced for monetized exchange, the purpose underlying these transactions is not always to make a profit. Examining the public sector, not-for-profit sector, cash-in-hand work and commercial sector, this chapter has revealed that there exist some very large economic spaces in the advanced economies that are not purely profit-motivated. Although the production and delivery of goods and services via the public sector are widely recognized to be in decline, the same cannot be asserted about the remaining spheres of monetized exchange considered here. As shown, the not-for-profit sector has grown throughout the advanced economies and now represents 4.6 per cent of GDP in the OECD nations. Cash-in-hand work, meanwhile, representing somewhere between 7 and 16 per cent of GDP, although often conceptualized as a profit-motivated sphere of monetized exchange, has been shown here in about three-quarters of cases to be underpinned by motives on the part of the seller and/or purchaser that are not profit-oriented. Even in the commercial sector of private businesses, moreover, this chapter has identified sectors and businesses that are not always motivated by the notion of profit, expansion and capital accumulation. The result, therefore, is that even if only the non-profit sector and that segment of cash-in-hand work conducted for reasons other than profit are included, one can estimate that at a very minimum some 10 per cent of GDP in the advanced economies is composed of monetary exchanges where the profit motive is absent. Over time, moreover, it appears that the profit-motivated commodified realm is constituting a smaller, rather than larger, segment of the monetized sphere given the relative growth of both cash-in-hand work and the not-for-profit sector.

Given this finding, it is now possible to conclude Part I of this book with a crude indication of the overall prevalence of profit-motivated monetized exchange in the advanced economies. In Chapter 3 it was revealed that non-exchanged work represents nearly a half of the total time that people spend working and is valued at between 50 and 120 per cent of existing GDP, whilst non-monetized exchange adds another 10–12 per cent to existing GDP. The unpaid sphere in total, therefore, contributes between 60 and 132 per cent to GDP in the advanced economies.

Not all paid work, however, as this chapter has shown, is commodified work in the sense of being conducted chiefly for the purpose of profit. To estimate the proportion of GDP that is profit-motivated monetized exchange, one needs to extract from the current GDP measure those goods and services produced for monetized exchange by not-for-profit businesses (4.6 per cent of GDP) and add on the hidden economy of cash-in-hand work where it is conducted primarily for motives other than economic gain (about 5–12 per cent of GDP).

Figure 5.1 provides a graphic representation of the results of doing so. The range of estimates for each realm have been achieved here by taking both the highest and the lowest estimates of its size and then comparing these with the lowest and highest estimates respectively for each other realm. This provides an estimate of the *maximum* and *minimum* ranges expected for each sphere in the advanced economies. It reveals that anywhere between 28 and 51 per cent of total GDP derives from non-exchanged work, between 4 and 7 per cent from non-monetized exchange, between 4 and 10 per cent from not-for-profit monetized exchange, and between 39 and 57 per cent from profit-motivated monetized exchange. The commodity economy, in sum, is far from hegemonic. Indeed, to name the 'advanced economies' as 'capitalist' or 'commodified' economies is a misnomer, for it obliterates from view vast swathes of work in these nations that are not profit-oriented monetized

Figure 5.1   The anatomy of the 'whole economy' in contemporary Western societies: maximum and minimum contributions of each sphere

Monetary exchange	Not-for-profit monetized exchange 4–10%	
	Profit-motivated exchange 39–57%	
Non-monetized work	Non-exchanged work 28–51%	Non-monetized exchange 4–7%

exchange. Commodified work is just one of a plurality of economic practices in the advanced economies.

Although the accuracy of these broad estimates can and should be questioned, and more detailed analysis is certainly required as stronger and more robust data become available, the intention underlying this thumb-nail sketch is simply to show that profit-motivated monetized exchange is just one of a plurality of economic practices used to produce goods and services in the advanced economies. This cannot be disputed.

For all of the talk of a commodified world, therefore, the first part of this book has revealed that the mode of economic organization in the advanced economies is far from being totally dominated by a hegemonic commodified economy. Rather, there exist a plurality of economic practices. As will be revealed in Part II of the book, however, commodification is an inherently uneven process. Although Part I has provided an overall indication of the extent to which working practices in the advanced economies have become commodified, there are some stark socio-economic, geographical and gender inequalities both in the degree to which commodification has taken hold and in the direction of change. In Part II, therefore, an attempt will be made to start to tease out some of these uneven contours of commodification in the advanced economies, as well as to show how the pace and extent of commodification differ between the advanced economies and the other major regions of the world.

PART II

The Uneven Contours of Commodification

6

Socio-economic Disparities

Part I of this book revealed that despite the hyperbole about a colonizing, victorious and all-pervasive commodified realm, there exists even in the heartlands of commodification – the advanced economies – a large and growing non-commodified sphere. In Western nations, there exists not a hegemonic commodified realm but rather heterogeneous economic practices, and, contrary to the commodification thesis, there is scant evidence that work is increasingly shifting into the commodified sphere. Until now, however, the focus of attention in this book has been only on providing an overall indication of the extent to which working practices in the advanced economies are commodified. In Part II, the emphasis turns towards charting the uneven contours of commodification within the advanced economies as well as how the pace and extent of commodification differ between the advanced economies and the other major regions of the world.

To commence this process of mapping the uneven contours of commodification, this chapter investigates how the penetration of the commodified realm varies across different socio-economic groups. Until now, the recurring assumption throughout the social sciences has been that relatively affluent populations in the advanced economies pursue more commodified lifestyles and that non-commodified work is concentrated among lower-income socio-economic groups. On the one hand, therefore, it is commonly believed that relatively affluent groups externalize their domestic workload to the commodified realm and reduce their own self-provisioning, as indicated by their use of nannies, gardeners, cleaners, painters and decorators and so forth. On the other hand, there is a widely held view that non-commodified work is the province of the poor and marginalized, who engage in such work as an economic survival practice.

This latter view is encapsulated in the long-standing 'marginality thesis', which assumes non-commodified work to be concentrated among the poor and marginalized, who are seen to engage in such work for unadulterated economic reasons (e.g. Button, 1984; Gutmann, 1978; Marcelli et al., 1999; Matthews, 1983; Rosanvallon, 1980). Over the decades, this marginality thesis has taken various forms. One recent and popular variant has been to embed this view of who engages in non-commodified work and why they do so into a structural economic explanation that views the persistence and growth of non-capitalist economic practices to be a result of a new post-Fordist regime of accumulation that is offloading the social reproduction functions of those surplus to the requirements of capital from the market sphere back onto the non-market sphere (e.g. Amin et al., 2002a, 2002b; Castells and Portes, 1989; Lee, 1999; Portes, 1994). In this reading, the breakdown of the post-war economic regulations and welfare state through deregulation and flexibilization of social relations of production and the trans-ferring of social services to private and communal hands (Pahl, 1984; Gershuny and Miles, 1983) is seen to have led to a process of decommodification. Non-commodified work, in this view, has expanded to occupy spaces of production (and reproduction) previously covered by the market and/or state. Here, therefore, it is the contradictions inherent in the commodification process itself that have led to decommodification. In order to compete in the global commodified economy, advanced economies have had to reduce social costs (see European Commission, 2000a). Activities associated with social reproduction have been decanted from the market or state spheres into the non-market realm. The result is a socio-spatial polarization of coping practices. The social reproductive functions of those populations working in the commodified sphere continue to be met through private or public-sector provision, whilst those excluded from work in the commodified realm are seen to be witnessing an offloading of their social reproduction onto the non-commodified sphere. From this post-Fordist economistic perspective, it is thus the poor and marginalized who engage in such non-commodified work and they do so out of economic necessity as they become separated from a commodified realm that views them as surplus to its requirements.

To evaluate critically this reading of the uneven socio-economic contours of commodification, the intention of this chapter is to seek answers to a number of questions. Is it the case that affluent social groups have more commodified lifestyles? And is non-commodified work concentrated among deprived populations who conduct such activity out of economic necessity? To answer these questions, this chapter explores, first, the extent to which commodification has penetrated the everyday lives of different socio-economic groups, and, second, the socio-economic disparities in the extent and nature of, and reasons for conducting, non-exchanged work followed by non-monetized exchange and cash-in-hand work. This will reveal that although relatively affluent populations do commodify a greater proportion of their household work practices, this does not mean that they abscond from engagement in non-commodified work. Instead, the finding is that they participate in more non-exchanged activity, non-monetized exchange and cash-in-hand work than lower-income groups. Examining the nature of this work, moreover, the finding is that their commodification of routine tasks appears to free them to engage in more creative, rewarding and non-routine forms of non-commodified work that they conduct out of choice rather than economic necessity. As such, the idea that non-commodified work is engaged in out of economic necessity does not suffice as an explanation. Although it is internally consistent and wholly coherent to view the reason for the persistence and even growth of non-commodified work among lower-income groups to be economic necessity, this is not the case with higher-income groups, who engage in such non-commodified work much more out of choice.

In this chapter, in consequence, it will be uncovered that if the uneven penetration of commodification is to be more fully understood, it is insufficient to use economic explanations. Instead, it will be revealed that although the persistence and even growth of non-commodified work among lower-income populations can be read in terms of economic constraints and interpreted as resulting from a new phase of capitalism where the costs and activities of social reproduction of those surplus to capitalism's requirements are being offloaded into the non-commodified sphere, such an explanation is insufficient on its own to explain the persistence and growth of the non-commodified sphere. Displaying how relatively affluent populations often make an active choice to engage in non-commodified work, this chapter reveals that 'cultures of resistance' to commodification appear to prevail among these socio-economic groups and that unless this anti-commodification ethic is recognized and incorporated into explanations for the growth of non-commodified work, then the uneven socio-economic contours of commodification cannot be fully understood. Here, therefore, the intention is to argue that neither a structural economic reading of non-commodified work nor an agency-oriented reading alone suffice for explaining the emergence of non-commodified work. Instead, a both/and approach is required sensitive to the different meanings of such spaces among different socio-economic groups.

Socio-economic Disparities in the Penetration of Commodified Work

A pervasive assumption across the advanced economies is that affluence leads to more commodified lifestyles. The perception is that as an individual and/or society accumulates wealth, a greater proportion of the workload will be commodified. Until now, there have been few attempts to evaluate directly this thesis regarding the socio-economic disparities in the extent of commodification. Indeed, there are few data sets available that can be used for such a task. For this reason, between 1998 and 2001 the author conducted 861 structured face-to-face interviews in higher- and lower-income urban and rural populations in England. These analysed 'household work practices' by taking the household as the unit of analysis (rather than the employment place, which is the usual unit analysed when exploring work practices) and examining the economic practices employed by households in order to undertake domestic service tasks (e.g. Nelson and Smith, 1999; Pahl, 1984; Sik, 1993; Smith, 2002; Wallace, 2002). Such an approach was adopted because once the plurality of economic practices is recognized, the conventional focus upon the employment place becomes redundant as the primary unit of analysis since it examines only one form of economic practice. Using the household as the unit of analysis, however, allows one to explore the diversity of economic practices used in daily life. Although such an approach does not cover the whole economy in that it fails to capture business-to-business transactions and concentrates on modes of domestic service provision, its value is that the economic pluralism characteristic of everyday household life is directly highlighted. Put another way, the method is fit for the purpose for which it is used here, which is to explore whether affluence leads to a commodification of working practices.

To investigate work practices, structured face-to-face interviews explored the mode of provision used to acquire 44 common domestic services, generated from the seminal study by Pahl (1984) on the Isle of Sheppey (see Table 6.1). Households were asked whether the task had been completed during the previous five years/year/month/week (depending on the activity). If so, they were asked who conducted the task the last time it was undertaken; whether the person had been unpaid, paid or given a gift, and if paid, whether it was 'cash-in-hand' or not, as well as how much they had been given. For each task completed, moreover, the respondent was questioned about why they had decided to conduct the work using that source of labour, so as to enable their motives to be understood. Following this, the supply of work by household members was examined. The interviewee was asked whether a household member had conducted each of these 44 tasks for another household and, if so, who had done it, for whom, whether they had received money, how much they had received and why they had decided to do the task.

Examining the sources of labour used in contemporary England by these 861 households, Table 6.2 displays that 18 per cent, or less than 1 in 5, of the 44 domestic tasks were last completed using commodified labour. This clearly displays the chasm between the present situation in the domestic sphere and a totally commodified domestic realm. In a fully commodified economy, the household services sector would be more than five times larger than its present

Table 6.1 List of tasks investigated in survey of English localities

Type of task	Specific tasks investigated
House maintenance	Outdoor painting, indoor painting, wallpapering, plastering, mending a broken widow, maintenance of appliances
Home improvements	Putting in double glazing, plumbing, electrical work, house insulation, putting in a bathroom suite, building a garage, building an extension, putting in central heating, carpentry
Housework	Routine housework, cleaning windows outdoors, spring cleaning, cleaning windows indoors, doing the shopping, washing clothes and sheets, ironing, cooking meals, washing dishes, hairdressing, household administration
Making and repairing goods	Making clothes, repairing clothes, knitting, making or repairing furniture, making or repairing garden equipment, making curtains
Car maintenance	Washing car, repairing car, car maintenance
Gardening	Care of indoor plants, outdoor borders, outdoor vegetables, lawn mowing
Caring activities	Daytime baby-sitting, night-time baby sitting, educational activities, pet care

size. However, this would require a commodification of the 71 per cent of tasks last conducted on a non-exchanged basis, the 5 per cent of tasks last conducted using unpaid labour from outside the household, and the 6 per cent of tasks using cash-in-hand labour. As such, these data provide a clear display of the limited extent to which the commodity economy has managed to penetrate everyday life so far as household work practices are concerned.

Here, nevertheless, what is of more interest is the degree to which different socio-economic groups pursue commodified working lives. Is it the case that as household income rises, a greater proportion of the workload is undertaken on a commodified basis? In

Table 6.2 Household work practices in contemporary England by household income

	Non-exchanged work		Non-monetized exchange		Cash-in-hand work		Formal employment	
	No.	*%*	*No.*	*%*	*No.*	*%*	*No.*	*%*
All households	14.7	71	1.0	5	1.1	6	3.7	18
>£275/week gross household income	15.9	66	1.3	5	1.4	6	5.5	23
<£275/week gross household income	13.9	74	0.7	4	1.0	5	3.3	18

other words, are higher-income populations more likely to employ gardeners, nannies, cleaners and formal craftspeople to undertake everyday household work? And does this externalization result in a net reduction in the amount of non-commodified work in general, and self-provisioning in particular, conducted by these households?

The first finding of this study is that a greater proportion of the domestic workload is commodified in higher- than in lower-income households (i.e. 23 per cent compared with 18 per cent). As such, this study superficially reinforces the common assumption that the relatively affluent have more commodified lifestyles and that lower-income groups rely more heavily on non-commodified economic practices. It might be thus assumed that as household income rises, a greater proportion of the domestic workload is externalized to commodified labour. To assert this, however, is only half the story. Although relatively affluent populations have more commodified coping practices, they also undertake a higher number of tasks on a non-commodified basis. As displayed in Table 6.2, despite externalizing to the commodified realm a wider range of activities, higher-income households still conduct some 20 per cent more tasks on a non-commodified basis than lower-income households. Externalization, in consequence, does not imply that relatively affluent households conduct less non-commodified activity than lower-income households.

Why is this the case? To find out, households were asked their reason for using the labour that they did when getting each task completed. The discovery is that the decision on whether or not to commodify work is not driven purely by economic constraints. To put it another way, households do not simply commodify work if they can afford to do so. Indeed, in only 43 per cent of cases where non-commodified work took place was cost or economic necessity the chief rationale. Other rationales beyond economic necessity are thus required to explain the different usage of commodified and non-commodified work by various socio-economic groups. As will now be shown, if the socio-economic variations in the usage of commodified and non-commodified economic practices are to be explained, it is the contrasting ways in which structure and agency influence decisions in different populations that need to be grasped. To see this, the contrasting reasons for different socio-economic groups participating in, first, non-exchanged work, second, non-monetized exchange and, third, cash-in-hand work, are analysed here.

Socio-economic Disparities in Subsistence Work

Is it the case that as household income rises, households engage in less subsistence work? The finding is that although a greater proportion of the domestic workload is commodified in higher-than in lower-income households in contemporary England, the relatively affluent still engage in a wider array of self-provisioning than lower-income populations. As Table 6.2 displays, higher-income households conduct 14 per cent more tasks on a subsistence basis compared with lower-income households (i.e. 15.9 tasks compared with 13.9 tasks). Consequently, although there is a relative shift of the workload in higher-income households towards the commodified sphere, this does not mean that the absolute amount of subsistence work decreases in such households. Rather, and as will now be shown, the contracting out of some routine self-provisioning enables these households to engage in more non-routine self-provisioning on a freely chosen basis.

The first issue that needs to be dealt with here, therefore, is how the character of non-exchanged work significantly differs in higher- compared with lower-income households. In lower-income households, which are more likely to contain a sick/disabled person or the retired, to be in rented accommodation and/or to be jobless, non-exchanged work is composed mostly of routine tasks (e.g. everyday housework) or essential tasks conducted when absolutely necessary (e.g. when a water leakage occurs, the cooker breaks down, the guttering leaks). Few such households engage in any significant range of more creative, rewarding and non-routine self-provisioning activities. For most of these households, such activity is conducted only when required and out of economic necessity.

For higher-income households, meanwhile, a greater proportion of subsistence work is composed of non-routine, creative and rewarding tasks (e.g. wallpapering, indoor painting and various other do-it-yourself activities) and conducted primarily out of choice rather than necessity. In contemporary English society, the outcome is that self-provisioning is often not a substitute for money income. It is the companion of money income. Unlike the marginality thesis, therefore, this study does not find that self-provisioning is a form of work turned to as a substitute for formal employment and a lack of cash. Instead, it finds that those without money are also unable to engage in self-provisioning, reinforcing rather than reducing their situation.

It might well be argued, however, that although some of the poorest socio-economic groups are excluded from self-servicing activity due to being unable to afford to engage in such work, there must be a level of affluence at which those who engage in self-servicing transfer this activity to the commodified realm. After all, if self-provisioning is viewed in economic terms as a cheaper way of achieving the same end product for those unable to commodify all of their household services, then at a certain level of affluence, self-provisioning should tail off as households become able to commodify nearly all of this work. The finding from this study of contemporary England, however, is that no level of affluence was identified at which the range of self-servicing activity declined as it became transferred into the commodified sphere. It seems, therefore, that self-servicing is not simply undertaken because one cannot afford to commodify the work. There appear to be other reasons also involved in the decision to conduct such work.

A Commodified World?

Table 6.3 Reasons for conducting domestic tasks on a self-servicing basis (%)

Reason for using self-provisioning	Lower-income groups	Higher-income groups
Economic	56	10
Ease	15	35
Choice/individuation	13	27
Pleasure	16	28

Why, therefore, do households engage in subsistence work? And are the motives the same among all socio-economic groups? Or do they vary? To answer this, each time a task was undertaken on a non-exchanged basis, interviewees were asked why the task had been conducted in this manner. The finding, as Table 6.3 reveals, is that just 56 per cent of self-provisioning in lower-income households was primarily motivated by economic necessity and merely 10 per cent in the higher-income groups. Put another way, just under half (44 per cent) of all self-servicing activity was conducted for non-economic reasons and/or out of preference in lower-income groups and 90 per cent of such activity in higher-income groups.

First, that is, the reason for some 15 per cent of all self-servicing in lower-income socio-economic groups and 35 per cent in higher-income groups was because it was felt to be *easier* to do the task on a self-servicing basis than to externalize the work. This applied to a wide range of activity, from routine housework to home improvement and maintenance. When routine housework was undertaken on a self-servicing basis because it was easier, the availability of domestic technologies (e.g. washing machines, dishwashers) and/or the problems in finding 'trustworthy' people to whom the tasks could be externalized were often cited. The demise in the prevalence of informal social networks through which cleaners and so forth could be found was also often cited. The domestic service firms in the commodified realm that had arisen to replace cash-in-hand cleaners and so forth, meanwhile, were seen to use labour of poor quality. While informal networks had been considered sufficient evidence of the trustworthiness of potential employees, the fact that these firms did not subject their employees to detailed police checks for their trustworthiness was seen as a major reason for not using them. In short, they did not want to use such firms. So far as home improvement and maintenance tasks were concerned, similar rationales prevailed. It was often stated, for example, that tradespeople were difficult to contact and even more difficult to persuade to come to do a job, so it was often easier simply to do the job oneself than to rely on them. In other words, a widespread distrust of professional tradespeople led households to do the work themselves.

Second, and in some 13 per cent of cases where self-servicing was last used in lower-income groups and 27 per cent of cases where it was last used in higher-income groups, self-servicing was the first *choice* of households rather than a last resort resulting from financial necessity. The perception was that by doing a task themselves, they could create an end product that was of a higher quality than would otherwise be the case or that the end product could be individualized in a way that suited their needs and/or desires. This displays that 'a largely unintended effect of a highly individualized and marketized society has been the intensification of social practices which systematically "evade the edicts of exchange value and the logic of the market"' (Urry, 2000: 146). Reflected in popular do-it-yourself home-decorating television programmes such as *Changing Rooms*, *House Doctor* and *House Invaders* that both cater to and fuel the desire for such self-servicing, this pursuit of individuation has led to the growth of self-servicing as a 'chosen space'.

Third and finally, self-servicing was often used due to the *pleasure* people got from doing the work themselves. Indeed, this reason accounted for some 16 per cent of cases where self-servicing was last used in lower-income groups and 28 per cent of cases where it was last used in higher-income groups. This rationale, moreover, did not relate purely to the more autonomously chosen do-it-yourself projects such as home improvement, although it was relatively concentrated in this realm. A significant minority did routine housework themselves because of the pleasure that they received from this activity. More often than not, these were employed women whose rationale entailed comparing the outputs of their housework with the products of their employment. As one employed woman put it, 'At least you are doing something productive and you can see what you have achieved at the end of it, unlike my job.' Or, as another employed women put it, 'Compared with my job, housework's great. You get a real buzz when you look at it when you have finished and see what you have achieved.' Although some non-employed women shared this view of routine housework as pleasurable, these were mostly older women, often of retirement age. For most people, however, it was non-routine self-provisioning that was perceived as pleasurable and this is the reason why pleasure was more heavily cited as a reason for self-servicing in the higher-income groups where a greater proportion of such non-exchanged work is of the non-routine variety.

In consequence, this study of contemporary England shows that the persistence of self-provisioning in the domestic realm is not simply the result of the financial inability of households to commodify these tasks. Households often prefer to undertake activities themselves due to ease, choice or pleasure. Indeed, this study is not alone in arriving at this finding. In one of the only other studies that explores the rationales for self-provisioning, Sundbo (1997) finds that in Denmark just 36 per cent of households would consider externalizing spring-cleaning, 33 per cent cleaning, 27 per cent gardening, 21 per cent advice about economic matters, 20 per cent household repairs, 17 per cent care of sick children, 13 per cent shopping, 13 per cent care of children in general, and 12 per cent the provision of meals. Two-thirds prefer to do these jobs themselves under all circumstances, never mind what price is charged. As such, he identifies a strong 'culture of resistance' to the externalization of activity, similar to the above study in contemporary England.

Whether 'cultures of resistance' prevail over economic necessity in determining the extent of self-provisioning, nevertheless, and as shown above, it differs across socio-economic groups. Different socio-economic groups have contrasting preference/necessity ratios. In higher-income groups, a larger share is conducted out of choice than out of necessity. Indeed, despite being financially able to commodify tasks, they choose only to commodify a narrow range of mostly routine, mundane and repetitive tasks and use some of the time released to engage in more non-routine, creative and rewarding self-servicing activity, often associated with home improvement, that they conduct out of preference rather than necessity. In lower-income populations, however, where self-servicing is composed mostly of essential and/or routine tasks, necessity tends to prevail to a greater extent.

It appears, therefore, that self-provisioning is being used especially in affluent populations to seek meaning, identity and a definition of self through work other than employment. People guard against externalizing activity in order to seek self-identity and worth other than through their formal jobs. Self-provisioning, it seems, provides one nexus through which people forge and display who and what they are and wish to be. The outcome is that the productive functions of the household, far from disappearing under capitalism, seem to be retained as an act of resistance to the notion of defining who and what one is through employment alone.

Of course, and just as in the commodified realm, the capabilities of people to use self-provisioning in this manner vary and the sizes of the rewards differ. Among lower-income households, self-provisioning is more routine and carries smaller material and psychological benefits. Such activity is compelled more by necessity than choice or an interest in the intrinsic satisfactions. It is much less about displaying an ability to manage on one's own and one's creative side and is much more about having to manage on one's own. In an already overburdened life where economic constraints severely impinge on one's opportunities to display who and what you are, self-provisioning represents, similar to the commodified realm, yet another sphere of constrained opportunities where choice is lacking and one's creative desires are stifled.

For more affluent populations, however, self-provisioning represents a sphere where needs can be fulfilled, capabilities developed and creative desires expressed, resulting in larger material and psychological benefits. In consequence, just as the material and psychological rewards of formal employment are unevenly distributed, the same applies to self-provisioning.

In sum, this investigation of subsistence work reveals not only that more affluent socio-economic groups engage to a greater extent in such activity and that the nature of the activity that they engage in is more rewarding, non-routine and creative than for poorer socio-economic groups but also that they carry out such activity out of choice rather than necessity. For these groups, therefore, such activity is more of a lifestyle choice. For relatively deprived socio-economic groups, however, such activity is not only more routine in nature but is also conducted more out of economic necessity than choice. It is obvious, therefore, that subsistence work cannot be universally seen as engaged in out of economic necessity. For affluent populations, such activity is much more a lifestyle choice; a sphere of resistance to the incursion of commodification in their lives and a means of finding material and psychological rewards from productive activity outside of commodified work.

In consequence, it appears that the argument that non-exchanged work is the outcome of a post-Fordist regime that is offloading the social reproduction functions of populations surplus to the requirements of capital does indeed tell only half of the story. Although such a description might well apply to lower-income groups, who are relatively unsuccessful compared with affluent groups at using the non-exchanged sphere as a coping mechanism, it does not explain the considerable level of engagement in non-exchanged activity among more affluent populations. To explain this, it is necessary, as shown above, to turn towards more agency-oriented explanations that see the realm of non-exchanged work as a site of resistance to commodification. For many affluent groups, it seems, there is a level of commodification beyond which they are unwilling to pass, and they find in the realm of non-exchanged activity an alternative source of self-identity and worth.

Socio-economic Disparities in Non-monetized Exchange

If non-exchanged work reinforces, rather than reduces, the socio-economic disparities produced by participation in the commodified sphere, is this also the case so far as non-monetized exchange is concerned? And do the reasons for engaging in non-monetized exchange differ across socio-economic groups?

Throughout the advanced economies, the common finding across all surveys of non-monetized exchange is that affluent populations engage in such activity to a greater extent than lower income socio-economic groups (e.g. Salamon et al., 1999). Take, for example, the UK. The National Surveys of Volunteering in 1981, 1991 and 1997 (Field and Hedges, 1984; Lynn and Davis Smith, 1992; Davis Smith, 1998) all identify that higher socio-economic groups are more likely to participate in unpaid voluntary activity than lower socio-economic groups, as well as a large fall over time in the participation rates of unemployed people, displaying a process of social polarization in the likelihood of participation in such activity. These socio-economic disparities in participation rates in non-monetized exchange are reinforced in all major surveys.

Take, for example, the 2001 National Adult Learning Survey (NALS) in the UK. The finding is that professionals and managers were the socio-economic group most likely to engage in voluntary activity (78 per cent). Those who were unemployed were less likely to be involved in any type of voluntary work (44 per cent), compared with 21 per cent of part-time employees and 22 per cent of the self-employed. Those with higher levels of household income were also found to be more likely than those with a low income to engage in voluntary activities. A third of those with household incomes of less than £10,400 per annum had no involvement, compared with 22 per cent of those with a household income of £31,200 or more.

This finding that affluent socio-economic groups are more likely to participate in non-monetized activity is not unique to the UK. In the USA, similarly, employed people are found to be more active socially and civically than those outside the paid labour force; and among those employed in the formal labour market, longer hours are often linked to more civic engagement, not less. People who report the heaviest time pressure are more likely, not less, to participate in community projects, attend church and club meetings, to follow politics, to spend time visiting friends, to entertain at home and the like (Putnam, 2000). As Putnam (2000: 193) thus concludes, 'People with lower incomes and those who feel financially strapped are much less engaged in all forms of social and community life than those who are better off.'

Table 6.4 Contributions to volunteering in South Australia (A\$ million), by employment status, 1995 and 2000

Employment status	1995	2000	1995–2000 % change
Employed full-time	292	563	93
Employed part-time	218	390	79
Unemployed	59	27	−54

Source: Ironmonger, 2002: Table 6.

Similar findings concerning the heavier engagement of the full-time employed are also identified both across the European Union (e.g. Paugam and Russell, 2000) and in South Australia (Ironmonger, 2002). Indeed, tracking the changes over time in South Australia, and similar to the National Surveys of Volunteering in the UK cited above, Ironmonger (2002) identifies a divergence rather than convergence between the employed and unemployed. As Table 6.4 reveals, between 1995 and 2000 those in employment increased the amount of time that they spent engaged in such activity, but among the unemployed such activity declined.

To understand more fully the socio-economic differences in participation in non-monetized exchanges, however, it is necessary to distinguish between, first, formal and informal non-monetized exchanges, or what is sometimes referred to as informal and formal volunteering, and, second, their reasons for engaging in such non-monetized activity. Organized or formal non-monetary exchanges involve unpaid participation in groups, associations and organizations. Informal non-monetized exchange, meanwhile, is where unpaid favours are provided on a one-to-one basis to friends, neighbours and kin who live outside the household. In nearly all studies in the advanced economies where these two forms of non-monetized exchange have been differentiated, the finding is that although affluent socio-economic groups are more likely to engage in both types of non-monetized exchange than other groups, their overall culture of engagement is oriented much more towards participation in organized non-monetized exchange than is the case in other socio-economic groups. For the most part, however, the

Table 6.5 Socio-economic variations in Britain in the extent of participation in formal and informal volunteering, 2000

	Involved in local organization with responsibilities in past 3 years	Involved in local organization without responsibilities in past 3 years	Had done a favour for a neighbour in the past 6 months	Received a favour from a neighbour in the past 6 months
By occupation				
Non-manual	18	9	78	77
Manual	9	6	73	69
By employment status				
All employed	13	7	75	74
Full-time employed	12	7	75	74
Part-time employed	16	8	77	75
Unemployed	7	4	67	60
Economically inactive	14	9	72	70
By tenure				
Owner occupier	15	9	77	76
Social renter	8	5	69	64
Private renter	8	5	59	57
No. of cars/vans available to household				
None	7	6	64	63
One	13	8	76	73
Two or more	17	8	78	76
All	13	8	74	72

Source: General Household Survey, 2000.

reason for the engagement of affluent groups in such organized forms of non-monetized exchanges is social in orientation, whilst the relatively greater participation of lower socio-economic groups in informal one-to-one exchanges is conducted more for the purpose of receiving and giving material aid. In consequence, and akin to non-exchanged work, economic necessity underpins the engagement of lower income groups whilst non-economic motives underlie the participation of more affluent social groups in more organized forms of voluntary action.

To help us start to see this, Table 6.5 examines data from the 2000 General Household Survey (GHS) in the UK on participation rates in formal and informal volunteering among different socio-economic groups. Just 7 per cent of unemployed respondents in the 2000 GHS had been actively involved in a local organization in the past three years, but 67 per cent had done a favour for a neighbour in the previous six months. Furthermore, although only 8 per cent of respondents in rented accommodation had formally volunteered in the past three years, some 69 per cent in the socially rented sector and 59 per cent in the privately rented sector had done a favour for a neighbour in the previous six months. There is thus a pre-existing culture of participation in acts of one-to-one aid among such deprived social groups, while participating in voluntary groups is relatively foreign to the vast majority of them. Similar results are identified in the European Union (Paugam and Russell, 2001), in the USA (Putnam, 2000), and in Australia (Ironmonger, 2002).

Given these socio-economic variations in participation in non-monetized exchange, it appears that engagement cannot be simply explained as a coping practice adopted out of economic necessity by the poor and marginalized. So far, however, and despite the wealth of data on participation rates, few studies have sought reasons for engagement in such work. Therefore, and to understand why people engage in formal and informal non-monetized practices, Williams and Windebank (2003a) in the UK asked respondents from different socio-economic groups for their rationale when both using and supplying non-monetized work. The finding is that among relatively affluent social groups, this is primarily viewed as a social activity, whilst among relatively poorer socio-economic groups this activity is conducted as a way of giving and receiving material aid. As such, if one examines only deprived social groups, the view in the marginality thesis that such work is a coping practice conducted out of economic necessity is reinforced.

Take, for example, non-monetized exchanges between kin who are not living in the same household. The finding in the UK is that such activity is a key component of their coping practices.

This is similar to what Paugam and Russell (2000) find in the European Union more generally. As they state,

> When a large part of the population shares the same unfavourable social conditions, familial solidarity does not arise from a logic of compensation nor from the logic of emancipation – it becomes a collective fight against poverty. Reciprocity in the exchanges is then functional. In order to face adversity, everyone gives and gives back, therefore everyone gives and receives. This is why we are more likely to find examples of lasting familial solidarity in these regions where unemployment and hardship are higher, because it is based on a reciprocity imposed by the need to resist collectively. (Paugam and Russell, 2000: 257)

Beyond kin, however, and unlike earlier studies (e.g. Young and Wilmott, 1975), the study of Williams and Windebank (2003a) found that norms of reciprocity were heavily imbued with payment, especially among lower-income populations. There was little desire to help others on an unpaid basis. This displays the 'inner–outer' logic in unpaid exchange relations and uncovers how the principle of non-equivalent, spontaneous balancing of needs cannot be generalized outside of the 'inner' sanctum of kin. Beyond this inner kinship space, indifference – even hostility – towards helping others exists. In the outer circle of friends, neighbours and others, unpaid help was not seen as something that should be provided.

Indeed, unpaid non-kinship exchange occurred only where it was felt to be unacceptable, inappropriate or impossible to do anything different. This tended to occur in four circumstances. First, it prevailed when it was considered unacceptable to pay somebody (e.g. when they lent you a saw). Second, it predominated when it was felt inappropriate to pay them (e.g. when a colleague from work did you a favour). Third, it occurred when payment was impossible (e.g. when somebody refused to be paid because they wanted an unpaid favour from you at a later date). And fourth and finally, it prevailed when the social relations prevented payment (e.g. when the recipient could not afford to pay and thus had no choice but to offer a favour in return).

Whenever feasible, however, interviewees avoided unpaid exchange. On the one hand, interviewees expressed great anxiety about owing people a favour if they accepted an unpaid offer of help from somebody. As one unemployed woman put it, 'I usually like to pay people who do work for me, so if I need to, I can feel free ... but a friend laid my carpet and wouldn't take money. I owe him now and I really hate that hanging over me.' On the other hand, they also expressed concerns that if they helped others, the favour would not be returned. As one respondent in a lower-income household asserted, 'most people don't return favours these days so I don't do anything for anyone else unless I'm paid for it.' Remarkably similar findings were identified in a separate study in small-town America. As one of the respondents Nelson and Smith (1999: 112) interviewed stated, 'We don't really like to owe anybody anything including favors because they can always come back on you in a negative way. So, whenever things are done it's usually been in exchange for pay.'

In consequence, the widespread preference was for money or gifts to be involved in one-to-one non-kinship transactions. This avoided any obligation 'hanging over you' to reciprocate favours, but at the same time the wheels were being oiled for the maintenance or creation of closer relations without being 'duty bound'. Seen in this light, the prevalence of unpaid exchange among lower-income populations is simply due to their inability to pay for help rendered. Accepting an unpaid favour from a friend or neighbour was a result of their lack of choice. It was not a choice born out of the existence of trust and/or close social relations (see Putnam, 2000). This perhaps explains why a far greater proportion of one-to-one help received by higher-income households is paid (79 per cent) than is the case in lower-income households (23 per cent). The prevalence of unpaid community exchange does not signify the persistence of trust and close bonds in deprived populations, as might have been previously assumed, but rather their inability to engage in monetized exchange.

In sum, the old-fashioned idea that lower-income populations help each other out using unpaid exchange is correct. It is not correct, however, that this occurs out of choice. Beyond kin, most people in most circumstances avoid using unpaid help and only do so when they cannot do the job themselves, afford to pay somebody, or when the social relations involved militate against payment. The result is that initiatives to develop reciprocity will need to reflect these circumstances. For these lower-income populations, the norm is to pay friends and/or neighbours so as to avoid any souring of their relationship if a favour is not returned. Initiatives to harness unpaid help beyond kin cannot avoid this desire for people to receive some form of payment, at least when the provision of material help is provided. Nor can one rely on existing community-based groups to harness such support networks. As shown, these are largely sociability vehicles for more affluent groups. They do not on the whole deliver material support to lower-income populations. The policy implications of such findings will be returned to in later chapters. For the moment, it simply needs to be recognized that the current focus throughout the advanced economies on harnessing non-monetized work through the development of community groups is perhaps not a suitable approach if the objective is to develop such activity as a form of material aid among lower-income social groups.

Socio-economic Disparities in Cash-in-Hand Work

The assumption in the commodification thesis is that as money has penetrated more areas of life, this has marched hand-in-hand with the profit motive. In the last chapter, however, it was shown that this is not always the case. There exist large spheres of activity where monetary transactions are not always imbued with the notion of economic gain. Here, the intention is to consider whether there are variations between socio-economic groups in the extent to which monetary exchanges are conducted for the purpose of economic gain.

To analyse this, the sphere of cash-in-hand work is here interrogated. As mentioned in Chapter 5, this is often seen to exemplify the more flexible profit-motivated exchange relations that have arisen under post-Fordist regimes of accumulation (Castells and Portes, 1989; Leonard, 1994; Portes, 1994; Sassen, 1989). Conceptualized as a form of low-paid peripheral employment conducted for unadulterated economic reasons, such work is assigned by proponents of the 'marginality thesis' to lower-income populations (e.g. Castells and Portes, 1989; Kesteloot and Meert, 1999; Portes, 1994). Here, however, such an economic reading of cash-in-hand work will be shown to be a misrepresentation of its distribution and a narrow interpretation of its diverse meanings, at least in the context of contemporary England (for an in-depth examination, see Williams and Windebank, 2001a).

As with previous studies (e.g. Fortin et al., 1996; Leonard, 1994; Pahl, 1984; Renooy, 1990), this study confirms the concentration of cash-in-hand work in higher-income populations. As Table 6.1 displays, it is higher-income households that are more likely to use cash-in-hand work. They are also more likely to be the suppliers of such work. In urban England, for example, higher-income households (24 per cent of the sample) supply 40 per cent of this activity. Comparing lower- and higher-income households, the average amount received for conducting a task on a cash-in-hand basis is £70.02 compared with £982. Moreover, the average hourly informal wage rate is £3.20 in lower-income households but £7.90 in higher-income households, and the mean annual household income from cash-in-hand work is £41.03 compared with £489.21. In consequence, higher-income groups are the major beneficiaries of such work both as customers and as suppliers.

However, if this study of urban England reinforces studies conducted elsewhere in the advanced economies concerning the socio-economic distribution of cash-in-hand work, it does not validate the assumption made in many previous studies that such work is primarily conducted for the purpose of economic gain. Instead, it finds that although this work is firmly embedded in unadulterated economic motives in higher-income households, this is not the case in lower-income households. In the latter households, much cash-in-hand exchange is conducted for and by close social relations for primarily social reasons or to help each other out in a way that avoids any connotation of charity. In higher-income households, meanwhile, such exchange is received more from self-employed people and firms for profit and is primarily used as a cheaper alternative to formal firms (for an in-depth examination, see Williams and Windebank, 2001c).

In lower-income households, it was found that less than a third (28 per cent) of all cash-in-hand exchanges used firms or unknown self-employed individuals, but such sources constituted 87 per cent in higher-income households. Therefore, in lower-income neighbourhoods cash-in-hand exchanges mostly involve transactions conducted by friends, neighbours or relatives, whilst they are between anonymous buyers and sellers in higher-income households. This is explained by the motivations of purchasers. In some 77 per cent of circumstances where cash-in-hand work was used in higher-income households, it was employed as a cheaper alternative to formal employment, but this is the reason for just 21 per cent of this work in lower-income households. In nearly all of these cases, it is firms and/or self-employed people not known by the household who conduct the work. When closer social relations are involved, it is either carried out for social reasons or seen as an opportunity to give money to another person in a way that avoids any connotation of charity (see Kempson, 1996).

Hence, just because cash-in-hand work is poorly reimbursed in lower-income households does not mean that it is a low-paid form of peripheral *employment*. Much is conducted for close social relations and, as will be shown below, the exchange relations are more akin to unpaid mutual aid among kin than an employer–employee relationship.

Social reasons tend to predominate when friends or neighbours (rather than kin) are involved. Indeed, it is in these cash-in-hand exchanges between friends and neighbours that one can see mutual aid that supposedly formerly took place on an unpaid basis. For participants, these exchanges are conducted in order to cement or consolidate social relationships. The exchange of cash is seen as a necessary medium, especially when neighbours or friends are involved, because it prevents such relations from turning sour if and when somebody reneges on their commitments. Cash thus provides the oil to lubricate mutual aid in situations where trust is missing. Indeed, many of the respondents, especially among lower-income populations, could not remember such relationships ever being any different. This, therefore, is not evidence of the commodification of previously unpaid reciprocal exchange. It is evidence that cash exchange does not have to be for economic gain and can be undertaken for other purposes. Put another way, monetary exchange relations do not necessarily have to be capitalist. And it is here in these lower-income groups that solid evidence is available of the existence of monetized exchange devoid of profit-motivated intentions and capitalist social relations.

Besides social reasons, another rationale for cash-in-hand exchange is redistribution. This mostly occurs when kin are involved. In these instances, it was either children or a relation such as a brother, sister or parent who was paid, normally in order to give them much-needed spending money, when, for example, they were unemployed. Indeed, using kin to do tasks so as to give them money was the principal rationale behind 12 per cent of all cash-in-hand work in the lower-income households. For these consumers, therefore, it was a way of giving money to a poorer relative in a way that avoided all connotations of charity, even if this was an intention underlying such exchange. This type of motivation, however, hardly existed in higher-income households, except when young children were involved who were paid by their parents to do a job.

In sum, cash-in-hand exchanges are largely driven by non-market motivations in lower-income households but by the profit motive in affluent households. As with self-provisioning and non-monetized exchange, therefore, participation in cash-in-hand work appears to have a varying logic in different socio-economic groups. Indeed, these contrasting logics mean that, although the profit motive has deeply penetrated monetary relations in higher-income households, which are usually heavily embedded in the formal labour market, some 28 per cent of all the monetary exchanges (both formal and informal) studied in these lower-income households were conducted for rationales beyond the profit motive.

The implications of this finding are potentially profound. It shows that even if there has been the deeper penetration of monetary relations in the advanced economies (see Harvey, 1989; Sayer, 1997), these are by no means everywhere driven by the social relations of capitalism. Monetary exchange is not everywhere based on profit-motivated market relations. Indeed, this study of cash-in-hand exchange, often taken as an exemplar of profit-motivated monetary exchange, displays how it is wholly feasible to have monetary transactions that are embedded in alternative social relations and motives. This study locates such work in the social as well as in the economic relations of poorer households. These transactions help maintain the social fabric and at the same time fill the gap left by the failure of markets in goods and services. As such, in these lower-income populations, as Zelizer (1994: 215) so eloquently puts it, 'Money has not become the free, neutral and dangerous destroyer of social relations.'

Conclusions

A pervasive assumption across the advanced economies has been that affluence leads to more commodified lifestyles. The perception is that as an individual or society accumulates wealth, a greater proportion of the workload will be undertaken on a commodified basis. In this chapter, this narrative has been evaluated critically. Although it is indeed found to be the case that higher-income households are more likely to commodify some tasks, especially of the routine and mundane variety, this is not found to reduce the overall amount of non-commodified work that they undertake. Instead, the externalization of such routine tasks is found to free time, some of which is used to engage in a range of non-routine, creative and rewarding forms of non-commodified work that is undertaken out of choice. Lower-income groups, meanwhile, are found to engage in only a relatively limited range of non-commodified work. The result is that higher-income groups carry out a wider range of non-commodified activity than their lower-income counterparts. Obviously, therefore, the notion that non-commodified work practices are adopted solely due to economic necessity needs to be reconsidered.

Examining subsistence work, it has been revealed that the externalization of some functions by affluent social groups does not reduce the overall amount of non-exchanged work that they conduct because some of the free time released is used to engage in more non-routine, creative and rewarding self-provisioning activity that is conducted more out of choice than economic necessity. Lower-income groups, meanwhile, find themselves unable to conduct a wide range of non-exchanged work due to economic constraints, and what work that they do conduct in this subsistence realm is routine in nature and undertaken more out of economic necessity than choice.

Similarly, examining the extent, nature and motives underpinning engagement in non-monetized exchange, and how this varies socio-economically, it has been revealed that affluent socio-economic groups not only engage in greater levels of non-monetized exchange than more deprived socio-economic groups but that the nature and motives underpinning this work also significantly vary. A greater proportion of non-monetized exchange among affluent socio-economic groups is conducted on an organized basis, and the motive underpinning engagement in such exchange is much more oriented towards social or community-building ends, whilst deprived socio-economic groups engage in less non-monetized exchange and a greater share tends to be conducted on a one-to-one (rather than organized) basis for material purposes associated with making ends meet. Again, therefore, economic necessity prevails among lower-income social groups, but a greater degree of choice among higher-income social groups.

Finally, and turning to the extent, nature and motives underpinning participation in cash-in-hand work, this chapter has investigated the case of the socio-economic disparities in cash-in-hand work. This has revealed significant variations in both the nature of cash-in-hand work and the motives underpinning it. Although such work is more likely to be conducted under commodified economic relations among affluent populations, among lower-income socio-economic groups a greater proportion of such work is akin to a form of mutual aid conducted for reasons beyond the profit motive. For the latter, therefore, cash-in-hand work represents a form of non-commodified work, whilst for the relatively affluent it is conducted under relations akin to commodified work.

In sum, this chapter has displayed that despite affluent socio-economic groups in advanced economies attempting to seize greater control over their work schedules by pursuing non-commodified practices of resistance to total immersion in the commodified realm, others surplus to the requirements of capitalism are finding themselves cast adrift from the commodified world and offloaded into the non-commodified sphere where such activity is conducted more out of economic necessity to make ends meet.

Non-commodified work, in consequence, is not solely a function of economic constraint. Instead, a more socio-economically sensitive understanding of such work is required that recognizes the prevalence of choice among the relatively affluent, and of constraint among lower-income groups. The non-commodified realm, in other words, means very different things to different socio-economic groups in the advanced economies.

7

The Uneven Geographies of Commodification

In the advanced economies, it is not only the case that the penetration of the commodity economy is unequal across socio-economic groups. It is also uneven geographically. Some places appear to be more heavily embedded in commodified work cultures than others. The aim of this chapter is to start to map out this uneven penetration of the commodity economy and to chart why it might be the case.

First, therefore, this chapter explores the uneven penetration of commodification *within* the advanced economies. To do this, answers will be sought at three spatial scales. Are urban areas more commodified than rural communities? Are affluent suburbs more commodified than deprived urban neighbourhoods? And are some cities more commodified than others? Given the lack of suitable detailed data available to answer these questions, this chapter concentrates again on the UK situation, where 861 face-to-face interviews in eleven higher- and lower-income urban and rural localities have been collected by the author. Throughout the chapter, however, evidence from other nations is reported where it is available so as to show that the results found in this study of the UK are not unique and that the uneven contours of commodification appear to display some common patterns throughout the advanced economies.

The finding, akin to the last chapter, is that it is far too simplistic to argue that the uneven geographical penetration of the commodity economy is purely a result of structural economic factors. Rather, human agency is shown to play a vital role, especially in more affluent localities. The argument here, therefore, and strongly resonating with the last chapter, is that a pluralistic and spatially sensitive both/and approach is required that explains the persistence of the non-commodified realm and its uneven geographical contours using both structural economic constraints and agency, with the weight given to each varying significantly according to the place under investigation. While cultures of resistance are far more influential than economic forces in sustaining a decommodified sphere in affluent suburbs and rural areas, more emphasis is given to economic forces when explaining the persistence of the non-commodified sphere in deprived and urban areas. The argument of this chapter, therefore, is that the slow, shallow and uneven advance of commodification can only be understood using both economic and cultural explanations and exploring how their role varies across space.

Examining the Uneven Geographies of Commodification

In popular discourse, there are some well-established beliefs about the extent to which commodification has penetrated various locality types. First, and based upon both the 'marginality thesis' that non-commodified work is concentrated among the poor and marginalized and the view that post-Fordism has resulted in the social reproduction of those surplus to the requirements of capital being offloaded onto the non-commodified sphere, there is a belief that the commodified sphere has penetrated more deeply in affluent areas and that deprived areas rely more heavily on the non-commodified sphere in their coping practices.

Moreover, and whatever way the highly contested concept of 'the rural' is defined, a widely held view is that commodification is less advanced in rural than in urban areas. This is not because rural areas are following a different development trajectory. It is seen to be a result of lagged adaptation. Nevertheless, commentators pinpoint a number of systemic changes that are driving rural areas towards a more commodified development path (e.g. Bradley, 1987; Hedges, 1999; Shucksmith, 2000). These include: increased mobility, gentrification and rapid population change (e.g.

Chapman et al., 1998); a trend towards commuting rather than working in the community (Chapman et al., 1998; Furlong and Cartnel, 2000; Pavis et al., 2000; Rugg and Jones, 1999; Storey and Brannen, 2000); the loss of younger people, not least due to high housing costs (Bradley, 1987; Chapman et al., 1998; Ford et al., 1997; Shucksmith, 2000); the decline of shared facilities such as shops, schools and pubs (Countryside Agency, 2000; Shucksmith, 2000); increasingly individualistic lifestyles (e.g. Shucksmith, 2000) and the loss of distinctive rural culture, language and dialects, as well as other intangible qualities (e.g. Countryside Agency, 2000; Shucksmith, 2000). The result, it is asserted, is that rural communities are becoming less close-knit, cooperative and supportive and the people less self-reliant, friendly and helpful. Put another way, they are slowly transforming into more commodified economic spaces, albeit lagging behind urban areas. So, despite rural areas retaining a greater sense of community spirit than urban areas (e.g. Chapman et al., 1998; Cloke et al., 1994; Findlay et al., 1999; Hedges, 1999; Shucksmith et al., 1996; Stratford and Christie, 2000), the socio-economic transformations in rural Britain, taken as a cumulative whole, suggest that a commodification process is under way. As people spend greater time outside of where they live, younger generations leave and incomers move in, self-reliance is seen to wither, and the depth and breadth of the social networks prevalent in these localities that provide the seedbed for the provision of informal support rupture. The result is that the non-commodified sphere is seen as a residual leftover of a bygone era that is slowly dwindling as commodification takes hold.

Here, a study is reported that set out both to analyse the uneven contours of commodification and to explain the persistence of non-commodified work in different locality types in contemporary England. Given that numerous studies show significant differences in the magnitude and character of non-commodified work between affluent and deprived localities as well as between urban and rural milieux (e.g. Felt and Sinclair, 1992; Jensen et al., 1995; Kestellot and Meert, 1999; Pahl, 1984; Renooy, 1990; Shaw and Pandit, 2001), between 1998 and 2001 a series of locality studies were conducted in affluent and deprived urban and rural localities in England (Williams and Windebank, 2001a, 2003a).

Table 7.1 English household work practices survey: localities studied

Area type	Locality	No. of interviews	Description of area
Affluent rural	Fulbourn, Cambridgeshire	70	Affluent 'picture postcard' rural village in high-tech subregion
Affluent rural	Chalford, Gloucestershire	70	Affluent rural village in Cotswolds
Deprived rural	Grimethorpe, South Yorkshire	70	Ex-pit village with very high unemployment
Deprived rural	Wigston, Cumbria	70	Deprived rural village with one factory dominating the local labour market
Deprived rural	St Blazey, Cornwall	70	Deprived rural locality in a tourist region
Affluent suburb	Fulwood, Sheffield	50	Affluent suburb in south-west Sheffield
Affluent suburb	Basset/Chilworth, Southampton	61	Only affluent suburb within the city of Southampton
Deprived urban	Manor, Sheffield	100	'Sink' social housing project with high unemployment
Deprived urban	Pitsmoor, Sheffield	100	Deprived inner-city area in deindustrializing city with high levels of private-sector rented accommodation and high unemployment
Deprived urban	St Mary's, Southampton	100	Deprived inner-city locality in affluent southern city with high levels of private-sector rented accommodation and high unemployment
Deprived urban	Hightown, Southampton	100	Deprived social housing project with high unemployment

First, therefore, a relatively affluent English city was selected that has witnessed strong service growth, resulting in low unemployment rates and high average wage rates – namely Southampton. Second, a relatively deprived English city was chosen that has witnessed deindustrialization and only weak service-sector growth, resulting in higher unemployment and lower wage rates – namely Sheffield. Three neighbourhoods were then selected for investigation in each city using the UK government's Index of Multiple Deprivation, which ranks all 8,000-plus wards in the UK in terms of their level of multiple deprivation (DETR, 2000). In both cities, the two wards with among the highest multiple deprivation were selected, which in both Southampton and Sheffield comprised an inner city neighbourhood with a high ethnic minority population and a 'sink' social housing project. In addition, and at the other end of the spectrum, the affluent suburb suffering the least multiple deprivation in each city was chosen. In rural England, similarly, and again using the 2000 Index of Multiple Deprivation, two affluent localities with low levels of multiple deprivation (Fulbourn and Chalford) and three contrasting rural localities suffering high levels of multiple deprivation (Grimethorpe, St Blazey and Wigton) were selected for investigation with a broad regional spread. Table 7.1 provides a brief summary of these localities.

To investigate the penetration of the commodity economy in each locality, it was apparent from the outset that one could not map the whole economy. To do so would be an unmanageable task. It would require every transaction or exchange in daily life to be identified and recorded. The decision was thus taken to focus upon one major sphere of activity in people's lives, namely the realm of household service provision. Some may assert, quite correctly, that such a choice is likely to result in the identification of a larger realm of non-commodified work than if goods transactions between firms was considered. However, for the purpose of identifying the extent to which commodification has penetrated the realm of final consumption, such a sphere represents a useful starting point.

To do this, and as described in the previous chapter, structured face-to-face interviews were conducted with 861 households. Having used maximum variation sampling to identify the localities to be surveyed, resulting in some of the most affluent and deprived neighbourhoods in urban and rural areas of England being studied, a spatially stratified sampling technique was then used to collect data in each of these neighbourhoods to ensure that the data were representative of the area and so that the contrasting localities could be compared. To collect data using this spatially stratified sampling method, every nth dwelling was targeted, depending on the number of households in the locality, in order to generate the set number of interviews. This provided a representative sample of each area in terms of tenure and type of housing and prevented any skewness in the sample towards certain tenures, types of dwelling and different parts of each area being interviewed. The results are reported below.

The Uneven Geographies of Commodification in Contemporary England

Before analysing the uneven geographies of commodification in contemporary England, it is important to note that across the 861 households surveyed in these eleven areas, just 18 per cent of the 44 tasks were last conducted using commodified labour, and that it is precisely the 'subsistence' work that Watts (1999) asserts has disappeared in the advanced economies that is the principal mode of provision. Those (mostly men) extolling the increasing dominance of commodification should thus perhaps turn their gaze away from their computer screens and reflect for a moment on the extent and importance of the subsistence work that, not least, enables them to work unimpeded on their advocacy of the commodification thesis. If they did so, they might start to understand the distance that the commodity economy has to travel before it penetrates every nook and cranny of our lives in Western economies.

Turning to the uneven development of the commodity economy, it might be expected that household services would be more commodified in affluent populations, which are more likely to use nannies, cleaners, gardeners and so forth, than in deprived populations. The data in Table 7.2 reinforce this finding. The

Table 7.2   Form of work last used to undertake 44 domestic services: by geographical area

% of tasks last conducted using	Non-exchanged work	Non-monetized exchange	Non profit-motivated monetized exchange	Com-modified labour	χ^2
All areas	72	5	6	18	–
Deprived rural areas	67	7	6	20	89.8
Grimethorpe	63	8	7	22	52.1
St Blazey	71	6	4	19	12.2
Wigton	68	8	5	19	24.3
Deprived areas Southampton	75	4	4	17	64.5
St Mary's	75	3	4	17	39.0
Hightown	75	4	5	17	26.7
Deprived areas Sheffield	77	4	5	13	174.2
Pitsmoor	76	4	6	14	67.5
Manor	79	4	4	13	127.5
Affluent suburb Southampton	71	2	7	20	29.9
Affluent suburb Sheffield	73	2	11	14	29.9
Affluent rural areas	63	8	4	24	28.9
Fulbourn	67	7	5	21	32.6
Chalford	60	8	4	27	137.1

Note: $\chi^2 > 12.838$ in all cases (with the exception of St Blazey), leading us to reject H_0 within a 99.5 per cent confidence interval that there are no spatial variations in the sources of labour used to complete the 44 household services.

commodification of domestic services is deepest in affluent localities. Over one in four (27 per cent) domestic tasks were last undertaken on a commodified basis in rural Chalford, 21 per cent in rural Fulbourn and 20 per cent in the affluent suburb of relatively wealthy Southampton. The penetration of the commodity economy is shallowest, meanwhile, in deprived localities such as the social housing project in the relatively deprived city of Sheffield where just one in eight (13 per cent) of these tasks were last conducted in a commodified manner.

The significantly deeper commodification of affluent compared to deprived areas in both urban and rural England will perhaps come as no surprise. Is it also the case, however, that rural areas are less commodified than their urban counterparts? It is widely assumed, as discussed above, that there is a process of lagged adaptation so far as the commodification of rural areas is concerned (see also Williams, 2002b). This was not identified in the study. Instead, affluent rural areas, where 24 per cent of domestic services are provided using commodified labour, are more commodified than affluent suburbs, where just 17 per cent of tasks were last provided on a commodified basis. Similarly, deprived rural areas are more commodified than their deprived urban counterparts (20 per cent versus 15 per cent).

How can these uneven contours of commodification be explained? One obvious suggestion is that commodification has more deeply penetrated affluent localities because these populations have the ability to pay for commodified domestic services. Does this economic determinism alone, however, explain all of the uneven contours of commodification? To evaluate whether this is the case, the motives for people using each form of non-commodified work are here analysed.

The Uneven Geographies of Subsistence Work

Do people undertake non-exchanged work mostly out of economic necessity? As Table 7.3 shows, this is not the case. In deprived urban and rural localities, only 44 per cent and 46 per cent of non-exchanged work, respectively, was primarily motivated by economic necessity, while in the affluent urban and rural localities this was the case for just 10 per cent and 11 per cent of such work.

If economic necessity is not the primary reason, why is such work conducted on a non-exchanged basis? As discussed in the last chapter when considering socio-economic disparities, three non-economic reasons exist, namely ease, choice and pleasure,

Table 7.3 Reasons for conducting domestic tasks on a non-exchanged basis (%)

Reason	Deprived urban	Affluent urban	Deprived rural	Affluent rural
Economic	44	10	46	11
Ease	18	37	24	40
Choice	21	24	18	22
Pleasure	14	32	12	27

and there are significant variations between localities in the degree to which each of these is the motive for engaging in subsistence work (see Table 7.3).

First, the fact that it was often felt to be *easier* to do a task oneself than to contract out the work was the reason for 18 per cent and 24 per cent of all non-exchanged work in deprived urban and rural neighbourhoods, respectively, and 37 per cent and 40 per cent in affluent urban and rural areas. It was often stated, for example, that tradespeople were difficult to contact and even more difficult to persuade to come around to do a job so it was often easier to do the job oneself than rely on them. This was particularly prevalent in rural areas, perhaps due to the lesser accessibility and/or availability of formal firms.

Second, the proportion of non-exchanged work that was conducted out of *choice* was 21 per cent and 18 per cent in deprived urban and rural neighbourhoods, respectively, and 24 per cent and 22 per cent of cases where it was last used in affluent urban and rural areas. As discussed in the last chapter, this clearly displays how some populations are using home-making as a form of identity politics (e.g. Miller, 2001) to enable them to define who and what they are outside of their formal jobs. The use of non-exchanged work for this purpose, however, was more frequent in affluent urban and rural areas than in deprived localities.

Third and finally, and related to the above factor, non-exchanged activity was used due to the *pleasure* people got from doing the work themselves. Indeed, this reason accounted for some 14 per cent and 12 per cent of cases where self-servicing was last used in deprived urban and rural localities, respectively, and 32 per cent and 27 per cent of cases where it was last used in affluent urban and rural areas. On the whole, it was non-routine self-provisioning that was seen to be pleasurable and this is the reason why pleasure was more heavily cited as a reason for engaging in non-exchanged work in affluent localities where a greater proportion of this work is of the non-routine variety and there is greater financial ability to engage in such activity.

In consequence, this study displays that the persistence of non-exchanged work in the domestic services realm is not simply the result of the financial inability of households to formalize these tasks. There is also a strong resistance to the transfer of activity to the commodified sphere. Households prefer to use self-servicing due to ease, choice or pleasure. Commodification, in consequence, is constrained not only by economic factors but also by 'cultures of resistance' to the edicts of commodification. The relative influence of economic constraints and agency in determining decisions to engage in non-exchanged work, however, varies over space, as displayed in the differential preference/necessity ratios. In affluent areas, non-exchanged work is much less a product of economic constraints than in deprived areas. Indeed, despite being financially able to commodify a wide range of activity, these households choose only to commodify a narrow spectrum of mostly routine, mundane and repetitive tasks and use some of the time released to engage in more non-routine, creative and rewarding self-servicing activity that they conduct out of preference rather than necessity. In deprived areas, however, where non-exchanged work is composed mostly of essential and/or routine tasks, necessity tends to prevail to a greater extent.

In relatively affluent localities, therefore, self-servicing acts to secure a definition of self that would be undermined by an exclusive reliance on commodified labour. Many people in these localities avoid externalizing activity in order to forge forms of self-identity and worth through this type of endeavour. Self-provisioning thus provides an alternative nexus to commodified work through which people forge and display who and what they are and wish to be. The outcome is that engagement in non-exchanged work seems to be retained as an act of resistance to the notion of defining who and what one is through employment alone (cf. Gorz, 1999; Rifkin, 1996).

Of course, and just as in the commodity economy, the abilities of different localities to use non-exchanged work in this manner vary and the sizes of the rewards differ. In deprived areas where self-servicing is compelled more by necessity, it is much less about choice and display, and much more about having to manage on one's own. In more affluent localities, however, non-exchanged work represents a sphere where needs can be fulfilled, capabilities developed and creative desires expressed, resulting in larger material and psychological benefits.

The Uneven Geographies of Non-monetized Exchange

To understand the geographies of non-monetized exchange, it is necessary first of all to distinguish between formal and informal community engagement. As Table 7.4 reveals, when this is done some significant cross-national variations within Western economies are revealed. In southern European nations, for example, there are low levels of formal engagement compared with northern European nations but the level of participation in informal engagement (i.e. talking with, meeting and receiving support from kin, friends and neighbours) is much higher. This indicates, therefore, that there are different cultures of community involvement in different regions within the advanced economies. In southern European countries, the participatory culture is more informally orientated than in northern European nations, whose culture is more formally orientated.

It is not only at the cross-national level, however, that these contrasting participatory cultures can be identified. There are also significant variations within countries both at the regional and the local level. Starting with regional variations, Table 7.5 documents the regional variations in the extent and nature of involvement in non-monetized exchange in the UK. This reveals that formal forms of non-monetized exchange are far more widespread in

Table 7.4 Indicators of formal and informal engagement in European Union nations (%)

	Talk to neighbours on most days	Meet friends and relatives not living in household on most days	Receive financial support or maintenance from relatives, friends or others outside the household	Participate in clubs or organizations
Denmark	32.4	26.4	8.3	58.8
France	41.4	64.5	3.6	48.5
Germany	35.1	23.6	0.8	51.8
Netherlands	19.0	19.3	4.7	50.0
Belgium	29.4	32.1	6.8	35.5
UK	42.1	36.4	5.5	48.5
Ireland	54.9	71.3	0.5	47.5
Italy	47.2	43.7	3.6	18.4
Spain	57.6	63.7	2.6	30.4
Portugal	56.4	37.6	1.2	18.3
Greece	75.5	57.8	4.7	12.9

Source: ECHP 1994 wave 1, reported in Paugam and Russell, 2001: synthesis of Tables 12.3, 12.5, 12.7 and 12.10.

some regions than in others. In the Southeast, East and London regions, for example, some 19 per cent, 17 per cent and 15 per cent of respondents, respectively, had been actively involved in at least one organization during the past three years, but this was the case for just 7 per cent of the population responding in the Northeast and 9 per cent in the Northwest. Community participation in the form of active engagement in local organizations is thus very much part of the participatory culture of regions such as the Southeast but is poorly developed in other regions such as the Northeast and Northwest.

Turning to how informal non-monetized exchange varies across regions, meanwhile, the 2000 GHS again provides a useful insight

Table 7.5 Regional variations in the extent of formal and informal community involvement (% of respondents)

Government office region	Involvement in local organization with respon- sibilities in last 3 years	Involvement in local organization without res- ponsibilities in last 3 years	Done favour for neighbour in past 6 months	Received favour from neighbour in past 6 months
Northeast	7	6	71	72
Northwest	9	9	77	74
Merseyside	11	7	77	73
Yorkshire and Humberside	13	6	74	74
East Midlands	14	10	74	71
West Midlands	17	5	71	69
East	11	8	73	73
London	15	7	70	65
Southeast	19	8	73	72
Southwest	13	8	78	79
Wales	15	9	75	73
Scotland	13	7	77	75
All regions	13	8	74	72

Source: Derived from Coulthard et al., 2002: Tables 2.14 and 3.14.

into the regional differences in participatory cultures. Although London, as mentioned, has relatively higher rates of participation in formal non-monetized work than other regions, it has the lowest rate of engagement in informal community involvement. While 72 per cent of respondents nationally had received a favour from a neighbour in the past six months, this was the case for just 65 per cent of Londoners (compared with 79 per cent in the Southwest). Similarly, while the Southeast displayed the highest rates of formal community participation, its rate of informal engagement is below

Table 7.6 Regional variations in time spent on formal and informal non-monetized exchange in the UK, 2000 (minutes)

Region	Formal non-monetized exchange	Informal non-monetized exchange
	Weekday	
North	3	11
Midlands	4	7
East	3	5
London and Southeast	5	5
Southwest	6	9
Wales	3	8
Scotland	3	10
Northern Ireland	–	9
Significance	F=2.49, p<0.05	F=7.68, p<0.001
	Weekend	
North	2	10
Midlands	1	13
East	4	8
London and Southeast	3	8
Southwest	4	7
Wales	5	6
Scotland	4	9
Northern Ireland	4	16
Significance	ns	ns

Note: One-way ANOVA test, ns = not significant.

Source: UK 2000 Time Use Survey (ONS, 2003).

the national average so far as receiving favours from neighbours is concerned. The Northwest, in contrast, despite having among the lowest rates of formal participation, is among those regions displaying the highest rates of engagement in informal forms of giving and receiving. In consequence, the participatory culture of some regions is orientated towards formal involvement and that of others towards informal engagement.

Table 7.7   Participation in volunteering in UK within the last 12 months, by level of deprivation in area (%)

	Least deprived			Most deprived			All
	I	2	3	4	5	6	
Informal volunteering	71	69	68	65	64	59	66
Formal volunteering	47	41	39	35	33	29	37

Source: HOCS 2001.

This is further reinforced by the 2000 UK Time Use survey (ONS, 2003). As Table 7.6 reveals, there is a tendency for the populations of the northern regions to spend more time engaged in informal non-monetized exchange rather than more formal forms of non-monetized exchange. Again, therefore, yet further evidence exists of these differential cultures of community engagement.

Similar findings about variable cultures of community engagement apply at other spatial scales. Using the Index of Multiple Deprivation produced by the Department of Local Government, Transport and the Regions (DLTR), the 2001 Home Office Citizenship Survey (HOCS) examines participation rates in formal and informal volunteering in six types of ward, ranging from the most to the least deprived (see Prime et al., 2002). The finding is that although participation in both formal and informal non-monetized work is significantly greater in more affluent areas, it is the proportion of people involved in formal engagement that differs by the largest margin when comparing the least and most deprived areas. As Table 7.7 displays, less than a third (29 per cent of people) engage in formal groups in the most deprived areas, compared with nearly half (47 per cent) of people in the most affluent areas. Consequently, while the proportion involved in formal groups differs by some 18 percentage points between the most and least deprived areas, the proportion involved in informal one-to-one aid differs by just 12 percentage points (71 per cent compared with 59 per cent).

Table 7.8 Spatial variations in the extent of participation in informal and formal volunteering in England and Wales: by Index of Deprivation (deciles)

% of respondents	Most deprived								Least deprived		All
	1	2	3	4	5	6	7	8	9	10	
Been involved in a local organization, with responsibilities	7	7	12	12	15	12	15	22	20	18	13
Been involved in a local organization without responsibilities	7	5	7	7	8	7	9	8	7	11	8
Done favour for a neighbour in past 6 months	65	72	73	78	76	74	71	77	77	78	74
Received favour from a neighbour in past 6 months	64	68	71	77	75	74	71	74	74	76	72

Source: General Household Survey 2000.

This finding is further reinforced by the 2000 GHS, which conducts a slightly finer-grained analysis by dividing wards into ten decile groups ranging from the least to the most deprived, again using the Index of Multiple Deprivation of the DLTR. Table 7.8 presents the results (Coulthard et al., 2002). In the most deprived 10 per cent of wards in England and Wales, for example, just 7 per cent of respondents had been involved in a local organization with responsibilities over the last three years (compared with 18 per cent in the most affluent wards) and 7 per cent without responsibilities (11 per cent in the most affluent wards). To seek to develop the voluntary sector by cultivating participation in voluntary groups is thus to attempt to harness a vehicle in which only a small proportion of the population of deprived areas engage.

This third sector approach has as its focus the development of a specific participatory culture that is relatively unfamiliar to most of the population in deprived areas and, at the same time, pays no heed to bolstering further that aspect of the voluntary sector in which two-thirds (65 per cent) of respondents in deprived areas are already involved, namely one-to-one aid.

There are also variations at other spatial scales. Although it is widely recognized that the size of place makes a difference, with non-monetized exchange being more common in smaller towns than in bigger cities (Horton Smith, 1994; Korte and Kerr, 1975; Piliavin, 1990; Putnam, 2000; Steblay, 1987; Wilson, 1985; Wolpert, 1993), there is lesser understanding of how the balance between formal and informal forms of non-monetized exchange differ between urban and rural areas. Williams and Windebank (2003a) find in their household work practices survey that urban areas tend to be more orientated towards formal forms of community engagement than their rural counterparts, suggesting that one-to-one aid is much more part of the culture of community engagement in rural than in urban areas.

Turning to the motives for participating in non-monetized exchange, the important finding of the data collected by Williams and Windebank (2003a) is that in relatively deprived localities and regions, non-monetized work is more commonly used for the purpose of giving and receiving material aid than in relatively affluent localities and regions, where it is principally engaged in for reasons associated with sociability. Here, therefore, similar arguments apply to those discussed in the last chapter when analysing the socio-economic disparities. There is thus no need to repeat them here. Instead, it is sufficient to state that while the culture of community engagement in affluent and southern regions is more grounded in formal involvement and loose ties so as to seek out opportunities for sociability, deprived and northern localities are more characterized by informal engagement in denser ties (especially with kin) in order to make ends meet. To concentrate on developing formal groups, therefore, is to feed the participatory culture of affluent and southern regions and to promote a form of non-monetized work used for social rather than economic purposes. This will be returned to in Part III.

The Uneven Geographies of Cash-in-Hand Work

How does the nature of cash-in-hand exchange, and how do its underlying motives, vary across space? Until now, cash-in-hand exchange has been seen to exemplify universally the more flexible profit-motivated exchange relations arising under post-Fordist regimes of accumulation (e.g. Castells and Portes, 1989; Leonard, 1994; Portes, 1994; Sassen, 1989) and to be a form of low-paid peripheral employment conducted in marginalized areas for unadulterated economic reasons (e.g. Castells and Portes, 1989; Portes, 1994). Here, however, such a reading is evaluated critically.

There is now a wealth of studies that have examined the geographies of cash-in-hand work in Canada (e.g. Fortin et al., 1996), the UK (e.g. Williams and Windebank, 2003a), the Netherlands (e.g. Renooy, 1990; Van Geuns et al., 1987) and Belgium (e.g. Kesteloot and Meert, 1999). These all reveal that such work is more prevalent in affluent than in deprived areas.

Nor is all of this work conducted for economic gain. In recent years, a greater spatial sensitivity has arisen regarding the motives underpinning engagement in such work. As Williams and Windebank (2003a) have shown in the UK, although such work is firmly embedded in unadulterated economic motives in affluent areas, in deprived localities much cash-in-hand exchange is conducted for and by close social relations for primarily social reasons or to help each other out in a way that avoids any connotation of charity.

In affluent suburbs, for example, 84 per cent of cash-in-hand transactions involved the use of firms or unknown self-employed individuals, and in 80 per cent of the instances where such work was sourced, it was used as a cheaper alternative to formal firms. In deprived urban areas, in stark contrast, 68 per cent of all cash-in-hand exchanges involved transactions conducted by friends, neighbours or relatives (16 per cent in affluent suburbs), and economic reasons prevailed in just 18 per cent of all instances where cash-in-hand work was employed. In all these cases where economic motives prevail, moreover, it was firms and/or self-employed people not known by the household conducting the work. When closer social relations are involved, the work is either conducted to maintain or build social networks, or is seen as an opportunity to give money to another person in a way that avoids any connotation of charity (see Williams and Windebank, 2001a). The same differences are found when cash-in-hand work is compared in affluent and deprived rural localities (see Williams and Windebank, 2003a). In affluent rural localities, it is again the case that cash-in-hand work is more likely to be conducted by firms and/or self-employed people for the purpose of economic gain, while in deprived rural localities it is much more the case that such work is conducted for friends, neighbours and kin for reasons associated with sociality and redistribution. As such, cash-in-hand work in affluent urban and rural areas is more akin to commodified work, while in deprived urban and rural areas it is more akin to mutual aid.

Similar to non-exchanged work, therefore, participation in cash-in-hand work appears to have a varying logic across space. Such contrasting local logics mean that the penetration of monetary relations by the profit motive is spatially variable. In affluent urban and rural areas, the profit motive has deeply penetrated monetary relations, with 96 per cent and 98 per cent, respectively, of all (formal and informal) monetary exchanges in the domestic services realm conducted for profit-motivated rationales. In deprived urban and rural areas, however, the penetration of monetary relations by the profit motive is shallower with just 70 per cent and 76 per cent, respectively, of all such (formal and informal) monetary exchanges being conducted for profit-motivated reasons. This displays the dangers of constructing generalizations from narrow experiential knowledge bases. The theory that profit-motivated monetary relations are penetrating every nook and cranny of social life (e.g. Harvey, 1989; Sayer, 1997), although applicable in the limited context of some affluent localities, is far from the reality elsewhere.

The implication is that even if there has been the penetration of monetary relations into every nook and cranny of social life, this is by no means everywhere driven by the motive of profit. Indeed, the study of cash-in-hand exchange, conventionally seen as the epitome of unbridled profit-motivated capitalism, displays how there exist monetary transactions that are embedded in alternative social relations and motives, particularly in deprived areas, that both help maintain the social fabric of such neighbourhoods and fill some of the gap left by the failure of markets.

Conclusions

This chapter has sought to delineate the uneven geographies of commodification, as well as the contrasting geographies of non-commodified work, within the advanced economies and to explore why this might be the case. In order to draw some conclusions about the uneven geographies of commodification and contours of work, this final section first synthesizes the above findings on the spatial variations in economic practices and then explores the nature of the relationship between the commodified and non-commodified realms.

Analysing how economic practices differ between urban and rural areas, it has been revealed that urban households rely to a far greater extent than their rural counterparts on using either commodified labour or their own endeavours to get work completed. There is a relative inability to draw upon the resources of wider community networks, especially in the form of one-to-one aid, in their coping practices. Rural households, meanwhile, although conducting less non-exchanged work, display a greater proclivity to draw upon broader community resources, especially in the form of one-to-one unpaid help and cash-in-hand work conducted by friends, neighbours and kin on a not-for-profit basis. Rural household economic practices thus use a wider mix of self-provisioning, unpaid and paid community exchange and commodified labour, whilst urban households adopt more bifurcated practices where either self-provisioning or formal labour is used.

Comparing affluent and deprived areas, meanwhile, both within rural areas as well as on an intra- and inter-urban level, economic practices again significantly vary, albeit not in the same manner as when urban and rural areas are contrasted. The first key distinction between affluent and deprived areas relates to the amount of work taking place. Affluent areas are here found to be more 'fully engaged' (or 'work busy') localities whilst deprived areas are relatively 'disengaged' (or 'work deprived') localities, with lower levels of both non-commodified and commodified work. However, it is not only the amount of work undertaken that differentiates them.

What also differentiates them is their work practices or 'work cultures', which differ in three respects. First, households in affluent areas are more formalized and monetized in the coping practices that they employ. Second, there are significant differences in the character of each form of work. In affluent areas, due to their greater externalization of routine self-provisioning to the formal and paid realm, a much larger proportion of self-servicing activity is non-routine, creative and rewarding in nature, whilst in deprived areas it is of the routine, mundane and less rewarding variety. Unpaid community exchange in affluent areas, meanwhile, is less conducted on a one-to-one basis and cash-in-hand work more carried out by and for people previously unknown on a profit-motivated basis. In deprived areas, in contrast, unpaid community exchange is largely of the one-to-one rather than the organized variety, and cash-in-hand work is much more a form of mutual aid conducted for social and redistributive purposes.

Third and finally, in affluent areas the work practices adopted are more likely to be a product of choice than of necessity, whilst in deprived areas this is much less the case. It has thus been shown here that it is too simplistic to argue that the uneven geographies of commodification are purely a result of structural economic conditions. Rather, human agency has been shown to play a vital role, especially in more affluent localities. Similar to the argument in the last chapter, therefore, a pluralistic and spatially sensitive both/and approach is thus required. This explains the persistence of the non-commodified realm and its uneven contours using both structural economic constraints and agency, but the weight given to each in explanations is seen to vary significantly according to the place under investigation. While cultures of resistance are far more influential than economic forces in sustaining a decommodified sphere in some areas (e.g. affluent suburbs, rural areas), more emphasis is required on economic forces in other localities (e.g. deprived urban neighbourhoods). Here, therefore, and rather than adopt either economic constraints or agency, it is argued that the slow, shallow and uneven advance of commodification can only be understood using both the structural economic and agency-orientated explanations and exploring how their role varies across space.

In sum, although affluent areas are more formalized, monetized and profit-motivated in their economic practices, they also engage in a much wider range of non-commodified work, much of which is out of choice. Meanwhile, if households in deprived areas are witnessing the offloading of their social reproduction functions onto the non-exchanged and non-monetized realm by a state and market sphere seeking to reduce social costs, this chapter displays that it would be erroneous to describe such areas as possessing an extensive and well-developed non-commodified sphere. Instead, a concomitant contraction rather than expansion of the non-commodified sphere appears to have occurred.

Viewing the non-commodified sphere as increasingly colonized, a substitute for, alternative to or by-product of the formal sphere, does not thus reflect its articulation in people's everyday lives. Given its size, the non-commodified realm cannot be seen as a leftover from precapitalist social formations. Neither can it be seen as a substitute for, or by-product of, the commodified sector that is confined to marginal populations. Nor can it be viewed always as an 'alternative' to the formal sphere by counterposing these two realms to each other in the belief that the growth of one (i.e. non-capitalist economic practice) can lead to the demise of the other (i.e. capitalism).

Instead, this chapter reveals that the commodified and non-commodified spheres coexist in a relationship of complementarity. Unlike those adopting a contrarian view of the relationship between these spheres, this study finds that contemporary society is not witnessing a polarization between an affluent core drawing upon formal provision in order to meet their needs and desires, and a deprived periphery increasingly engaged in non-commodified practices in response to their exclusion from the formal sphere. Rather, it identifies the existence of 'work busy' localities relatively fully engaged in a plurality of economic practices, and 'work deprived' localities relatively disengaged from both the commodified and the non-commodified spheres.

This has important implications for understanding both the nature of uneven development and the changes required to resolve it. So far, and based on a contrarian view of the interrelationship between the commodified and non-commodified realms, the degree of formalization and commodification has been popularly portrayed as differentiating affluent from deprived populations, and the solution has been to try to insert deprived populations into the commodity economy so that they can earn money in order to acquire commodified goods and services to meet their needs and desires. Here, however, the identification of a distinction between localities more fully engaged in a plurality of economic practices and those disconnected from both commodified and non-commodified coping practices suggests that it is important not only to insert people into commodified economic relations but also to develop their capacities to engage in non-commodified work.

Of course, if it is believed that a change in a locality's commodified sphere causes a change in its capacity to engage in non-commodified economic practices, then there will be no need for a raft of initiatives to harness the commodified realm. However, whether such a one-way cause-and-effect approach applies is very much open to question. It appears that a non-reductive approach that recognizes the co-constitutive complementary relationships between commodified and non-commodified economic practices is a more accurate portrayal (see also Smith, 2002). This will be returned to in Part III. Here, it will suffice to say that there are large question marks over the policy option of seeking solely to develop the commodity economy as the principal route to salvation for deprived areas.

8

Gender and Commodification

The last two chapters outlined the uneven socio-economic and spatial contours of commodification, highlighting how lower-income populations have less commodified lifestyles and participate in non-commodified work mainly out of economic necessity, unlike affluent populations, which conduct a wider range of non-commodified work more as a matter of choice. In this chapter consideration is given to gender differences. Are men's work patterns more commodified than women's and how is this changing? Is it the case, as might be assumed, that although men's work patterns have been historically more commodified than those of women, women are leading increasingly commodified lives and men more decommodified lives? In other words, is a process of convergence taking place? And what are the gender disparities in the extent and nature of non-exchanged work, non-monetized exchange and cash-in-hand work? This chapter seeks to answer such questions.

Here, some marked gender variations in the degree of commodification and the direction of change will be identified. While the working lives of men in the advanced economies will be shown to be witnessing a process of decommodification, quite the opposite is revealed to be happening for women. For them, a process of commodification is taking place. Until now, it will be revealed, few commentators writing from the perspective of women's position have seen such a trend in a negative light. It has been widely assumed that the commodification of women's working lives is the route to their liberation. Few have thus stopped to consider whether advocating the greater subjugation of women by capitalist social relations, especially given the low-paid nature of women's employment, is the route to their liberation, doubtless because they equate, or maybe confuse, this with financial independence from men. This chapter, however, starts to evaluate critically whether women's further immersion in the commodity economy is the path to independence. Showing that even though women have entered the commodified realm, they remain responsible for much of the subsistence work, non-monetized exchange and cash-in-hand work, especially of the routine, monotonous and unrewarding variety, this chapter finds that perhaps greater attention needs to be placed on resolving the gender disparities in the non-commodified realm by encouraging men to engage more in such activity rather than solely seeking to immerse women in commodified work.

To show this, the chapter first charts the gender disparities in formal employment and how this is changing over time. Second, the shifts in the work schedules of men and women are analysed in terms of how the paid/unpaid work balance is changing for both genders. Following this, the gender disparities in, first, subsistence work, second, non-monetized exchange and, third, cash-in-hand work will be evaluated. This will reveal that although there is evidence of a convergence in work schedules so far as the paid/unpaid work balance is concerned, women remain responsible for non-commodified work, especially that which is routine, monotonous and unrewarding in nature. To conclude, therefore, some crucial questions are raised about the direction of change and its implications for men and women.

Gender Disparities in Formal Employment

To begin to chart the extent to which men and women lead commodified working lives and how this is changing over time, this section investigates one of the most noticeable features in the formal labour market throughout the advanced economies, namely the changing gender composition of the labour force. Over the past half-century, the employment participation rates of women and men have steadily converged and are now approaching parity.

At the turn of the millennium in the UK, for instance, some 75 per cent of the total population of working age was in employment, but 70 per cent of women of working age compared with 80 per cent of men.

Indeed, during the past decade or so, the particular life-cycle pattern of women's participation in employment that was so evident in the past has disappeared (Gregg and Wadsworth, 1996), even if the pay rates and hours that have long distinguished women's employment remain. Until recently, that is, a graph of women's participation rates by age would have revealed two peaks: among young women until their mid-twenties, after which rates declined until they peaked again by about the age of 40. Presently, however, this line is almost flat, paralleling that of men's participation, but about 10 per cent below it. A significant change in women's participation, therefore, which has been evident since about 1975, is that women in their thirties with dependent children are now almost just as likely to be in the labour force as women of other ages. Although there remain marked gender differences in hours of employment, with women constituting the vast majority of part-time employees and also their pay being lower (e.g. Gardiner, 1997; Himmelweit, 2000; McDowell, 2001), the widespread view is that employment represents a route to their liberation. All that is seen to be now required are fairer conditions of employment to match those of men.

For men of working age, meanwhile, the last decades have seen a decline in overall participation rates in the UK from 91 per cent in 1979 to 84 per cent by the end of the 1990s, an absolute decline of 3.5 million men in waged employment. This fall has been particularly noticeable for men over 50 years old, whose average participation rates now match those for women of their age. This 'lost generation' of men aged 50 to 65 is the result of both corporate de-layering and downsizing, as well as a continuing decline of male-dominated manufacturing industries, similar to many other advanced economies. Overall, therefore, the patterns of employment for men and women are moving in markedly different directions. However, it is not solely the participation of men and women in formal employment that is undergoing significant change.

Gender and the Commodification of Working Time

With the immersion of women in formal employment and men's increasing exclusion, is it the case that men and women are also converging in terms of the proportion of time that they spend engaged in paid and unpaid work? Table 8.1 investigates the changing ways in which men and women spend their working time in twenty countries. This reveals that while women have witnessed a commodification of their work schedules, there has been a decommodification so far as men are concerned. The share of unpaid work in men's total working time has increased from 19.4 per cent in 1960–73 through 22.0 per cent in the period 1974–84 to 26.4 per cent from 1985 until the present. For women, in contrast, there has been a process of commodification, at least if the period from 1985 to the present is compared with 1960–73. The share of women's total work time that is occupied by unpaid domestic work has reduced from 64.6 per cent to 62.7 per cent. Nevertheless, nearly two-thirds of women's total working time is spent engaged in domestic work, whilst for men under a quarter of their total working time is spent in this realm. Importantly, moreover, and contrary to popular myth, the reduction in the proportion of time that women spend in unpaid work is not due to an increase in the time spent in employment. Rather, it is mostly due to the decrease in the time spent on domestic work.

There appears to be, therefore, a slow convergence of men's and women's work patterns, even if there is an extremely long way to go before they fully converge. It is important to highlight, however, that this convergence is taking place within the context of an over-arching process of decommodification, not commodification.

From these data, it is far from evident that 'the commodification of domestic labour ... has continued to expand' (McDowell, 2001: 457). Merely pointing a finger at the expansion of paid domestic workers, as McDowell does along with others (e.g. Anderson, 2001a, 2001b), provides no clue about whether or not there is an overall process of commodification. It is only by comparing the amount of unpaid relative to paid work that this can be understood, and the overwhelming evidence presented in Table 8.1 is of a process of decommodification.

Table 8.1 Distribution of working time in twenty countries, by gender

Minutes/day	Mean	1960–73	1974–83	1985–present
Men and women				
Paid work	297	309	285	291
Domestic work	230	237	212	235
% of working time spent on domestic work	43.6	43.4	42.7	44.7
Women				
Paid work	196	198	193	196
Domestic work	339	362	310	329
% of working time spent on domestic work	63.4	64.6	61.6	62.7
Men				
Paid work	403	424	382	391
Domestic work	115	102	108	140
% of working time spent on domestic work	22.2	19.4	22.0	26.4

Source: Gershuny, 2000: Table 7.1.

At this point, it might be argued, as shown above, that it is necessary to differentiate the experiences of men and women. In order to do so, therefore, the following sections analyse the gender disparities in the extent and nature of non-exchanged work, non-monetized exchange and cash-in-hand work. This will reveal the marked differences in both the extent and the character of the non-commodified work undertaken by men and women.

Gender Disparities in Subsistence Work

Analysing the data in Table 8.1 further, it is apparent that there has been little renegotiation of the gender division of domestic work. In the period 1960–73, women conducted 362 minutes of domestic work per day on average compared with 102 minutes by men. As such, the total time spent in domestic work by men was just 28.2 per cent that of women. By 1974–83, although the time spent by women had fallen to 310 minutes and men's had risen to 108 minutes, the time spent by men was still only just over a third (34.8 per cent) of the time spent by women. Studies conducted between 1985 and the present day, meanwhile, reveal continuing progress in that, despite women's time spent on domestic work rising to 329 minutes, men's contribution had risen to 140 minutes, meaning that the time that they spent on domestic work was now 42.5 per cent of the time spent by women. As such, women still spend well over twice the amount of time as men on subsistence work. Non-exchanged work, therefore, remains chiefly women's realm, even if there appears to be a slight redistribution of this work towards men as the decades have rolled on.

Such aggregate data on total time spent engaged in subsistence work, however, mask some important underlying trends so far as men's contribution to the domestic workload is concerned. On the one hand, as will be shown below, women still conduct the vast majority of the routine domestic work, and much of the growth in men's participation in subsistence work can be put down to the growth in their participation in non-routine domestic work (e.g. DIY activity). On the other hand, and more qualitatively, there is the issue of whether men have taken responsibility for domestic work or whether they just 'help out' more than they did in the past.

Starting with the issue of the nature of men's participation in routine (cleaning and cooking) and non-routine (childcare, shopping, odd jobs) subsistence work, the finding is that in 1960–73, men conducted 20 minutes of core domestic work compared with women's 236 minutes and thus spent just 8.5 per cent of the time of women on routine domestic activity. By 1974–84, however, women spent 198 minutes per day compared with men's 31 minutes (15.6 per cent of the time spent by women), and from 1985 to the present, the 180 minutes spent by women was matched by men's 40 minutes per day (22.2 per cent of the time spent by women). On one level, therefore, there has been some renegotiation of the routine domestic workload, albeit from a very low base level so far as men are concerned. Men now spend just over one-fifth of the time of women on routine domestic work.

Turning to participation in non-routine domestic work (childcare, shopping, odd jobs), meanwhile, one sees a far greater surge in men's contribution. Men's 82 minutes in 1960–73 was matched by 126 minutes by women. By 1974–85, men were spending 75 minutes compared with women's 112 minutes, and from 1985 to the present, men have been spending 100 minutes compared with women's 109 minutes. There is a clear need, therefore, to distinguish the types of domestic work engaged in by men when considering the fact that the time that they spend in this sphere has increased.

It is not only the fact that women still conduct the vast majority of the routine domestic work. There is also the issue of who takes responsibility for the domestic workload. It might well be the case that men are doing more of the shopping, for instance, than was the case in the past, especially the grocery shopping. However, what needs to be considered is whether responsibility for this work is also shifting towards men. In the case of grocery shopping, for instance, one needs to ask who makes the list of what items are required? Is that men or women? Similarly on the issue of childcare, one needs to consider that even if men are now more engaged in caring for children, is it simply so that women can be released in order to go out to their jobs and thus relieve them of their role as principal 'breadwinner', and who cares for the child when both are present and available? The split-shift system, for example, whereby men and women engage in employment at different times of the day is a growing trend. Men's increased contribution in the realm of childcare, therefore, may well simply be a result of women's dual responsibility. Moreover, it may well be also a product of the demise of availability of other women (e.g. grandmothers) to care for children. Indeed, there is some evidence that it is only when men are forced through necessity that they undertake more subsistence work (see, e.g., Windebank, 1999), indicating the value attached to such work in the wider society.

Overall, therefore, the time-budget data on men's increased contribution to the domestic workload hide some important trends so far as the nature of the work of men and women is concerned. Women remain responsible for the vast majority of the routine domestic work, and there is little evidence that there has been any significant shift of responsibility for subsistence work from women to men over the past few decades.

This has clear implications for the issue mentioned earlier, that non-commodified work often goes unnoticed and is frequently not even seen to be a form of work (see Chapter 2). Of course, one reason why this may be the case is because of who does it. Women's share of the total time spent on routine domestic work is 81.8 per cent (Gershuny, 2000: Table 7.1). The commodification thesis, therefore, is perhaps just one more portrayal of how male scholars who scribe texts asserting that there is a commodification of life appear oblivious to the necessary work taking place around them that allows them to partake in their mistaken musings. It is thus perhaps no accident that the majority of those actively selling the commodification thesis are men. Subsistence work, however, is not the only sphere of non-commodified work in which there are significant gender disparities.

Gender Disparities in Non-monetized Exchange

Examining the data on men's and women's participation in non-monetized exchange, it becomes quickly apparent that women engage in far greater levels of such unpaid exchange than men. This is the case across nearly all advanced economies. Indeed, examining the evidence collected by the Johns Hopkins University Comparative Not-for-Profit Sector project, it is shown that in all nations studied women undertake a greater amount of non-monetized exchange than men (Salamon et al., 1999).

Take, for example, the case of the UK. Using data from the 2000 UK Time Use Survey (ONS, 2003), Table 8.2 reveals that women spend more time involved in unpaid community exchange, whether of the formal or informal variety, than men. Indeed, at weekends women spend 50 per cent more time than men on formal community involvement and 37 per cent more time on informal forms of community engagement.

Table 8.2 Average time spent on informal and formal
community engagement in the UK, by gender

	Formal volunteering	Informal volunteering
Weekdays		
Men	4 mins	6 mins
Women	4 mins	9 mins
Significance	ns	p<0.001
Weekend		
Men	2 mins	8 mins
Women	3 mins	11 mins
Significance	ns	p<0.05

Notes: Information is for main activity only. Differences between means tested using T-test:
p<0.001 very significant, p<0.05 significant, ns= not significant.
Source: 2000 UK Time Use Survey.

It is also the case that when measured in terms of participation
rates a greater proportion of women than men engage in such
non-monetary work in the UK. The 2000 UK Time Use survey,
for example, identifies that in the four weeks prior to interview
some 13 per cent of women compared with 11 per cent of men had
engaged in formal forms of community engagement, and 33 per
cent of women compared with 27 per cent of men in informal one-
to-one aid. This finding that it is women rather than men who are
likely to engage in non-monetized exchange in the UK is further
reinforced by a multitude of other surveys conducted in recent
years, including the British Crime Survey, Home Office Active
Citizenship Survey and General Household Survey (Coulthard
et al., 2002; Kershaw et al., 2000; Krishnamurthy et al., 2001;
Prime et al., 2002). It appears, therefore, that women conduct
both more formal and more informal non-monetary work than
men. It is also the case, and returning to an issue considered in
the previous chapter with reference to socio-economic and spatial
disparities, that women have a more informal culture of community
engagement than men. Examining Tables 8.2 and 8.3, it is clear
that women's participation in unpaid community engagement is
more oriented towards informal forms of engagement than is the

Table 8.3   Percentage of adults who engage in formal and informal volunteering, different time periods

Volunteering[1]	In the past four weeks[2]			On the diary day[3]		
	Men	*Women*	*All*	*Men*	*Women*	*All*
Formal	11	13	12	3	3	3
Informal	27	33	31	7	11	9

1 Main activity only, for weekends and weekdays combined.
2 Using the individual questionnaire.
3 Using the time-use diaries.

Source: UK 2000 Time Use Survey.

case with men, who are more oriented towards formal forms of engagement.

Such findings about the gender disparities in both the extent and the nature of non-monetary work are not unique to the UK. In South Australia, for instance, Ironmonger (2002) finds that in 2000, women contributed the equivalent of A$945 million dollars in the form of both organized and unorganized community engagement compared with A$865 million from men (i.e. 9 per cent higher than men). In the United States, meanwhile, and as Putnam (2000) reveals, men are found to be more likely to participate in formal forms of community exchange and women in informal community exchange. As Putnam (2000: 95) puts it, 'keeping up with friends and relatives continues to be socially defined as women's work'. Women, therefore, represent the social glue that maintains informal social ties.

In sum, it is not solely in the sphere of non-exchanged work that there are significant gender disparities in both the extent and the character of non-commodified work. The same applies to unpaid community exchange. Again, women not only conduct a disproportionate amount of such work but also tend to be more likely to engage in informal forms of engagement compared with men, whose culture of engagement is oriented towards more formal forms of community engagement. Is this also the case, however, when cash-in-hand work is evaluated?

Gender Disparities in Cash-in-Hand Work

The commodification thesis assumes that money transactions are always profit-motivated. In Chapter 5 it was revealed that this is not always the case. Here, therefore, the issue of whether money transactions are more likely to march hand in hand with the profit motive when men rather than women are involved is evaluated. To investigate this, the case of cash-in-hand work is analysed.

Until now, and reflecting the view that cash-in-hand work is market-like exchange undertaken for the purpose of economic gain (e.g. Castells and Portes, 1989; De Soto, 1989; Lagos, 1995; Maldonado, 1995; Matthews, 1983; Rosanvallon, 1980; Sassen, 1989), women cash-in-hand workers have been largely viewed as engaged in low-paid forms of exploitative market-oriented work for the purpose of making additional money 'on the side' so as to help the household get by (e.g. Howe, 1990; Jordan et al., 1992; Leonard, 1994; MacDonald, 1994; Morris, 1987, 1995; Rowlingson et al., 1997). Men, meanwhile, have been viewed as relatively better paid for their cash-in-hand work and more likely to see their money as 'extra cash' for their personal spending. Here, however, this view of the character and motives of women's cash-in-hand work is evaluated critically.

Until now, few studies have investigated either the character or the motives underpinning engagement in such work. Instead, it has been simply assumed that this is profit-motivated exploitative employment. Here, therefore, it is again necessary to draw upon the results of the English household work practices survey in order to understand this issue. Drawing upon the interviews conducted with 400 households in UK lower-income urban neighbourhoods (reported in depth in Williams and Windebank, 2003c), it will be revealed here that for men, cash-in-hand work is more likely to be undertaken under social relations akin to employment for profit-motivated purposes, whilst the vast bulk conducted by women is undertaken for and by friends, kin and neighbours under non-market relations for reasons associated with redistribution and sociality. This thus reveals the need for a less totalizing and more gendered conceptualization of this form of monetary exchange. Although some cash-in-hand work conducted by women in these

Spring cleaning	2	2	89	13	72	15
Do the shopping	1	1	80	14	50	36
Wash clothes/sheets	1	1	88	11	73	17
Ironing	1	1	80	11	71	18
Cook the meals	1	1	88	12	54	34
Wash dishes	1	1	83	17	53	30
Hairdressing	8	8	80	22	75	3
Administration	1	1	50	28	59	13
Making and repairing goods	**2**	**3**	**94**	**10**	**89**	**1**
Make clothes	0	0	100	9	91	0
Knitting	0	0	100	2	98	0
Repair clothes	0	0	100	7	91	2
Make furniture	6	1	50	61	39	0
Make garden equipment	33	0	0	50	50	0
Make curtains	8	2	100	3	97	0
Car maintenance (last year)	**9**	**12**	**11**	**78**	**15**	**8**
Wash car	6	3	50	68	20	13
Repair the car	19	8	13	100	0	0
Car maintenance	4	2	0	84	12	4
Gardening (last year)	2	3	58	32	59	9
Indoor plants	0	0	86	18	76	6
Outdoor borders	3	2	40	34	53	12
Outdoor vegetables	0	0	100	41	47	13
Lawn mowing	4	2	50	52	38	10
Caring (last month)	**8**	**11**	**92**	**11**	**63**	**26**
Babysitting (day)	12	5	100	5	74	21
Babysitting (night)	12	5	92	11	68	21
Courses (e.g. piano lessons)	0	0	100	22	67	11
Pet care	2	1	50	15	50	35
All	**5**	**100**	**56**	**26**	**58**	**16**

Table 8.4 Gender divisions of cash-in-hand work and unpaid domestic work in UK lower-income urban neighbourhoods, by task

	% of work conducted using cash-in-hand exchange	% of all cash-in-hand exchange	% of cash-in-hand exchange conducted by women	Unpaid domestic work % conducted by		
				man alone	woman alone	shared
House maintenance (last 5 years)	**8**	**24**	**19**	**49**	**37**	**15**
Outdoor painting	10	4	23	65	22	13
Indoor painting	7	4	19	36	43	21
Wallpapering	6	4	18	39	45	16
Plastering	12	4	11	74	20	6
Mending broken window	7	2	17	93	7	0
Maintenance of appliances	11	6	33	75	23	2
Home improvement (last 5 years)	**10**	**19**	**3**	**74**	**25**	**1**
Double glazing	7	2	0	67	33	0
Plumbing	13	6	0	76	24	0
Electrical work	12	4	0	68	29	3
House insulation	1	0	0	100	0	0
Put in bathroom	24	2	0	100	0	0
Build a garage	0	0	50	100	0	0
Build an extension	0	0	0	100	0	0
Convert attic	25	0	0	100	0	0
Put in central heating	9	1	0	100	0	0
Carpentry	9	4	0	72	0	1
Routine housework (last week)	**3**	**28**	**85**	**17**	**63**	**21**
Do housework	2	2	93	13	65	22
Clean the house	2	2	86	25	65	11

lower-income urban neighbourhoods is indeed low-paid market-orientated work conducted for unadulterated economic reasons, the vast majority is for and by friends, kin and neighbours for motives more associated with redistribution and sociality than economic gain.

To commence this analysis, it is useful to provide some indication of the types of work conducted on a cash-in-hand basis. In deprived UK urban neighbourhoods, just under half (45 per cent) of all tasks conducted on a cash-in-hand basis were found to be concentrated in six tasks (window cleaning, hairdressing, car repair, appliance maintenance, plumbing and childcare). Looked at another way, some tasks are much more likely to be conducted using cash-in-hand labour than others. Notable here, as Table 8.4 displays, are making garden furniture, bird tables and suchlike (which in 33 per cent of cases was conducted on a cash-in-hand basis), attic conversions (25 per cent conducted on a cash-in-hand basis), putting in a new bathroom suite (24 per cent), car repair (19 per cent), plumbing (13 per cent), electrical work and plastering (both 12 per cent) and nighttime and daytime babysitting (both 12 per cent). Indeed, the prominence of babysitting here is important since there is now a lot of evidence that Britain relies on a low cash-in-hand system of childcare where grandmothers, mothers, sisters, aunts and other women are looking after employed women's children (for a review, see Windebank, 1999). This study shows that at least some of this childcare is reimbursed on a cash-in-hand basis.

More interesting, perhaps, especially in terms of the gender divisions of cash-in-hand work, is that women undertake tasks on a cash-in-hand basis for which they are also largely responsible so far as the gender division of domestic work is concerned. This has been intimated before in studies conducted in Canada (Fortin et al., 1996), Germany (Hellberger and Schwarze, 1986, 1987), the USA (Jensen et al., 1995), Italy (Mingione, 1991) and the UK (Leonard, 1994; Pahl, 1984). Indeed, the data presented above indicate that the gender segregation of tasks in the realm of cash-in-hand work is, if anything, stronger than the gender segregation of unpaid domestic work. For example, women alone conduct 63 per cent of all routine housework tasks when unpaid domestic work is used, but 84 per cent when carried out as cash-in-hand work. In contrast, women conduct 37 per cent of house maintenance tasks when domestic work is used, but only 19 per cent when carried out as cash-in-hand work. The inequalities prevalent in the gender divisions of domestic work, therefore, are extenuated in the cash-in-hand sphere.

Take, for example, the task of doing the housework. The last time that this was conducted on an unpaid self-provisioning basis, it was a woman alone in 65 per cent of instances. When conducted on a cash-in-hand basis, however, in 93 per cent of instances it was a woman who had undertaken this work. Payment for such work appears to reinforce the gender segmentation of tasks, not reduce it. This applies to nearly every task surveyed in Table 8.4. It seems, therefore, that women are employed on a cash-in-hand basis to do tasks 'traditionally' associated with women's work, and men to do tasks conventionally associated with men's work. Monetization, in consequence, seems not to reduce, but to consolidate, gender divisions of labour at least so far as paying on an informal basis is concerned.

Beyond the 44 tasks in Table 8.4, furthermore, Williams and Windebank (2003c) identify numerous instances of women engaging in cash-in-hand work for businesses. For example, several women were employed as waitresses at rates as low as £2.00 per hour or £12.00 for two nights' work, and a number of others worked as bar staff in public houses for rates of £3.00 per hour, well below the national minimum wage of £3.60 per hour. Others worked as ice-cream vendors for £2.50 per hour and on canteens on a building site for £2.00 per hour. These low wage rates are not confined to the organized cash-in-hand work conducted by women. Overall, women working on a cash-in-hand basis tend to be paid even less than in formal employment (i.e. 60 per cent of the average wage rate of men), as previously identified in other nations (Fortin et al., 1996; Hellberger and Schwarze, 1986; Lemieux et al., 1994; McInnis-Dittrich, 1995). In these lower-income UK urban neighbourhoods, women received an average wage rate per hour of just £2.60 (compared with £4.20 for men), well below the minimum wage rate in formal employment of £3.60.

Reinforcing previous assertions, therefore, this study finds that women participate in cash-in-hand work to a slightly greater extent than men, engage in tasks mostly associated with their domestic roles, and receive low wage rates. Can one thus conclude that this is low-paid market-like work? Although most of the literature takes low wage rates as a surrogate indicator that this must be the case, a deeper investigation of the social relations and motives underlying this work reveals that the reality is richer and more complex than has been assumed, as will now be shown.

To evaluate critically the so far unchallenged assumption that this low-paid form of work conducted disproportionately by women is market-like work undertaken for the purpose of economic gain by both employers and employees (De Soto, 1989; Castells and Portes, 1989; Matthews, 1983; Sassen, 1989), first the social relations involved in these exchanges are unravelled, and second the motives of the employers and employees.

Who do women work for on a cash-in-hand basis? For example, do they work for organized businesses? Examining the evidence from these low-income UK urban neighbourhoods, the finding is that just 5 per cent of women's cash-in-hand work was undertaken for formal businesses (12 per cent of men's cash-in-hand work) and only 10 per cent (37 per cent among men) on a self-employed basis for people previously unknown to them. The vast majority (85 per cent) of women's cash-in-hand work (compared with 51 per cent of men's) is either for relatives, friends or neighbours. When women conducted work on a cash-in-hand basis for kin, friends and neighbours, moreover, it was in 95 per cent of cases other women who had employed them. Breaking down this cash-in-hand work conducted for close social relations, 45 per cent is undertaken for kin (mostly sisters, aunts, grandmothers, cousins) and 40 per cent for friends and neighbours (nearly always other women). Men, in contrast, are more likely to engage in cash-in-hand work that is market-like and conducted for people that they do not know.

Turning to the motives underpinning the decision of men and women to engage in cash-in-hand work, the conventional view is that this work is conducted for the purpose of economic gain, such as to earn some extra cash in order to help the household get by (Howe, 1990; Jordan et al., 1992; Leonard, 1994; MacDonald, 1994; Morris, 1987, 1995; Rowlingson et al., 1997). In this study of UK lower-income urban neighbourhoods, however, some stark gender variations in the rationales of men and women are identified. Only 18 per cent of the cash-in-hand tasks conducted by women are undertaken purely to make money, compared with 72 per cent of the cash-in-hand tasks conducted by men. This rationale predominates when women and men work for firms or engage in self-employed activity for people they do not know well. It does not prevail, however, when they work for friends, relatives and neighbours, which constitutes 85 per cent of all cash-in-hand work conducted by women and 47 per cent of all such work conducted by men.

First, and given that many women knew the people for whom they worked, 49 per cent of the tasks conducted on a cash-in-hand basis were undertaken for 'redistributive' reasons (compared with just 22 per cent of the tasks undertaken on an informal paid basis by men). The supplier knew the recipient needed to carry out the task and that they would be unable to get the work completed unless they were helped. This was either because they could not afford to get it done or because they were unable to do it due to age, illness and so forth. The price charged was often well under the market price. Indeed, the closer the social relations, the more likely was the price to diverge from market norms. The fee charged when close social relations were involved, although more than a token gesture, was well below the normal market price. Given that these rationales prevailed for some 50 per cent of all women's cash-in-hand work, it is not difficult to see one of the principal reasons why women are poorly paid for their cash-in-hand work.

Besides redistributive rationales, another reason women engage in cash-in-hand work revolves around community building. Over one-third (35 per cent) of the cash-in-hand work conducted by women (compared with 6 per cent undertaken by men) is carried out for this reason. Conducting a job informally for a small payment was a way of mixing with and helping people one knew, and at the same time making a little money on the side. As one respondent explained her act of helping out her neighbour with childcare:

> I did it because it was a good chance for 'Josh' [her son] to get to
> know her kids so it was a bit selfish I suppose. But I suppose the main

reason was to sort of help her out so she would return the favour one day when I needed one. I didn't really know her that well so it sort of got us started off. I think she paid and paid me near enough proper rates to show that she wasn't trying to play on my good nature

When the work was conducted for somebody fairly well known to them in order to develop closer bonds, payment diverged from market norms to a greater extent than for all other forms of cash-in-hand work. However, when conducted for somebody less well known to them the price was often set at just below the market price. This is because there is a keen sense of not wanting to insult the person either by charging too much (in which case they might see you as 'ripping them off') or too little (in which case they might realize you are expecting something in return). Instead, the aim is to charge an amount that leaves the way open to reciprocity but does not oblige it.

As such, and similar to other forms of non-commodified work, there are gender disparities in both the extent and the nature of cash-in-hand work in the advanced economies. Not only are the gender divisions in the nature of cash-in-hand work more acute than is even the case with unpaid domestic work, but the motives of men and women when conducting this work are significantly different. For men, cash-in-hand work is much more likely to be conducted under social relations akin to commodified labour and conducted for the purpose of profit. For women, however, such work is more akin to mutual aid in terms of both the social relations within which it is conducted and the motives underpinning it.

Conclusions

This chapter has revealed that women conduct a disproportionate share of non-commodified work. They not only conduct a greater proportion of subsistence work and non-monetized exchange than men but they are also more likely to undertake cash-in-hand work when it is not conducted under commodified economic relations. This might well start to explain why non-commodified work remains unvalued and largely unrecognized. Such work, it could be suggested, is unvalued and unrecognized not only because of the nature of the work (i.e. it is not commodified) but also because of who does it. Indeed, this is an argument that has been posed by feminist analysts of work for some decades. Since the early 1970s, it has been continuously asserted that non-commodified work in general, and subsistence work in particular, are not recognized or valued in society because they are seen as 'women's work'. The route to liberation for many has thus been to insert women into the formal labour force. However, whether employment is the route to women's liberation is open to question.

While the working lives of men in the advanced economies have been shown to be undergoing a process of decommodification, quite the opposite is revealed to be happening for women. For them, a process of commodification is taking place. Until now, few commentators writing from the perspective of women's position have read such a trend negatively. It has been widely assumed that the commodification of women's working lives is liberating. Few stop to consider whether advocating the greater subjugation of women by capitalist social relations, especially given the low-paid nature of women's employment, is the route to 'gender progress', doubtless because they equate, or maybe confuse, this with financial independence from men. This chapter, however, has shown that even though women have entered the commodified realm, they remain responsible for much of the subsistence work, non-monetized exchange and cash-in-hand work, suggesting that perhaps greater attention needs to be placed on resolving the gender disparities in the non-commodified realm by encouraging men to engage more in such activity rather than solely seeking to immerse women in commodified social relations. As such, this chapter has begun to uncover the need to consider the possibility of alternative futures beyond further immersion in the commodity economy as the path to independence for both men and women.

9

Beyond the Advanced Economies

Until now, attention has been placed on deconstructing the discourse of commodification in the so-called 'advanced economies'. The aim in so doing has been to show, first, that these societies are less commodified than has been perhaps popularly assumed and more composed of a plurality of economic practices, and second, that they are by no means universally pursuing a linear and unidimensional trajectory of economic development towards a commodified world. The result is that the future of working life in these advanced economies has been shown to be much more open than was previously considered to be the case.

In this chapter, attention turns away from deconstructing the discourse that those countries at the front of the queue in the race towards commodification, and towards those that have been viewed as further behind and consequently as premodern, thwarted, under-developed and/or traditional in their economic practices. These are the ex-socialist economies of central and eastern Europe and the 'majority world' nations, or what is more often called the third world. Here, the intention is to seek answers to two key questions. To what extent are economies in these areas of the world com-modified? And should it be assumed that they are pursuing an inexorable shift towards commodification?

To answer these questions, I first consider the so-called 'transition economies' of central and eastern Europe. Second, I turn attention to what I here prefer to call the majority world nations, but that are more commonly referred to as 'developing', 'undeveloped', 'underdeveloped' or 'third world' countries. In each case, both the degree to which their economies are commodified and whether the trajectory of economic development is towards commercialization will be evaluated. Before setting out on this exploration of the penetration of commodification beyond the 'minority world' of the Western economies, however, it is well worth briefly noting how the terminology used when discussing these regions of the world is itself very much grounded in the commodification thesis. While the West is viewed as 'advanced' due to the supposed extent to which commodification has permeated its economic practices, both the terms 'transition' and 'developing' economies construct these nations as becoming commodified. As will be shown throughout this chapter, however, this is by no means certain. When Harvey (2000: 23) states how 'the uneven insertion of different territories and social formations into the capitalist world market has created a global historical geography of capital accumulation whose character needs to be well understood', he thus encapsulates precisely the motives underlying this chapter.

Here, it will be shown that it is far too simple either to depict a universal development path towards commodification or even to divide the world up into a first, a second and a third world based on their relative position in the queue shuffling towards a commodified world. To speak of a group of advanced economies, transition economies or a third world is both inappropriate and invalid because the countries within these blocs are pursuing markedly different development trajectories and are profoundly diversified. As already shown in the case of the advanced economies, Western nations display markedly different levels of commodification and whilst some are commodifying, others are decommodifying. Whether this is also the case in the context of the transition and the third world nations is here investigated.

Until now, by depicting a linear and unidimensional development path towards commodification, the story of development has involved designating most of the world as poor and attempting to instil and install capitalist production worldwide in the name of eradicating poverty. The effect of defining development in terms of one form of economy and seeing all others as non-existent or deficient is that recognition of difference and the possibility that working life might be other than commodified has been lost. In this chapter, therefore, an attempt is first of all made to recapture the sense of diverse development paths. Rather than overlay onto this a hierarchical narrative of 'progress' and 'moving backwards', a story of heterogeneity and diversity is instead depicted.

Second, the intention is to show that, just as in the advanced economies a plurality of economic practices exists both at the societal and at the household level, the same applies in these transition and majority world nations. Moreover, the persistence of economic plurality and engagement in non-capitalist economic practices is not simply always to be interpreted as a refuge for marginalized populations who cannot access commodified practices (the marginality thesis). Instead, there appears to be a heterogeneous non-capitalist sphere with *a hierarchy of its own*. This hierarchy, moreover, seems to reproduce, rather than mitigate, the inequalities prevalent in the commodified sphere, as already uncovered in the advanced economies. Those heavily embedded in the commodified realm appear to be those able to benefit most from their participation in the non-commodified sphere. For them, such engagement is much more a matter of choice, whilst those disengaged from the commodified sphere appear to be not only most reliant on the resources of the non-commodified sphere but also least able to benefit from it. To see this, first, the situation in the so-called 'transition' economies is considered and, second, the majority world is put under the spotlight.

The Transition Economies

In this section I wish to evaluate critically the changes in the mode of economic organization in the transition societies of central and eastern Europe. What has been the nature of the transformation in these economies? To what extent have they undergone a transition towards the market? And how far have they progressed, if at all, in this direction?

Until now, the widespread assumption has been that the transition economies are uniformly undergoing a process of commodification. The demise of the state as a direct provider of goods and services in favour of the formal market economy, even if the state continues to regulate, albeit in poorer ways and with less developed and appropriate legislation than in Western economies (Sik, 1993, 1994; Neef, 2002; Wallace and Haerpfer, 2002), is often taken as evidence. Here, however, it is argued that such a trend towards privatization within the formal sphere is insufficient to inform an understanding of whether or not an overall process of commodification is taking place. If, for example, subsistence work, non-monetized exchange and the cash-in-hand economy were found to be growing relative to the combined state and market sphere, then commodification would not be occurring.

To evaluate critically the degree to which the transition economies are commodified and the view that such economies are pursuing a linear and unidimensional trajectory of economic development towards commodification, two data sources are analysed here. First, time-budget studies that have been conducted in various transition economies are interrogated so as to provide a measure of the degree to which subsistence work persists in these nations. Second, and so as to analyse the direction of change, the New Democracies Barometer (NDB) surveys are analysed, conducted in the years 1992, 1994, 1996 and 1998 in eleven countries: Poland, the Czech Republic, Hungary, Slovakia, Slovenia, Croatia, F.R. Yugoslavia, Romania, Bulgaria, Belarus and Ukraine (see Wallace and Haerpfer, 2002). In each country, face-to-face interviews were conducted with a random survey of 1,000 people in each of these years by established national institutes that regularly undertake nationwide representative surveys.

The penetration of commodification in transition economies

To start to measure the extent to which the transition nations have progressed along the path towards becoming commodified economies, and akin to Chapter 3 in relation to the advanced economies, time-budget studies are here reviewed in order to evaluate the persistence of subsistence work. As Table 9.1 reveals, across the six transition economies for which data is readily available, some 45.6 per cent of total working time is spent engaged in subsistence work. This suggests, therefore, that these transition economies are far from a state of being totally commodified (even

Table 9.1 The paid/unpaid work balance in central and eastern European nations

Country	Paid work (mins)	Domestic work (mins)	% of work time spent on subsistence work
Transition economies			
Hungary	345	254	42.4
Poland	332	244	42.4
Bulgaria	285	245	46.2
Czechoslavakia	320	272	45.9
East Germany	298	276	48.1
Yugoslavia	308	292	48.7
Mean	314	263	45.6
Advanced economies			
Canada	291	210	41.9
Denmark	283	155	35.4
France	297	246	45.3
Netherlands	265	209	44.0
UK	282	204	41.9
USA	304	231	43.2
Finland	268	216	44.6
Mean	284	210	42.5

Source: Derived from Gershuny, 2000: Table 7.1.

if one assumes that all paid work is commodified work). Indeed, there remains a long way to go before these economies approach the status of commodified states.

Comparing the degree to which paid work has penetrated these transition economies relative to advanced economies, however, some fascinating findings emerge. Despite the common perception that the Western 'advanced' economies are more commodified than their transition country counterparts, Table 9.1 reveals that monetization has permeated people's work schedules to only a slightly greater extent in advanced than in transition economies.

Table 9.2 Primary sphere relied on by households in central and eastern Europe, 1992–98

Country		1992	1994	1996	1998
NDB mean	Formal economy	68	67	70	68
	Household economy	22	22	21	22
	Cash economy	7	7	6	6
Czech Rep.	Formal economy	80	82	88	85
	Household economy	17	15	9	11
	Cash economy	7	2	2	2
Hungary	Formal economy	80	77	80	83
	Household economy	16	19	15	14
	Cash economy	2	3	4	3
Slovenia	Formal economy	71	64	59	80
	Household economy	25	33	37	11
	Cash economy	3	3	4	7
Slovakia	Formal economy	78	80	82	70
	Household economy	20	15	14	25
	Cash economy	2	3	3	4
Poland	Formal economy	82	82	67	70
	Household economy	13	12	21	21
	Cash economy	3	4	7	5
Bulgaria	Formal economy	67	67	63	69
	Household economy	24	22	28	24
	Cash economy	7	9	5	4
Belarus	Formal economy	71	59	78	64
	Household economy	14	26	12	26
	Cash economy	11	10	7	6
Ukraine	Formal economy	26	52	58	57
	Household economy	59	30	30	33
	Cash economy	5	10	7	8
Romania	Formal economy	61	55	59	46
	Household economy	26	29	33	47
	Cash economy	10	11	3	5
Croatia	Formal economy	69	66	71	69
	Household economy	7	13	11	18
	Cash economy	21	17	14	10
F.R.Yugoslavia	Formal economy	–	–	–	68
	Household economy	–	–	–	16
	Cash economy	–	–	–	14
		10,160	10,709	10,069	11,296

Source: Wallace and Haerpfer, 2002: Table 1.

However, it is also important to point out that just as there are cross-national variations in the degree to which paid work has permeated work schedules in the advanced economies, the same applies in central and eastern European nations. In Hungary and Poland, some 58 per cent of working time is spent in paid work, which is far higher than in many Western nations. For nations such as East Germany and the former Yugoslavia, meanwhile, a relatively smaller amount of time is spent in the paid sphere than in the average advanced economy. This first set of data on the allocation of working time, therefore, does not provide clear evidence that the advanced economies are to any great extent more formalized than the transition economies so far as the paid/unpaid work balance is concerned, thus questioning whether their depiction as 'advanced' economies due to their greater level of commodification is valid.

These data on the amount of subsistence work relative to paid work thus provide a clear indication of the lack of penetration of paid work in the transition economies. Another data set that clearly indicates the relatively low level of permeation of formalization in general, and commodification in particular, is to be found in the New Democracies Barometer (NDB) survey. In response to the question, 'Which activity on this card is the most important for the standard of living of you and your family?', Table 9.2 reports the primary sphere that households rely on in these eleven transition economies, and Table 9.3 reports the results of asking households for both the primary and the secondary sources relied upon.

Commencing with the primary sphere on which households rely for their standard of living, Table 9.2 shows that this is the formal sphere for only just over two-thirds (68 per cent) of households. A third of households, therefore, primarily rely on sources other than the formal realm. Such an overall statistic, however, masks considerable cross-national variations. Comparing different central and eastern European nations in 1998, the proportion of households primarily dependent on the formal sphere ranges from 46 per cent in Romania to 85 per cent in the Czech Republic.

These data on the primary sphere relied on to maintain standard of living, furthermore, mask the degree to which households in practice draw upon the resources of both the formal and the

Table 9.3 Primary and secondary spheres relied on by households in central and eastern Europe, 1992–98 (%)

Combinations	1992	1994	1996	1998
Household and household	4	5	5	6
Household and social	3	2	3	2
Household and cash	3	3	3	4
Household and formal	11	10	11	11
Social and household	1	1	1	1
Social and social	0.4	1	0.3	0.4
Social and cash	1	1	1	1
Social and formal	1	1	1	1
Cash and household	2	2	1	2
Cash and social	1	1	1	1
Cash and cash	1	2	1	1
Cash and formal	3	3	3	2
Formal and household	36	33	36	32
Formal and social	8	9	11	8
Formal and cash	13	14	13	16
Formal and formal	11	11	10	13
N =	10,160	10,709	10,069	11,296

Source: Wallace and Haerpfer, 2002: Table 2.

informal spheres. As Table 9.3 reveals, when both the primary and secondary spheres upon which they rely are analysed, the finding is that just 11 per cent of households across these countries rely on the formal sphere. Some 57 per cent of households draw on both the formal and the informal spheres while 32 per cent state that the formal sphere is neither the primary nor the secondary most important sphere for maintaining their standard of living. For a third of the population of these countries, therefore, the formal sphere plays only a minor role in their coping practices, and for a further half of the population, the resources gained from the formal sphere are combined with informal resources in their coping practices. To refer to these societies as commodified when only one-tenth of households define themselves as reliant on the formal sphere would be a misnomer. Most households in these transition economies adopt heterogeneous economic practices.

Until now, such a survey of the primary and secondary sphere relied upon has not been conducted in the advanced economies. Given the relatively minor differences between advanced and transition economies in the proportion of time spent on paid and unpaid work outlined in Table 9.1, it is here considered that such a survey might well shed far greater light on the economic plurality that characterizes the advanced economies than has so far been the case. It is to be hoped, therefore, that in the near future such a survey can be used in the advanced economies to investigate the relative importance of these spheres in household coping practices.

Returning to the transition economies, one of the most fascinating aspects of this data set are the revelations concerning which informal spheres are relied upon to the greatest extent to maintain living standards. As Table 9.3 reveals, in 1998 over one-fifth (21 per cent) of households relied primarily on subsistence work, 3.4 per cent on the social economy and 7 per cent on cash-in-hand work. In these central and eastern European nations, therefore, one-fifth of households are primarily reliant on subsistence work to maintain their standard of living and 6 per cent on subsistence work as both their primary and secondary resource. It appears, therefore, that even where subsistence economies are defined in the very narrow sense of meaning economies where households are reliant primarily on subsistence production for their livelihoods, such economies are alive and well in the transition economies. One in five households are of this variety.

In these central and eastern European nations, moreover, even where the formal sector is used as either a primary or a secondary means of livelihood, it is nearly always combined with some other kind of non-commodified economic practice. A heterogeneous portfolio of economic practices is the norm rather than the exception for the populations of these transition economies in that around 90 per cent rely on sources other than the formal sphere as either their most important or second most important source of livelihood.

These data thus clearly portray the limited importance of the formal sector (i.e. where goods and services are provided through paid employment), never mind the commodity economy (where this formal provision is conducted by private-sector firms for profit-motivated purposes rather than the public sector or not-for-profit enterprises). Unfortunately, to repeat, similar survey data have not been collected in the 'advanced economies', doubtless based on the assumption that the result would merely show the dominance of the formal sphere. These data from central and eastern Europe, however, certainly cast a shadow over whether this would indeed be the case. Given that time-budget studies indicate that, in terms of work schedules, these nations are only a little less formalized than their Western counterparts, there certainly appears to be a case for at least attempting a small-scale study along the same lines in Western nations in the near future.

Here, however, attention needs to turn to a second issue so far as these central and eastern European nations are concerned. This is the matter of their trajectory of economic development and whether a process of formalization in general and commodification in particular can be identified.

The trajectory of economic development in the transition economies

As Table 9.2 reveals, there is scant evidence of a formalization of the transition economies. Between 1992 and 1998 there was little overall change in the proportion of households primarily reliant on the formal sphere for their living standards. However, these aggregate data mask considerable variations between nations. Of the ten countries for which longitudinal data are available, the proportion of households primarily reliant on the formal sphere rose in five nations over this six-year period (Czech Republic, Hungary, Slovenia, Bulgaria, Ukraine), remained stable in one country (Croatia) and fell in four nations (Belarus, Romania, Slovakia, Poland).

An alternative way of depicting the differences is to divide these countries into three groups according to both the reliance on the formal sphere and their trajectories. In the first group of countries

(Czech Republic, Hungary and Slovenia), a large proportion of households (more than 80 per cent in 1998) depend on the formal economy as their main source of support and these countries are undergoing a process of formalization. In the second group of countries (Slovakia and Poland), although a similar proportion of all households previously relied on the formal sphere as their primary source of support, as in the first group of countries, these nations are witnessing fluctuations and even informalization over time. In the third group of countries (Bulgaria, Belarus, Croatia, Ukraine, Romania), meanwhile, formalization is relatively low and again fluctuating.

As a whole, therefore, the development trajectories of these eastern and central European nations are not following a linear and unidimensional path towards formalization. Instead, heterogeneous development paths can be identified. If by 'transition' economies is thus meant nations that are undergoing a process of formalization, then this term is inappropriate and inadequate to describe the plurality of development paths being pursued by nations in this region of the world.

So, too, is it invalid to assume that there is a race towards dependence on the formal sphere. As Table 9.3 reveals, in 1992 just 11 per cent of households relied on the formal sphere as both their primary and their secondary source of livelihood. By 1998, this had risen to just 13 per cent. Meanwhile, the proportion of households relying on both the formal and the informal spheres declined from 57 per cent to 56 per cent between 1992 and 1998, and the share that did not rely on the formal sphere as either their principal or secondary source of support declined from 32 to 31 per cent.

Indeed, households themselves appear to be pursuing a plurality of divergent coping practices in these transition economies. Examining the principal and secondary sources of support used by households to secure their livelihoods, Table 9.3 reveals that although the share of households relying on the formal sphere alone increased from 11 to 13 per cent of all households between 1992 and 1998, the proportion of households relying on subsistence work alone increased from 4 to 6 per cent over this time period and those using a combination of the formal sphere as a principal source of support and cash-in-hand work as a secondary source increased from 13 to 16 per cent in the same time frame. Consequently, just as there is a divergence between nations in terms of their trajectories of economic development in these transition economies, the same appears to apply to households that are adopting a plurality of economic practices, and this heterogeneity shows no sign of abating over time.

In sum, and as many have previously shown, different regions in post-communist Europe have pursued different paths of transition (Boren, 2003; Piirainen, 1997; Rose and Haerpfer, 1992; Wallace and Haerpfer, 2002). Similarly, and on a household level, the heterogeneity of coping practices employed appears to show no sign of withering. Who, therefore, relies on these informally orientated coping practices and who relies on more formally oriented practices?

Socio-spatial disparities in the penetration of formalization

Until now, and as already shown in relation to the advanced economies, a popular assertion has been that non-commodified economic practices are concentrated among marginalized populations that use such activity as a survival strategy. This became known, to repeat, as the marginality thesis. Here, I evaluate critically whether this applies in the transition economies.

Table 9.4 reveals that the use of the informal sphere, although more likely to be relied on as the primary source of livelihood by the poorest sections of the population, is by no means confined to the poorest quartiles of the population. A large proportion of those in the most affluent (fourth quartile) sections of the population also rely on the informal spheres as their principal source of livelihood. In consequence, participation in the informal sphere and reliance on it as a principal source of livelihood are not confined to the poorest sections of the population. Participation in such activity as a principal means of livelihood occurs across the spectrum of socio-economic groups.

In sum, the transition nations have economies that are heterogeneous in nature and most households draw upon a plurality of

Table 9.4 Primary sphere relied on by households in central and eastern Europe: by socio-economic group, 1998 (%)

	Formal	Household	Social	Cash
Household income quartile Cramers V = .083 p<000				
First quartile	20	32	27	22
Second quartile	24	25	19	26
Third quartile	26	25	26	26
Fourth quartile	30	18	28	26
N =	4,996	1,968	202	499

Source: Wallace and Haerpfer, 2002: Tables 4 and 5.

economic practices in their daily lives (see Piirainen, 1997; Rose and Haerpfer, 1992; Wallace and Haerpfer, 2002). Neither is it clear-cut that all of these economies are following a linear and unidimensional trajectory of economic development towards formalization in general, and commodification in particular. Instead, it appears that a multitude of trajectories are being pursued both at the level of the nation-state and at the level of the household. It is thus far too simplistic to describe these transition economies as being composed of nations on a uniform and linear development path towards commodification. If the transition economies are thus composed of heterogeneous economic practices and trajectories, is this also the case when the majority world is analysed?

The Majority World

The origins of the study of non-capitalist economic practices in the so-called 'developing' nations lie in the work on the 'informal sector' of Hart in Ghana over three decades ago (Hart, 1973), thus mirroring the separate interest shown in this form of employment in the advanced economies at about the same time by feminists (e.g. Oakley, 1974). Despite equally long histories, there has been relatively little exchange between these two bodies of knowledge. Instead, the two literatures remain disconnected, with commentators rarely venturing into the others' territory. This is doubtless because of the vast size of each of two sets of literature, as well as the fact that they emanate from within separate disciplines. It is also because of the deep and entrenched divide between the study of 'developing' and 'advanced' economies. The study of commodification is no exception. Here, therefore, I intend not only to set foot in a realm seldom entered by analysts who study the advanced economies but also to seek out whether there are similarities concerning commodification in developing nations in both the way in which the subject is theorized and the phenomenon on the ground. To do this, I pose the same key questions in relation to the majority world as have been already addressed with reference to the advanced economies.

Are the developing economies witnessing commodification, as modernization theory assumes, or is there a process of decommodification taking place? Alternatively, is such an either/or choice too simplistic to capture the diverse experiences of this large portion of the total world population? Moreover, is the 'marginality thesis' applicable across the entire developing world? In other words, is such economic practice merely a response to economic austerity and confined to marginalized groups or is there a heterogeneous non-capitalist sphere with a hierarchy of its own? If so, does it mitigate or reinforce the socio-spatial divisions prevalent in the commodified sphere? In asking these questions concerning the magnitude and character of commodified and non-commodified spheres, the intention is not necessarily to provide comprehensive answers. Instead, it is merely to explore whether there is a need to question commodification not only in the advanced economies and transition economies but also in the majority world. To analyse this, I evaluate first the penetration of the commodified sphere and the trajectory of economic development, and second the socio-spatial variations in these areas.

The penetration of commodification and trajectories of economic development in the majority world

The commodification thesis asserts that as economies develop and mature, there is a shift of economic activity from the non-commodified to the commodified sphere. Indeed, much of the

discourse in economic development is so embedded in this theorization that commodification is often the 'measuring rod' used
to define an economy as either 'modern' or 'backward' (e.g.
Rostow, 1960). However, there are good reasons for believing
that this trajectory of economic development is neither natural
nor inevitable.

First, there is the evidence already presented in Chapters 3–5
from the advanced economies. This shows that by no means all
advanced economies can be seen as pursuing a trajectory towards
ever more commodified economies. Instead, there appear to be
heterogeneous trajectories in different places. Second, and the focus
of attention here, there is the evidence from the majority world.
Unlike the advanced economies, and as the International Labour
Office (1996) states, it is often the case that national data are not
even available to indicate whether formal employment is decreasing
or increasing, never mind the level of non-commodified work. In
the majority world, therefore, the evidence is even patchier than
in the so-called advanced economies.

The little evidence available, however, suggests that the assumption of a progression from non-commodified to commodified
activity is by no means universally applicable. Instead, heterogeneous trajectories can be identified. Take, for example, East and
Southeast Asia. This is often assumed to be a region of the world
that has undergone a widespread commodification of economic
life due to the new international division of labour (NIDL) that
has increasingly dispersed physical production functions, and more
recently call centres, into this region whilst retaining the control
and command functions in a network of global cities in advanced
economies (e.g. Sassen, 1991). During the 1970s and 1980s, the beneficiaries of the NIDL were the middle-income nations such as the
Republic of Korea, Hong Kong and Singapore, which have now
purportedly joined the ranks of the advanced economies and been
replaced by a second wave of middle-income countries including
Malaysia, Thailand and Indonesia (Hall, 1996). It appears, therefore, that commodification is a widespread phenomenon in this
region of the world. Indeed, the evidence on employment growth
seems to support this assertion. Between 1986 and 1993 in East
and Southeast Asian nations, with the sole exception of Indonesia,

employment rose at more than 3 per cent per annum, well in excess of the rate of increase in the labour force (International Labour Office, 1996: 143).

However, there is also evidence to question whether the process of commodification is as clear-cut as is sometimes assumed in discussions of these 'tiger' economies. For example, examining Hong Kong, Singapore, South Korea and Taiwan, Cheng and Gereffi (1994) highlight the way in which informal modes of production have played a major role in their recent economic development and growth. In Taiwan, for instance, very weak regulation of the small-firms sector has enabled the growth of cash-in-hand work that has been a central pillar in the country's success at pursuing export-led development. As Cheng and Gereffi (1994) clearly show in the case of both the Hong Kong and Taiwanese economies, formal jobs have not replaced informal work. Rather, they have grown in tandem. Whether the remarkable growth rate of formal jobs in East and Southeast Asia can thus be taken as an indicator of formalization is extremely doubtful. Instead, it appears that there are different processes in different nations. For example, whilst in Hong Kong and Taiwan informal work seems to have expanded alongside formal jobs, in the more highly regulated economies of South Korea and Singapore such work appears to be both limited and, if anything, contracting relative to formal employment.

In Latin America and the Caribbean, similarly, the same heterogeneity of development trajectories can be identified. As Table 9.5 shows, there is little if any evidence in this region of a universal process of either formalization or informalization. On the one hand, some nations appear to have witnessed a process of informalization during the 1990s, albeit at different rates and to varying extents. In the already heavily informalized nation of Honduras, for example, the share of non-capitalist economic practices in non-agricultural employment declined rapidly from 54.2 to 51.9 per cent between 1990 and 1994, whilst in the previously more formalized economy of Panama the share of informal work declined at only a marginal rate from 40.4 to 40.2 per cent. On the other hand, however, there are also nations witnessing a process of informalization, again at very different rates and from contrasting base levels. Already heavily informalized Paraguay, for instance,

Table 9.5 Share of informal sector in non-agricultural employment, Latin America, 1990 and 1994 (%)

	1990	1994
Paraguay	61.4	68.9
Colombia	59.1	61.6
Bolivia	56.9	61.3
Mexico	55.5	57.0
Honduras	54.2	51.9
Brazil	52.0	56.4
Peru	51.8	56.0
Ecuador	51.6	54.2
Chile	49.9	51.0
Argentina	47.5	52.5
Costa Rica	42.3	46.2
Panama	40.4	40.2
Venezuela	38.8	44.8

Source: International Labour Organization, 1996: Table 5.5.

further increased its share of informal work in non-agricultural employment from 61.4 to 68.9 per cent between 1990 and 1994, whilst the more commodified nation of Chile saw informality increase at a slower rate from just 49.9 to 51.0 per cent.

Indeed, Table 9.5 suggests not only that there is a pattern of heterogeneous development in Latin America but that this heterogeneity increased in intensity during the 1990s. Of those Latin American nations that were formalizing, the countries doing so at the quickest rate during the 1990s were generally those with already relatively high levels of commodification (e.g. Panama). Similarly, of those Latin American nations pursuing informalization, it was again the countries which were already heavily informalized that were moving along this development path at the fastest speed (e.g. Paraguay). The implication, therefore, is that there is an increasing polarization of development trajectories; a divergence is taking place.

In other regions of the world, despite the evidence being patchier, it is sufficient to conclude that there is neither uniform formalization nor informalization. In sub-Saharan Africa, the data that exist on formal jobs show that out of 13 nations, 5 have witnessed negative employment growth, and in another 3 job growth has been significantly below the growth rate of the labour force. Of the remaining 5 that have seen jobs increase at a faster rate than the available labour force, 2 (Mauritius and Botswana) have displayed significant growth rates in formal employment. Similar heterogeneous trends are identified in the Middle East and North Africa (International Labour Organization, 1996).

Such evidence of heterogeneous development paths is applicable not only on a cross-national level but also on an intra-national level. Numerous studies have revealed significant local and regional variations in development trajectories. In Nigeria, for instance, Anheier (1992) compares the cities of Lagos and Ibadan, concluding that the very different development trajectories of these two areas are the result of the contrasting urban and regional economies in which they are embedded. A study of six metropolitan areas in northeast Brazil (Rio, São Paulo, Belo Horizonte, Recife, Salvador, Fortaleza), similarly, finds significant differences in the magnitude, growth and character of informal work (Schuster, cited in Lautier, 1994). In a study of Mexico, in addition, PREALC show significant differences between Guadalajara, Monterey and Mexico City in terms of both the extent and the nature of informal work, which they put down to the rather limited variable of the contrasting industrial structure of the three areas (see Roberts, 1990). Martin (1996), again in Mexico, also identifies significant differences in the intensity to which, and how, informal work is employed in household work strategies in urban and rural areas.

In sum, the evidence available suggests that, similar to the advanced economies, there are varying processes in different places in the majority world. Formalization in general, and commodification in particular, therefore, cannot be assumed to be evenly and continuously occurring in a universal manner across all localities, regions and nations. Neither, moreover, can informalization and decommodification. Rather, heterogeneous development appears to be occurring.

Socio-spatial allocation of non-commodified work in the majority world

Uncommodified work in the majority world has often been caricatured as a form of work that is the last resort for peripheral populations, which are obliged to perform it as a means of survival (e.g. Fashoyin, 1993; Lagos, 1995; Lubell, 1991; Maldonado, 1995). For example, Fashoyin (1993: 90) argues that 'the informal sector has demonstrated that it can serve as employer of last resort' whilst Lubell (1991: 12) concludes that 'informal sector participants usually constitute the vast bulk of the urban working poor so that informal activity is ... often a last resort for urban survival'.

Here, however, the validity of this marginality thesis is questioned. Arising out of findings in the advanced economies, first, the view is examined that uncommodified work is a form of marginal work and, second, the socio-spatial configuration of the uncommodified sphere in the majority world is explored. The objective, in so doing, is to question whether the uncommodified sphere in the majority world is really a sphere for the marginalized or whether it is more accurate to view it as a heterogeneous sphere that has a hierarchy of its own which normally reflects and reproduces the socio-spatial inequalities prevalent in the commodified sphere.

The origins of the formal/informal dichotomy in the development studies literature, to repeat, is usually accredited to Hart (1973), who used it as a way of understanding the vast amount of activity taking place which was at odds with conventional wisdom in 'western discourse on economic development' (Hart, 1990: 158). For him, informal work was not solely composed of marginal activities and neither was it a remnant from some precapitalist period that would disappear as 'development' ensued. Instead, it was composed of a diverse range of activities and had its own dynamic in the sense that such work was seen as a contemporary phenomenon rather than as an anachronism. Subsequently, however, this heterogeneous and dynamic view of the sphere was quickly lost as the concept became not only institutionalized into and operationalized by international organizations such as the International Labour Organization (ILO), PREALC and the World Bank but also simplified by a range of commentators.

For many, the view has been that there is a separate uncommodified 'economy' or 'sector' inhabited by the marginalized, who use such low-paid work as a means of survival (e.g. Fashoyin, 1993; International Labour Organization, 1972; Lagos, 1995; Lubell, 1991; Maldonado, 1995). For example, the International Labour Organization (1972: 23–6) distinguished this uncommodified or informal 'sector' as possessing the following characteristics: (a) ease of entry; (b) reliance on indigenous resources; (c) family ownership of enterprises; (d) small-scale of operation; (e) labour-intensive and adopted technology; (f) skills acquired outside the formal school system; (g) unregulated and competitive markets. The formal sector, by contrast, was seen to possess the opposite characteristics. This 'dual economy' thesis, however, has subsequently been extensively criticized both in the advanced economies and in the majority world. That is, although general differences in wage rates, contractual status, ease of access, protective legislation and security, capitalization and size of operation are to be witnessed between formal and informal employment, the above characteristics are no longer viewed as exclusive to the informal sphere and are seen to imply a misleading homogeneity of both commodified and uncommodified economic practice (Bromley and Gerry, 1979; Connolly, 1985; Dasgupta, 1992; Meagher, 1995; Lautier, 1994; Peattie, 1980; Portes et al., 1986; Rakowski, 1994; Sharpe, 1988; Tokman, 1978). Instead, informal work is increasingly viewed as a form of economic activity that is part of a larger structure that also includes formal or commodified markets (Bromley and Gerry, 1979; Frank, 1996; Peattie, 1980; Richardson, 1984; Sanyal, 1991; Tokman, 1978). In this sense, the definition and conceptualization of uncommodified work have taken a similar path in both the advanced and developing economies. Both sets of literature have recognized the heterogeneity of such activity, its interdependent relationship with the commodity economy and its non-traditional nature (e.g. Castells and Portes, 1989; Rakowski, 1994).

Indeed, much of the evidence is that the informal sphere can no longer be seen as marginal work solely for those excluded from commodified labour who use it as a last resort. Although the non-commodified sphere is used by those excluded from the commodified sphere, it is also extensively used by those already inserted into the commodified realm. Take, for example, cash-in-hand work. Although informal wages are on average lower than formal ones (see De Pardo et al., 1989; Guisinger and Irfan, 1980; Roberts, 1989, 1990), there is a significant overlap in the wage rates of formal and informal workers.

Examining the distribution of monthly incomes in formal and informal employment in Lima, for instance, Table 9.6 shows that although the mean formal income is higher than the mean informal income (392,379 soles compared with 263,458 soles), informal incomes often match or exceed those of formal incomes. So, despite informal incomes being skewed towards the lower end of income levels to a greater extent than formal incomes, with 63.9 per cent having informal incomes less than 250,000 soles compared with just 39.1 per cent of formal incomes, nearly one in five informal workers earn above the mean formal income. In consequence, paid informal work can no longer be seen as the lowest paid form of work conducted by marginalized groups as a last resort. Neither can such paid informal work simply be seen as a way of exploiting cheap labour.

These findings in Lima are not an exception to the rule. Tokman (1986) finds in Costa Rica, Colombia and Peru substantial differences in informal income between owners of informal shops, the self-employed, workers in informal workshops and domestic servants. Indeed, the variation in income is such that, for some categories of informal worker such as shop owners, earnings are higher than for formal workers. Portes et al. (1986) discover much the same situation in Montevideo, Uruguay. In East Asian nations, meanwhile, Cheng and Gereffi (1994) uncover that informal work is not a phenomenon of unemployment or underdevelopment but instead is highly productive rather than subsistence-oriented, and dynamically linked to the growth of national economies. Therefore, to define informal work solely as a marginal activity for the poor and excluded would be to do an injustice to the large number of informal workers who earn above the average formal wage and for the considerable number of formal employees who earn less than the average informal wage.

Paralleling the theoretical developments in the advanced economies, therefore, such data on cash-in-hand work call seriously into

Table 9.6 Monthly income distributions for formal and informal sectors in Lima, 1983

Monthly income (soles)	Formal sector		Informal sector	
	No.	%	*No.*	%
0	17,260	2.08	33,520	7.13
1–49,999	20,417	2.47	40,433	8.61
50,000–99,999	30,756	3.71	50,914	10.84
100,000–249,999	255,192	30.82	175,487	37.35
250,000–349,999	174,341	21.05	78,307	16.67
350,000–499,999	134,539	16.25	34,982	7.45
500,000–749,999	104,687	12.64	28,548	6.08
750,000–1,499,999	80,268	9.69	22,278	4.74
1,500,000–2,999,999	8,525	1.03	4,498	0.96
3,000,000–4,999,999	1,226	0.15	592	0.13
5,000,000 +	911	0.11	287	0.06

Source: Paredes Cruzatt, 1987: 3, cited in Thomas, 1992: Table 4.4.

question the marginality thesis. Informal labour markets in developing nations appear to be heterogeneous entities with their own hierarchy. For example, studies reveal that although the formally employed often work informally only on a part-time basis due to their formal job commitments, the work they do is higher paid than that conducted by those without a formal job who undertake full-time informal employment at lower wage rates. Simon (1997), for example, shows this to be the case in his study of informal retailing in the city of Kaduna in Nigeria. Here, part-time retailing is practised by formal wage employees such as civil servants to supplement their salaries at higher rates of pay than those earned by the non-employed, who have to work long hours so as to secure sufficient income to get by. As such, he claims that the paid non-commodified realm is composed of a dual labour market in this specific context. This indicates, therefore, that a segmented non-commodified realm exists in which there is a well-paid core informal workforce of people who often also have a job, and a peripheral informal workforce of frequently non-employed people who tend to engage in the more exploitative lower-paid forms of such employment.

A common presupposition in studies of the informal sphere in the majority world, nevertheless, is that individuals are formal or informal workers, not both. This is due to the belief that informal work is for those excluded from the commodified sphere. As already shown in the advanced economies, however, this is not always the case. Individuals engage in both spheres in their daily lives and the tendency is for affluent households to engage in a wider range of non-commodified work, especially of the creative, rewarding and non-routine variety, than poorer households.

The evidence is that a similar tendency exists in the majority world (see Gilbert, 1994; Lautier, 1994; Roberts, 1990). As Gilbert (1994: 614) puts it, 'if the informal sector has acted as a sponge, there are equally clearly substantial hurdles preventing some unemployed workers from entering it. These barriers are especially high in the more remunerative areas of informal self-employment.' For Gilbert (1994), therefore, it is necessary to distinguish between different types of non-commodified work. While it is easy to enter what Lautier (1994) calls 'survival' activities, it is much more difficult to get into those kinds of activities which require skills, capital, know-how or contacts.

One question that remains unanswered, however, concerns the contrasting motivations for engaging in the non-commodified realm. Until now, the assumption has been that all informal workers are purely economically motivated. There is a need, however, in future research, for this aspect of the non-commodified sphere to be examined in greater depth in a majority world context. What makes both formally employed and non-employed workers engage in the non-commodified realm and how do their motivations differ? And is this reflected in the types of non-commodified work that they undertake, and, if so, how?

In the advanced economies, as shown, economic rationales tend to be primary among more deprived populations, and cultures of resistance primary among those from more affluent groups. Do similar motives appear in the majority world? Are there those in these nations who engage in such activity not only due to economic motives but also as a way of resisting the shift towards 'modernization' in their countries?

There is now plenty of evidence in a multitude of books written from the perspective of an anti-capitalist agenda that specific initiatives are being undertaken as a way of opposing the penetration of the commodity economy in general and the associated notion of globalization, which refers to the ongoing incursion of the commodity economy (e.g. Bennholdt-Thomsen et al., 2001; Escobar, 1996; Esteva, 2001; Goldsmith et al., 1995; Hines, 2000; Norberg-Hodge, 2001; Shiva, 2001).

However, for the majority of the poor who use non-commodified work, such a rationale is far from the case. As Quijano (2001) has shown in relation to Latin America, it is nonsense to conceptualize the non-commodified realm as an alternative to capitalism. He shows that this is not some chosen site of resistance so far as most Latin Americans are concerned but, rather, an economy into which those no longer needed by capital tend to be subsumed in order to gain their welfare and livelihood. Indeed, he focuses upon paid informal work and argues that, to greater or lesser degrees, this sector is centred around waged work and around groups unequally situated in relation to control of the means of production and thus to production or profits. Their activities are geared to the acquisition of profits and accumulation, and they consequently operate, completely or in part, within the logic of capital. In many cases this amounts to a 'capitalism of the poor' according to Quijano (2001: 160). Referring to the wider non-commodified realm of subsistence work and reciprocity conducted by the poor, moreover, Quijano (2001: 161) argues that 'only with difficulty could we accept that it amounts to an alternative economy' in the sense of an alternative to capitalism. Although this is correct, great care should be taken, however, not to assign such motives to all non-commodified work. There remains little doubt that such activity represents in some circumstances a site of resistance to the forces of capitalism and its associated bedfellow of globalization. To see this, one has only to consider the local currency experiments in Argentina (e.g. Powell, 2002) or the commentaries of Esteva (2001) on Latin America.

In consequence, caution needs to be taken when considering commodification in relation to the majority world. By viewing the trajectory of economic development towards commodification as natural and inevitable, this discourse has acted not only to define as 'backward' those nations that are less commodified but also to provide a clear prescription of the direction in which they need to develop. The result, as Escobar (1995) has tellingly revealed, is that this Eurocentric perspective on the direction of change has a devaluing and disabling effect on the majority world. For him, the 'third world' – that collection of countries whose populations came to be represented as poor, illiterate, malnourished, underemployed, requiring aid, and in need of Western models of development – is a social construction. The third world was the problem for which 'development' was the solution – through the establishment of a range of institutions, practices and experts that were empowered to exercise domination in the name of the scientifically justified development project. Escobar's close reading reveals how the practice of identifying barriers to growth and prescribing development pathways has in effect violently 'subjected' individuals, regions and entire countries to the powers and agencies of the development apparatus. The subjects produced within and by this discourse are ill equipped both to think outside this presumed order and truth of the economic development story and to reject a vision of the 'good society' emanating from the West. Escobar's Foucauldian approach to development discourse has thus opened the way towards 'unmaking' the third world, by highlighting its constructedness and the possibility of alternative constructions. Importantly, his work points the way towards a repositioning of subjects outside a discourse that produces subservience, victimhood and economic impotence (Gibson-Graham and Ruccio, 2001).

Conclusions

In both the transition economies of central and eastern Europe and the third world, the shallow penetration of commodification has often been seen as a mark of their 'underdevelopment' and something that will naturally and inevitably disappear with economic advancement as they make the 'transition' to the market and 'develop' their economies. In this chapter, however, it has been argued that rather than view the trajectory of development through the eyes of the West, in which the 'advanced economies' position themselves at the head of the queue and view others as backward because they are different (i.e. less commodified), there is a dire need to recognize the heterogeneity of economies and how not all economies may be following the same development path as the West.

It has been revealed here that there is neither universal formalization nor informalization in the transition and developing economies but, rather, different processes in varying places. The result is that the future is much more open than has so far been considered. There is, after all, no natural and inevitable drift towards commodification. In Part III, therefore, the various policy options available and their implications are considered.

PART III

Future Options and Their Implications

10

Towards a Commodified World

E valuating critically the recurring assumption that late capitalism involves an inevitable and natural shift towards a commodified world under the market-driven search for corporate profit, Parts I and II of this book have revealed that for all of the hyperbole of a hegemonic, enveloping, dynamic, pervasive and totalizing commodified realm, there is little evidence that this is indeed the case. Instead, it was revealed in Part I that even in the heartlands of commodification – the Western economies – a non-commodified sphere exists that is not only as large as the commodified sphere but is growing relative to it.

Examining the uneven contours of commodification, Part II then uncovered that, contrary to popular prejudice, it is not simply populations marginalized from the commodified sphere that engage in non-commodified work as an economic survival strategy. Although the growth of the non-commodified sphere is in part the result of social reproductive functions being moved back into the non-commodified realm in order to compete effectively in a globalized economic order, it is also in part the result of a 'culture of resistance' to commodification. Indeed, examining the socio-economic and spatial disparities, it was revealed that although affluent populations lead more commodified working lives, this does not mean that they undertake less non-commodified work. Instead, commodified and non-commodified work display a complementary, rather than a substitutive, relationship. The result is that affluent populations undertake a wider range of non-commodified work than deprived populations, and are more likely to conduct such work out of choice rather than constraint.

In this part of the book, in consequence, the future options with regard to this large and growing non-commodified realm are evaluated. What is to be done about the non-commodified sphere? Should attempts be made to repress such work so as to move towards a commodified world? Should a laissez-faire approach be adopted towards it? Or should an attempt be made to work with the grain of current trends by pursuing the cultivation of such activity? To begin to answer these questions, this chapter deals with the implications of pursuing the first policy option, namely seeking to *repress* such work.

The argument will be that, at least in the advanced economies, there is surfacing a commodified/non-commodified balance beyond the limits of which populations do not seek to pass and capitalism seems incapable of transcending. These blockages to the advance of commodification are not only the result of populations attempting to seize greater control of their destiny by pursuing non-commodified practices of resistance but also due to the inherent contradictions within capitalism that prevent its deeper penetration. In this chapter, in consequence, the idea that there is an inevitable and natural drift towards commodification is called into question. The implication of doing this is that it reveals how pursuing a commodified world then becomes a political choice rather than some organic inevitability about which there is little choice but to go with the flow. Evaluating whether one should choose to commodify work, the argument developed here is that repressing non-commodified work is both impractical and undesirable. It is impractical because non-commodified work is deeply embedded in everyday life and the evidence points towards a decommodification rather than commodification of economic activity. It is undesirable because this work is often the preferred means by which people conduct activities.

First, therefore, this chapter will highlight how, despite the recurring assumption that the shift towards a commodified world is inevitable, this represents a choice (albeit one not always seen as such) that has been taken and one that is currently facilitated and engendered by a multitude of government policy decisions throughout the advanced economies. Following this, the feasibility and desirability of pursuing this policy option will be evaluated, displaying how its impracticality and undesirability are due to the economic constraints that prevent its further advance and the preferences of people to engage in non-commodified economic practices rather than commodify each and every facet of their economic life.

Towards a Commodified World: Inevitability or Choice?

Unless the myth that commodification is a natural and inevitable process is dispelled, there are no options regarding the future of work. When commodification is viewed as natural and inevitable, nations and populations perceive themselves as having little choice but to accept a future in which the commodity economy penetrates ever wider and deeper. In this first section, therefore, it is necessary to show that commodification is far from being inescapable and unstoppable.

First, there is the issue of the inevitability of commodification. It is to be hoped that earlier chapters of this book have made it very clear that a future of commodification is not cast in stone. Over the past forty years or so, the advanced economies have witnessed a process of decommodification. Thus, to assert that commodification is unavoidable is to fly in the face of the macro-level changes occurring in Western economies.

Second, there is the issue of whether commodification is an organic or natural process. To believe this is to view the market sphere as an autonomous sector that grows with little or no help. This, however, is blatantly not the case. Over half a century ago, to repeat, Polanyi (1944: 140) recognized that 'the road to the free market was opened and kept open by an enormous increase in continuous, centrally organized, and controlled interventionism.' As such, the commodification of economic life has been energetically facilitated and sustained by a barrage of state intervention that has actively sought to promulgate the growth of the market. Bearing this in mind, one has to wonder quite how widely and deeply the market would have penetrated economic practices without such active intervention and encouragement by the state. If the market has only captured such a minor share of all economic activity even when governments have so actively intervened to encourage its growth, then one does wonder quite how expansive the market would have been if left to its own devices.

To see how the governments of Western economies have actively encouraged and supported the growth of the commodity economy, while non-commodified work has been at worst repressed, and at best ignored, one needs look no further than the issue of tackling poverty. In Western economies, the widespread approach is that inserting people into the commodified sphere in particular, and formal employment more generally, is the best means of alleviating poverty (Beck, 2000; Giddens, 1998; Williams and Windebank, 2003a). The outcome has been an employment-centred social policy agenda that has actively pursued the insertion of people into the formal labour market (see Levitas, 1998; Lister, 2000; Williams and Windebank, 2003a). Examining this poverty agenda, moreover, it becomes quickly apparent that the intention is not to insert these 'job seekers' into waged employment in the public or third sector unless absolutely necessary. This is often derided as a 'make work' approach that does not create 'real jobs'. Instead, the policy is to seek to insert them into the commodified sphere wherever possible. To achieve this, the 'workfare' approach that commenced in the USA and has now spread to many other Western nations is used, which deliberately creates an environment that encourages people to enter the commodified sphere (Moller and van Berkel, 2002; Peck, 1999, 2001). In this approach to poverty alleviation, therefore, the whole focus is upon using 'sticks' and sometimes 'carrots' to attach people to commodified work. Little, if any, emphasis is put on encouraging participation in non-commodified work as a route out of poverty.

It is not only in the policy realm of poverty alleviation, however, that state intervention has confined itself to facilitating insertion into the commodified sphere rather than harnessing the non-commodified realm. Regional and local economic policy is a realm of public policy more or less entirely devoted to encouraging the development of private-sector firms. To see this, one needs only to glance at the economic development strategy of any locality or region, which tends to be almost entirely focused upon providing incentives to help develop the commodified sphere. Seldom do economic development strategies give consideration to cultivating public-sector employment, and where not-for-profit enterprises are considered worthy of attention, the intention is solely to use them to fill some of the gaps left by the private and public sectors. No consideration at all, meanwhile, is given to harnessing non-exchanged work and non-monetized exchange. Again, therefore, one can see that the continuing prevalence and development of private-sector enterprise has been maintained by an enormous amount of 'continuous, centrally organized, and controlled inter-ventionism' (Polanyi, 1944: 140).

Indeed, wherever one looks, public policy is actively engaged in supporting the development of a commodified economy as the path to progress. Given this continuous and ongoing nurturing and support by government, it is thus obvious that commodifica-tion is not an organic process. Once this is recognized, then the future of work becomes more open. Seeking to develop the market sphere through controlled interventionism and paying little heed to the development of the non-commodified sphere become clearly recognized as but one option available to late capitalist societies, albeit one that is often seen to be anything but a choice.

Repressing Non-commodified Work

Recognizing that facilitating a shift towards a commodified world is a choice rather than a societal inevitability, the issue that then comes to the fore is whether this policy option should be pursued. Here, and in order to evaluate this chosen path, the consequences are analysed of repressing non-commodified work so as to pursue commodification.

Before doing so, however, it is first necessary to outline briefly what such a policy option entails. In this approach, the desire is to commodify work. The intention is thus to transfer work currently conducted using subsistence work, non-monetized exchange and not-for-profit monetized exchange into the commodified sphere. Unpaid activities associated with housework, child-rearing, do-it-yourself activity and volunteering would all be subjected to commodification. This is because the non-commodified sphere has no place in the future. Instead, it is seen at worst solely as a sphere ripe for commodification, and at best as a sphere that is important only in the sense that it can provide a springboard for workers to enter the commodified realm.

In this latter view, for example, volunteering is important not because it meets needs and desires unmet by the market but because it provides a means by which volunteers can develop self-confidence as well as acquire and maintain skills and competencies that will enable them to enter the commodified sphere. Indeed, this 'capitalocentric' (Gibson-Graham, 1996) reading of non-commodified work that defines its importance only in relation to how it can help the commodified sphere develop is now widely adopted throughout the Western economies and beyond. Tabak (2000: 1), for example, encapsulates this current perspective towards non-commodified work when he states,

> Elevated from its former 'marginal' to its current 'leading' economic-sector status, the informal economy now looms large as the breeding ground for the micro-enterprise (*microempresa*) system and as a potential site for robust economic growth. As a result, the transition of the informal economy from an obstacle to an asset to development has been surprisingly smooth.

In this approach towards the non-commodified sphere, adopted by supra-national agencies such as the World Bank in the transition economies and majority world, non-commodified work is important only in the sense that commodifying it may aid and abet the transformation to a commodified economy. The non-commodified sphere is not seen as important in itself.

Indeed, such a discourse on non-commodified work is also apparent in the advanced economies. Rather than seeing it as an obstacle to development, a view has emerged that non-commodified work needs to be harnessed by turning it into commodified activity. Take, for example, the raft of policy initiatives seeking to develop the 'social economy' or 'third sector'. Their whole thrust is to use the third sector as a means of creating additional employment, as witnessed by the fact that the major European Union initiative in relation to this sector is entitled 'Third System and Employment' (see ECOTEC, 1998; Haughton, 1998; Westerdahl and Westlund, 1998).

The rationale for such an approach is that in an age of decoupling of productivity increases from employment growth the private sector can no longer be relied upon to create sufficient jobs. Neither, moreover, can the post-war corporatist welfare state model be expected to spend its way out of economic problems. The 'fiscal crisis' of the state, widely predicted in the 1970s (Habermas, 1993; O'Connor, 1973), is now seen as firmly established. The 'social economy' is thus bolted onto conventional job creation and training programmes and policies so as to fill the 'jobs gap' left by the private and public sectors (Archibugi, 2000; Community Development Foundation, 1995; ECOTEC, 1998; European Commission, 1996b; Fordham, 1995; OECD, 1994).

This is also the approach adopted towards the non-commodified sphere by the New Labour government in the UK. Through its urban and neighbourhood regeneration policies masterminded by the Social Exclusion Unit (SEU) and the Neighbourhood Renewal Unit (NRU), the UK government has shown itself to be genuinely supportive of third-sector initiatives and community enterprises. This, however, is only so in the context of markedly deprived areas and as a stepping stone back into the formal economy (Amin et al., 2002a). The third sector is something to be cultivated to aid those excluded from employment, to be either directly reincorporated into the formal labour market or indirectly so by improving their employability. Indeed, in the UK, a recent government advertisement for a position in the office of the deputy prime minister to forge policy on the informal sector explicitly states that the aim of the post-holder is to find ways 'to encourage residents of disadvantaged areas to move out of the informal economy into formal and legitimate employment' and 'how more people might be helped to move out of the informal economy' (ODPM, 2003). Little consideration is thus given in this capitalocentric approach to the idea that non-commodified work might be in itself a means of livelihood, and to the associated notion that this work could be cultivated rather than turned into commodified work.

Critical Evaluation of the Repressive Approach

Once it is recognized that commodification is a choice rather than an inevitability, the question that arises is whether this normative policy approach should continue to be pursued. To evaluate this repressive policy approach, therefore, two crucial issues need to be considered. On the one hand, there is the matter of whether it is in fact possible to eliminate non-commodified work. On the other hand, there is the issue of whether it is desirable to eradicate such work. These two interrelated issues are now considered. This will show that pursuing a policy of eradication of the non-commodified realm is both impractical and undesirable. It is impractical because the direction of change is towards a decommodification of economic life, and it is undesirable because such non-commodified economic practices are often used out of preference in the advanced economies. As such, seeking to commodify working life not only goes against the grain of the current trajectory of economic development but also against the preferences of the populations of the advanced economies.

Feasibility of eradicating non-commodified work

Once the pursuit of commodification is recognized as a societal choice rather than inevitable, the issue arises of whether it is feasible for commodification to penetrate deeper and wider than at present. To explore this, the idea of 'blocked exchanges' (Walzer, 1983; Block, 1990, 2002; Bloch and Parry, 1989) is considered here, which refers to the existence of constraints on the feasibility of further commodification.

Walzer (1983) argues that in capitalist societies, although some goods and services are sold on the market, other types of exchange are blocked and this impedes an ongoing commodification of society. To see that norms and sometimes laws block exchanges from taking place in the commodified sphere, one has only to consider, for example, that Western economies prohibit the sale of political offices on the market, as well as body parts. Indeed, many of the most intense political debates in recent decades have been over whether certain exchanges should or should not be blocked. Many conservatives want to outlaw the purchase of abortion services and cultural products with sexual themes, for instance, while liberals often favour stricter rules governing gun sales and tighter controls over campaign contributions. Debates about decriminalizing drugs and prostitution are also precisely about this issue of what exchanges should or should not be blocked.

Indeed, such blockages have been the main theme underpinning some 'blockbuster' movies. One such example is the 1993 film tellingly entitled *Indecent Proposal*. Starring Robert Redford as a Las Vegas playboy who pays $1 million to spend the night with Woody Harrelson's wife, Demi Moore, despite her initial protest 'The dress is for sale, I'm not', this movie deals with one particular type of 'blocked exchange'. Indeed, the fact that this type of exchange remains 'blocked' a decade later is evident from the wide media coverage given to a case in the UK involving a married multimillionaire who had supposedly offered a husband the sum of £1 million if his wife spent the rest of her life with him. The publicity surrounding the case and the fact that this 'market exchange' reached the High Court reflect the fact that this remains a 'blocked exchange' that crosses the boundaries of what is an acceptable transaction.

Other examples of how profit-motivated transactions are blocked can be seen in the fact that society expects professionals such as doctors, lawyers and architects not simply to maximize their incomes, but to obey a series of ethical injunctions. Of course, professionals might sometimes ignore these ethical considerations: journalists may slant their coverage in exchange for personal favours or gifts; or surgeons may recommend the same lucrative operation to patients whether they need it or not. The point, however, is that the effective functioning of these institutions is compromised if these ethical injunctions are disregarded. If, for example, accountants were simply to charge a little extra to approve a firm's balance sheet no matter how much financial fraud is involved, economic activity would quickly grind to a halt because investors would no longer be able to trust the financial information that they were receiving.

Another way to see how some transactions are blocked in contemporary society is to consider whether there are barriers to the flow of money between people in certain circumstances. Domains can be identified where, although money may not be completely excluded, its use is often highly constrained or restricted. Take, for example, the exchange of gifts. Although gift-giving is universal, its pattern and meaning vary cross-culturally (Bloch and Parry, 1989; Carruthers and Espeland, 2001). In many Western societies, gift exchange tends to be personal and altruistic relative to impersonal and self-interested commodity exchange. As Gregory (1982: 12) states, 'commodity exchange is an exchange of alienable things between transactors who are in a state of reciprocal independence ... Non-commodity (gift) exchange is an exchange of inalienable things between transactors who are in a state of reciprocal dependence.' Gift exchange establishes and/or maintains a social relationship between the giver and the recipient. A gift invokes an obligation – a relationship of indebtedness, status difference or even subordination. As such, the meaning of the gift must be appropriate to the relationship. And in contemporary advanced economies, money is seldom seen as an appropriate gift. As Carruthers and Espeland (2001: 301) state,

> some exchanges are protected from monetarization and commodification because of their inappropriate ethos. Money in our society is so strongly identified with market exchange that its attachment to something brings with it strong 'economic' connotations that may be deemed unsuitable. In many situations, the use of money violates and endangers the spirit of gift-giving. Consequently, money is generally inappropriate as a gift, and even when it is used as such, all kinds of restrictions, framings, markings, and reinterpretations come into play.

Another example of such blockages is that one would never offer money to somebody who invited you to dinner as a substitute for returning the favour. The debt is personal and direct and must be repaid in kind. Norms of exchange evolve, however; they are not timeless and unchanging. What is inappropriate at one time period or place can become acceptable later or elsewhere. Indeed, and as argued in Chapter 5, it is perhaps the case that payment for favours is now becoming much more widely acceptable in Western societies, especially in deprived populations, even if such payments do not mean that the relationship has been commodified.

It appears, in consequence, that the notion that all goods and services can be commodified confronts blockages. These blockages are normative and temporally and spatially fluid. Let us take one example found in the UK localities study that was reported earlier. In some deprived localities, there was an overwhelming perception that painting the outside of one's house was a task to be undertaken on a self-provisioning basis, doubtless a response to the lack of money available to pay commodified labour. Indeed, some who had the money to do so reported that they would not employ formal labour because neighbours would think that 'they had more money than sense'. In some affluent suburbs, however, quite the opposite was found. The 'norm' was to employ external labour to do this task and some respondents reported that 'they had received funny looks and strange comments' from their neighbours when they had decided to do this task themselves rather than employ somebody. The upshot was that they felt pressured socially to commodify the task in the future. For them, the perception they created by doing it themselves was that 'we couldn't afford to employ somebody' and 'didn't fit in'.

Similarly, there persists in some liberal middle-class circles a perception that one should not employ 'domestic workers' to undertake one's housework since this is seen as an unacceptable exploitative practice that smacks of domestic servitude. The point quite simply is that blockages are always present. Although these blockages change over time and space, there are always blockages of one form or another. Reinterpreting the argument of exponents of commodification, it is perhaps the case that the spheres subject to blocked exchanges are dwindling in number over time as the tentacles of commodification stretch ever deeper and wider. As this book has shown, however, this notion that the scope of unblocked exchanges is growing wider is not borne out by the evidence. If the extent of the size of the non-commodified realm is any measure of where the lines are being redrawn, then even if unblocked exchanges are becoming more common it does not appear that the populations of the advanced economies are taking advantage of this unblocking. Instead, quite the opposite appears to be occurring.

Put another way, there are blockages to commodification and they might well be expanding rather than contracting their coverage. The resulting question is whether it is in fact possible and/or desirable to eliminate such blockages. What has been shown throughout this book is that any attempt to eradicate non-commodified economic practices will confront 'cultures of resistance'. Many do not wish to reduce their non-commodified work and to see the incursion of commodification into ever more areas of their everyday life and it will be difficult to persuade them to do otherwise. Such activity is deeply embedded in everyday social life.

The desirability of eradicating non-commodified work

It is not only blocked exchanges, however, that suggest the impracticality and undesirability of a commodified future. Throughout the advanced economies, there appears to be a deep division between government policy and individual attitudes. In policy-making circles, the desire seems to be to make employment the central focus of people's lives. Indeed, many left-wing commentators who quite correctly used to bemoan the exploitation inherent in employer–employee relationships and profit-motivated exchange relations are now among the principal advocates of inserting people precisely into this relationship. How this is meant to represent a path that transcends capitalism and socialism is hard to decipher, at least so far as the capitalism side of the coin is concerned.

Similarly, many 'old style' feminists who were quick to point out the dangers of patriarchal subjugation when women were confined to the home seem quite happy for their sisters to enter subjugation under capitalist social relations by advocating employment as the principal route to their liberation (e.g. McDowell, 2001). Few stop to consider whether advocating the greater subjugation of women by capitalist social relations, especially given the low-paid nature of women's employment, is the route to their liberation. Perhaps this is because these analysts are so immersed in their own 'careers' that they do not consider it may not be the same for others. Perhaps it is because they themselves are the employers of their sisters as cleaners and nannies. Perhaps, however, it is because they can see no feasible alternative future beyond a commodification of economic life. If this is indeed the case, then such academics, like their political counterparts, perhaps need to start to listen to the population at large.

At the very moment that the 'employment ethic' in particular, and the 'commodification ethic' more generally, has moved to centre stage in both policymaking circles and academic theories, however, it has become evident that many people are starting to redefine the importance of commodified work in their lives (e.g. Cannon, 1994; Coupland, 1991; Franks, 2000; Maffesoli, 1996; Gorz, 1999; Schor, 1991; Sue, 1995; Zoll, 1989). Gorz (1999), for example, cites two surveys conducted in France on young graduates of the Grandes Écoles. A 1990 survey showed that 'what comes out way ahead of everything else is the possibility of working when it suits them, so as to be able to devote more time to personal activities'. In 1993, moreover, a survey of current and past students at the prestigious École Polytechnique confirmed this disaffection regarding careers and the general preference for multi-activity and part-time working. As Gorz (1999: 62) summarizes, 'the relation to work [employment] is growing looser because life goes on elsewhere' and particularly in 'unpaid activities which are regarded as socially useful'.

There is thus a marked decentring of the idea about the growing involvement and identification of the whole person with his/her job. This disaffection with formal employment is the case in all countries and throughout the entire working population, however obsessed people become with income and fear losing their job. In Germany, only 10 per cent of the working population regard their employment as the most important thing in their lives. In the USA, the proportion is 18 per cent, as against 38 per cent in 1955 (*Gallup Monthly*, September 1991, cited in Gorz 1999: 63). Among Western Europeans aged between 16 and 34, 'work' or 'career' trails far behind five other priorities in the list of 'things which are really important to you personally' (Yankelovich, 1995). The five priorities are: having friends (95 per cent), having enough free time (80 per cent), being in good physical shape (77 per cent), spending time with one's family (74 per cent), and having an active social life (74 per cent). Only 9 per cent of those questioned (and

7 per cent of young people between 13 and 25) cited work as 'the main factor for success in life' (Sue, 1995). The gulf between 'work' and 'life' thus seems greater than ever: 57 per cent of Britons, for instance, 'refuse to let work interfere with their lives', as against only 37 per cent of those aged between 45 and 54 (cited in Pahl, 1995). In a sample of upper-middle-class full-time employees in the USA, meanwhile, Schor (1991) finds that 73 per cent take the view they would have a better quality of life if they worked less, spent less and had more time for themselves. The outcome is that some 28 per cent of those questioned had indeed chosen to 'downshift' (i.e. voluntarily earn and spend less) in order to lead a more meaningful life.

It seems, in consequence, that a cultural turn has occurred and that much of the political (and academic) world has not caught up with it. People are in employment because the danger is that if they lose it they will lose their income and all the opportunities for activity and contact with others. Employment is valued, therefore, not for the satisfactions that the work itself brings, but for the rights and entitlements that have been attached to employment and to employment alone (Gorz, 1999). Whilst governments continue to confine citizens' rights to employment rights, this situation seems likely to continue.

This is reinforced in evidence on the motives of US women workers. Putnam (2000: 197) asserts that 'virtually all the increase in full-time employment of American women over the last twenty years is attributable to financial pressures, not personal fulfilment'. Let us interrogate DDB Needham Life Style data. Women were asked whether they are full-time employees, part-time employees or full-time homemakers. Those employed on a full- or part-time basis were then asked whether they work primarily for personal satisfaction or primarily for financial necessity. Full-time homemakers, meanwhile, were asked whether they stay at home primarily for personal satisfaction or primarily to take care of children. People have complex feelings about work, and the simple 'choose to/have to' dualism fails to capture these fuzzy, mixed and complex motives and attitudes. In the real world, such decisions are doubtless a mixture of all these motivations and others. However, as a crude first cut, the standard question distinguishes between women who

Table 10.1 American women: employed out of choice or necessity, 1978–99

% of all women	Financial necessity/ children	Personal satisfaction
Employed full time	31	11
Employed part time	11	10
Homemakers	8	29

Source: Putnam, 2000: 197.

are working (or not working) mainly because they want to and those who are working (and not working) mainly because they must. Table 10.1 displays the results.

Over the last two decades, 31 per cent of women have taken full time employment out of financial necessity. This is misleading because their numbers almost doubled from 21 per cent of all women in 1978 to 36 per cent in 1999. The proportion of all women working full time out of personal satisfaction, meanwhile, has not changed over the past two decades, meaning that of all women employed full time the share doing so for financial reasons has risen from two-thirds to more than three-quarters.

For part-timers, it is again the case that although roughly equal proportions do so out of choice or necessity, this hides a modest increase over time in those doing so for financial gain. Some 8 per cent of all women are homemakers who stay at home for childcare reasons. This declined from 11 per cent in 1978 to 7 per cent in 1999. The proportion of women who stay at home for reasons of personal satisfaction has fallen from 37 per cent of all women in 1978 to 23 per cent in 1999. These represent women at different stages of the life cycle. Stay-at-home mothers are ten years younger than the national average, while personally satisfied homemakers include a large number of retired women, and this category is ten years older than the national average (Putnam, 2000).

In the UK context, the controversial figure of Hakim (2000) has similarly explored work–lifestyle preferences among men and

Table 10.2   Classification of work–lifestyle preferences in the twenty-first century

Home-centred	Adaptive	Work-centred
20% of women 10% of men	60% of women 30% of men	20% of women 60% of men
Children and family life remain the main priorities throughout life	Diverse group including those who want to combine work and family, plus unplanned and unconventional careers, drifters and innovators	Main priority in life is employment or equivalent activities (e.g. politics, sport, art)
Prefer not to engage in competitive activities in the public domain	Want to work, but not totally committed to work career	Committed to employment or equivalent activities in the public domain
Qualifications obtained for intellectual value, cultural capital or as insurance policy	Qualifications obtained with the intention of working	Large investment in qualifications for employment or other activities, including extra education during adult life
Responsive to family and social policy	Very responsive to all policies	Responsive to employment policies

Source: Adapted from Hakim, 2000: Tables 1.1 and 9.1.

women. Table 10.2 presents her results. This divides men and women into three broad categories: 'home-centred' people for whom family life remains the main priority throughout life; 'adaptive' people who seek to combine work and family; and 'work-centred' people whose main priority in life is their employment or similar activities. For Hakim (2000), a strict gender division in terms of the work–lifestyle preferences exists. While women are predominantly adaptive, men tend to be more employment-centred. As Hakim (2000) reveals, only about one-fifth of women and one in three men pursue employment-centred lifestyles. Whatever the gender divisions and proportions allocated to each category, the important point that Hakim (2000) makes (see Table 10.2) is that employment is not always centre stage and that many people are seeking a better balance between employment and family life (see also Mauthner et al., 2001).

In sum, it is often taken for granted among many academic commentators and policymakers that a principal role of government is to provide people with the opportunity to enter formal employment if they wish to do so. However, it appears that what many people want is not the right to employment but the opportunity to choose between commodified and non-commodified forms of work, to combine them in ways that suit them rather than the market. The only conclusion, therefore, is that reconsideration is required of whether the 'employment ethic' should remain at the core of economic and social policy, or whether a 'work ethic' based on a broader conceptualization of economic practices is required. Just as people are recognizing and valuing work beyond employment, there appears to be a case for economic and social policy following suit.

Indeed, one outcome is that few of the commentators who have considered the future of work conclude that there is only one future and that it is a future characterized by greater commodification. As Comeliau (2002: 94) has asserted about those who have studied the future of work:

> they are all opposed, in one way or another, to the logic of capitalist modernity and its neoliberal globalization, which claims to know no other criterion for decisions than indefinite accumulation of the maximum profit. The future of work is thus one of the most essential problems of our societies – both because of the human issues involved, and because of the obstacle that it inevitably runs up against in the logic of the system itself. Solutions will remain mere 'tinkering' so long as they fail to distance themselves from that logic – so long as political reflection, debate and action fail to recognize that we live in societies too complex for regulation by a single criterion, even such a fundamental one as individual interest and the accumulation of profit.

Conclusions

In sum, this chapter has evaluated the policy option of pursuing commodification. Conventionally, grounded in the view that there is a natural and inevitable process of commodification taking place, few have seen this as a matter of choice. Rather, it has been seen as an organic and indelibly mapped-out future from which it is impossible to digress. By showing that commodification is not a natural or inevitable future, however, this chapter has made clear that commodification is a matter of choice.

To assess both the feasibility and the desirability of choosing a commodified future, this chapter has brought to the fore how there are blockages to commodification throughout the advanced economies. If these blockages were purely a product of economic constraint, then perhaps this policy option of commodification could be seriously considered. After all, if the only barrier to commodification were the existence of economic constraints, especially among the poor, that prevent them from enjoying the fruits of a commodified world, then policy would need to consider seriously whether it is feasible to tackle these blockages.

However, in practice, blockages to commodification are also the result of choice on the part of the population. People do not wish many goods and services to be commodified, and resist the encroachment of the market. As such, there are social limits to commodification. Indeed, with the overarching thrust of public policy being to promote the market, such social limits might seem currently to have been surpassed in some spheres, as witnessed by the strong present-day desire of many to roll back the frontiers of commodification so as to strike a greater balance between the commodified and non-commodified spheres. Certainly, the present debates in Western societies about the work–life balance seem to suggest strongly that this is the case. In the next chapter, therefore, an alternative option is considered: doing nothing.

11

Doing Nothing

In this chapter the implications of 'doing nothing' with regard to non-commodified work are explored. After all, the option of making a non-decision and doing nothing is one choice available to Western nations. Indeed, it might seem to some that this is a viable option. Given the cultures of resistance to commodification, adopting a laissez-faire approach towards the non-commodified sphere to allow those who wish to engage in such activity to do so seems superficially to be something of a feasible option. The problem, however, as will be argued here, is that those offloaded from the commodified realm are not thriving in the non-commodified realm at present, and for this large segment of the population 'doing nothing' is not an option. Such a non-decision will serve merely to leave intact the current socio-spatial disparities that result in marginalized populations that have been decanted from the commodified sphere into the non-commodified realm without the capacities to pursue alternative means of livelihood.

To show this, this chapter first outlines what is meant by a laissez-faire approach towards non-commodified work and the possible rationales for pursuing this policy option. Second, the implications of pursuing this approach are evaluated critically so as to display that doing nothing is not a feasible policy option if those being offloaded onto the non-commodified sphere, by a commodified sphere that no longer has a use for them, are to be helped to pursue effective and adequate coping practices.

A Laissez-faire Approach towards
Non-commodified Work

By a laissez-faire approach towards non-commodified work, I here
refer to an approach that does not intervene in non-commodified
work in either a repressive or an enabling manner, but instead
adopts a neutral or 'do nothing' stance. This approach can be
adopted for a variety of reasons. On the one hand, it might be
pursued by those left of centre politically. For these analysts, who
might assume that marginalized populations are already drawing
upon non-commodified work as a coping practice, this approach is
adopted in order to enable what they see as a 'business-as-usual'
approach. By ignoring the fact that marginalized populations
engage in non-commodified work, some legal and some illegal
(e.g. cash-in-hand work), the view is that this would enable such
populations to maintain their current coping practices.

On the other hand, this approach might be adopted by neoliberals. For these right-of-centre analysts, non-commodified work
is not only an indicator of how the commodified sphere might be
organized if it were deregulated and allowed to operate unhindered
but also a means by which the unemployed and marginalized are
currently getting by in the advanced economies (e.g. Matthews,
1983).

Common to both approaches, therefore, is the view that a
laissez-faire approach towards non-commodified work is a feasible
policy option. The problem, however, is that just as in the commodified sphere 'the hidden hand of the market is not an even
hand' (Peck, 1996: 2), it is the same in the non-commodified sphere.
As Part II of this book highlighted, marginalized populations
are less able to engage in non-commodified activity than more
affluent populations. The result is that a laissez-faire approach
towards non-commodified work will merely reinforce, rather than
reduce, disparities. Those currently least able to engage in non-
commodified work will remain unable to perform such activity as
a coping practice. The net result of a 'do nothing' approach is
thus that current socio-spatial inequalities are perpetuated. Those
marginalized populations that are already least able to engage in
non-commodified work as a coping practice will be left bereft of

Table 11.1 Labour force participation rates, 1960, 1973 and 1999

Country	Total participation rate			Growth (+) or decline (−)
	1960	1973	1999	1960–99
Finland	77	71	67	−
Sweden	75	75	71	−
Denmark	74	75	76	+
UK	72	73	71	−
Austria	71	69	68	−
France	70	68	60	−
Germany	70	69	65	−
Ireland	68	64	63	−
Greece	66	57	55	−
Italy	65	58	53	−
Netherlands	64	61	71	+
Spain	61	60	52	−
Belgium	60	61	59	−
Portugal	58	64	67	+

Source: ILO, 1997: Table 2.2; European Commission, 2001: Annex 1.

alternative means of livelihood. This would not be a problem perhaps if these populations were going to be fully integrated into the commodified sphere. The issue, however, is that this appears increasingly unlikely.

To see the implications of pursuing a 'do nothing' approach, therefore, it is first necessary to highlight how a large and increasing proportion of the population are becoming excluded from access to the formal sphere in general, and the commodified sphere in particular, how the welfare safety net to support such populations is being 'stripped away' in advanced economies, and also how such populations fail to find salvation in non-commodified work.

Starting with the degree to which the populations of the advanced economies are directly immersed in the formal labour market (which might be commodified or might be conducted on a not-for-profit basis), one might believe, listening to politicians, that advanced economies are nearly at a stage of 'full employment'. This, however, does not mean that nearly everybody is employed, at least in the language of the politicians. Indeed, examining employment participation rates in the advanced economies, the current situation is far from a state of full employment, if by that is meant a situation in which all people of working age are in jobs (see Table 11.1).

Take, for example, the European Union. In 1999, 147 million of the 375 million inhabitants of the EU were in employment (40 per cent of the population). Some 60 per cent of the EU population were thus being supported by the remaining 40 per cent and it is widely agreed that this will deteriorate as the 'baby boom' generation reaches retirement age. For the working-age population, meanwhile, the employment participation rate in the EU was just 61 per cent (European Commission, 2000b). Nearly two in five (39 per cent) of working-age people in the EU were thus without a job. To achieve full participation, two new jobs for every three currently in existence are needed (a 66 per cent increase in the number of jobs). For some EU nations, nevertheless, the 'jobs gap' is narrower than for others. In Denmark, the country with the highest employment participation rate in the EU (75.3 per cent), a mere 33 per cent rise in the number of jobs would suffice. In Spain, the country with the lowest employment participation rate (49.7 per cent), however, the number of jobs would need to double (European Commission, 2000b).

Is it the case, nevertheless, that the employment problem is reducing over time? Analysing the official data, this is not the case. As Table 11.1 shows, over the past four decades few EU nations have managed to close the 'jobs gap'. Indeed, just three nations have made any progress at all. Denmark managed to raise employment participation rates from 74 per cent to 76 per cent, the Netherlands from 64 per cent to 71 per cent, and Portugal, starting from the low base level of 58 per cent participation, to 67 per cent. These, however, are the exceptions. Most nations went backwards; the 'jobs gap' widened. Indeed, some falls were quite dramatic. Employment participation rates in Finland slid from 77 per cent in 1960 to 67 per cent in 1999. In France they fell from 70 per cent to 60 per cent, in Greece from 66 per cent to 55 per cent and in Italy from 65 per cent to 53 per cent. The view that there is a long-term trend towards full employment, therefore, must be treated with considerable caution. It is not borne out by the evidence.

Is it any different elsewhere in the Western economies? In the USA, the major competing trading bloc that provides the 'baseline' against which the EU measures its progress on employment participation rates (see European Commission, 2001a), the employment participation rate is higher. Even here, however, it is only 73 per cent, meaning that one job needs to be created for every three that currently exist if full participation is to be achieved (European Commission, 2000b). A 37 per cent increase in the number of jobs in the US economy is thus required. In Japan, similarly, the employment participation rate is 70 per cent, necessitating a 43 per cent growth in the number of jobs to achieve full participation (European Commission, 2000b).

Across Western nations, in sum, a wide gap exists between current employment levels and a situation of full participation. Nor is the trend narrowing over time. Advanced economies, therefore, are far from a steady state of full employment and many are moving ever further away from such a situation. Indeed, the principal historical lesson is that full employment was achieved for at most thirty years or so following World War II in a handful of advanced economies (Pahl, 1984). Even here, however, this was only full employment for men, not women (Gregory and Windebank, 2000). As Beveridge (1944: 18) put it, full employment is a state in which there are 'more vacant jobs than unemployed *men*' and where there are jobs 'at fair wages, of such a kind, and so located that the unemployed *men* can reasonably be expected to take them' (my emphasis). Although this language was, of course, based on the widely accepted sexist discourse used at the time, Beveridge was correct to refer to the full employment of men alone. Any talk of returning to a 'golden age' of full employment is illogical if by that is meant an era of full employment for both men and women. Such an era has never existed, so to seek its return is meaningless.

Even this gloomy portrait of employment participation rates, however, does not tell the full story. It omits to mention that over time an increasing proportion of those in employment are

Table 11.2   The polarization of employment between
households, OECD nations, 1983–94

% of all households	Jobless households			Mixed employment status households			Households where all are in employment		
	1983	1990	1994	1983	1990	1994	1983	1990	1994
UK	16.0	14.3	18.9	30.1	22.0	18.6	53.9	63.7	62.1
US	13.1	10.0	11.5[d]	32.3	24.9	24.9	54.6	65.1	63.6
Germany	15.0[a]	12.8	15.5	32.5	27.7	25.6	52.5	59.5	58.9
Netherlands	20.6[b]	17.2	17.2	39.1	31.9	27.0	40.3	50.9	55.7
France	12.5	14.4	16.5	30.6	28.3	27.9	56.9	57.4	55.7
Belgium	16.4	18.0	19.6	41.8	33.7	28.8	41.8	48.3	51.6
Australia	11.9[c]	14.5[e]	–	32.6	28.3	–	55.8	57.2	–
Portugal	12.7[c]	10.8	11.0	38.3	32.9	32.6	49.0	56.4	56.4
Canada	15.2	12.5	15.1	35.7	37.0	35.9	49.1	50.6	49.0
Ireland	17.2	20.0	22.3	47.3	40.8	36.9	35.5	39.3	40.9
Greece	16.0	16.9	17.6	46.3	40.1	38.9	37.7	43.0	43.5
Luxembourg	10.9	9.3	10.5	47.3	42.1	39.0	41.8	48.7	50.5
Italy	13.2	14.3	17.2	47.4	43.1	42.8	39.4	42.6	40.0
Spain	19.4[c]	15.2	10.8	54.5	51.6	48.1	26.2	33.2	31.8

a 1984 data.   *b* 1985 data.   *c* 1986 data.   *d* 1993 data.   *e* 1991 data.

Source: Gregg and Wadsworth, 1996: Table 1.

part- rather than full-time employed (e.g. European Commission,
2000b; Thomas and Smith, 1995; Townsend, 1997). In the EU, for
example, the share of part-time employment increased from 14 per
cent of all employment in 1990 to 17 per cent in 1998 (European
Commission, 2000b). This historical shift in employment contracts
from full to part time is prevalent across the advanced economies.
The outcome is that using employment participation rates alone to
analyse whether or not there is a move towards full employment
masks the extent to which underemployment is rising.

   Who, therefore, are the non-employed? Using data from the
mid-1990s, Hirsch (1999) in the UK identifies the nature of the 10
million working-age jobless. He finds that about 2 million are in

full-time further and higher education, 3 million are women who are married or cohabiting and not employed, and 5 million are adults living in households without anybody in a job (which also contain just over 2 million children). Of these, slightly under 2 million are actively looking for jobs, 3 million are disabled people not working and not looking for work, and around 1 million are non-employed lone parents (see also Dorsett, 2001).

In consequence, half of the non-employed are not wives of employed spouses and/or those who are in education. These 5 million people are living in jobless working-age households. Indeed, this is similarly the case throughout the advanced economies. One of the most significant contemporary labour market trends is the demise of the single-earner household and the polarization of society into no-earner and multiple-earner households. Examining the distribution of employment across prime age (20–59) households for fourteen OECD countries between 1983 and 1994, Table 11.2 displays how the growing polarization of society into households where no member is in employment and households where all are in employment is prevalent across all OECD nations (with the exception of Canada). However, in only seven out of the fourteen nations did the proportion of jobless households increase between 1983 and 1994. In the remaining nations, social polarization has been a consequence of the increasing share of households where all are in employment. Although this social polarization of households is thus a near universal trait, the rise in the proportion of jobless households is not.

Indeed, examining what has happened since 1994, Table 11.3 reveals that the proportion of the population living in jobless households has slightly declined in most nations. In major part, this is due to a concerted effort by governments to resolve the problem of jobless households. Nevertheless, across the EU in 2000, some 13.6 per cent of the population remained living in jobless households with no attachment to the formal labour market. A significant minority of the population is thus in households excluded from the labour market, ranging from 15.4 per cent of the total population in the UK to just 6.3 per cent in Portugal.

The existence of such a large number of no-earner households might not be so damning if the people living in them were being

Table 11.3 Percentage of persons living in jobless households in EU nations

	1995	1997	2000
Belgium	16.9	16.9	15.2
Germany	14.3	15.9	15.3
Greece	11.2	10.8	10.7
Spain	16.3	15.1	11.3
France	11.4	12.0	11.2
Ireland	16.1	15.0	–
Italy	12.2	12.4	11.3
Luxembourg	10.3	10.2	9.7
Netherlands	14.3	12.6	11.5
Austria	8.0	9.0	9.9
Portugal	8.1	8.4	6.3
United Kingdom	17.7	16.8	15.4
EU 15	15.2	15.0	13.6

Note: No data for Denmark, Finland and Sweden.

Source: Eurostat Labour Force Survey, cited in European Commission, 2001b: 14.

supported by the welfare state and not living in continuous poverty. It would show that governments were at least ameliorating the plight of these households. In the UK, however, Dickens et al. (2000) find that in 1996 some 70 per cent of jobless households had less than half the mean household income whilst the figure for jobless households with children was 90 per cent. Moreover, taking the poverty line to be where annual incomes fall below 50 per cent of the median of household disposable income adjusted for household size, Oxley (1999) finds that 91 per cent of the continuously poor live in jobless households in the UK. Indeed, the average income of UK no-earner households is only 28 per cent of that in multiple-earner households (Harkness, 1994). It can thus be concluded that the welfare state is not currently being used to ameliorate the plight of those cast out of the formal labour market.

Given the significant gap between the current employment situation and a full-employment scenario, moreover, there appears to be little hope either in the near future or even beyond that a full-employment scenario will be achieved. Most governments in advanced economies have recognized this problem even if they have not made it explicit to their electorate. Why else, for example, did the EU member states at the Lisbon European Council in March 2000 decide to redefine what is meant by full employment? At this meeting, although the overarching objective of 'full employment' was maintained and reiterated, it became redefined to mean 'To realise Europe's full employment potential by working towards raising the employment rate to as close as possible to 70% by 2010' (European Commission, 2000b: 15).

What no government has so far explained, however, is what is to be done with this 30 per cent of the EU population of working age who are not envisaged as potential employees? How are these 75 million people of working age to make a living? This is a crucial issue. As seen in earlier chapters, it is certainly not the case that they are able to turn to non-exchanged work, non-monetized exchange or cash-in-hand work to provide them with alternative means of livelihood.

What, therefore, is to be done? If policymakers leave the goal of fuller employment in place and seek separate solutions for this large segment of the population excluded from the labour market, then the outcome will be a 'dual society'. The 70 per cent will continue to find their salvation through the formal labour market while the 30 per cent excluded will have to be given some alternative coping mechanism. This might be a passive welfare benefits system or it might be payment for active citizenship or a reinvigorated non-commodified sphere through which they can pursue alternative means of livelihood. However, a policy approach that maintains the goal of full employment but introduces alternative work and welfare practices for those falling by the wayside is not here considered the appropriate solution. Rather than deliberately create a 'dual society', it is perhaps more appropriate to question the current goal of full employment and consider whether some alternative goal can be put in its place. It is not just the jobs gap that leads me to this conclusion.

Disparities in Non-commodified Work

As Part II of this book clearly showed, not to intervene in the non-commodified sphere is to leave in place a realm of activity that is highly uneven in terms of participation and mirrors the inequalities in the formal sphere. Previous writing on non-commodified work often assumed that such activity was undertaken by marginalized populations and thus provided an alternative means of livelihood for those excluded from the commodified realm. However, and as displayed in Part II, this is not the case. Such populations are less able to participate in non-commodified work, and what work they conduct on a non-commodified basis tends to be routine, monotonous and unrewarding activity. Affluent populations, in contrast, are able to partake in a wider range of non-commodified work and a greater proportion is of the non-routine, creative and rewarding variety. The consequence, therefore, is that the non-commodified sphere does not reduce the inequalities wrought by the commodified sphere. Instead, it consolidates the socio-spatial inequalities.

For marginalized populations, that is, self-provisioning does not provide a substitute for their inability to externalize necessary work to the commodified sphere. Rather, such populations are less able to engage in self-provisioning than relatively affluent groups and the activity that they conduct is routine and carries smaller material and psychological benefits. Non-monetized exchange, similarly, although often assumed to be a realm of activity more heavily used by marginalized populations, is in fact concentrated among affluent groups who use it for sociability purposes. For marginalized populations, meanwhile, the little activity that does take place is primarily undertaken in order to make ends meet. This pattern whereby non-commodified work mirrors the commodified sphere is again replicated in the case of cash-in-hand work. As Chapters 6 and 7 showed, the fruits of cash-in-hand work are largely concentrated in affluent populations. For deprived populations, meanwhile, cash-in-hand work is much less prevalent.

Indeed, it is not only the extent and nature of non-commodified work that vary between affluent and deprived populations. There are also significant variations in the motives for engaging in such activity. Based on the commodification thesis that there is a natural and inevitable shift towards profit-motivated monetized exchange, a popular assumption has been that non-commodified work is predominantly engaged in out of economic necessity and that if populations had the opportunity they would undertake this work on a commodified basis. Such economic essentialism with regard to explaining participation in non-commodified work is manifested, for example, in the 'marginality thesis' that views non-commodified work as engaged in by mostly marginalized populations out of economic necessity.

It is also reflected in the more recent view of non-commodified work that conceptualizes its resurgence as the product of a new post-Fordist regime of accumulation that is decanting the functions of social reproduction from the commodified realm back into the non-commodified sphere (e.g. Castells and Portes, 1989; Lee, 1999; Portes, 1994). In this perspective it is the contradictions inherent in the commodification process itself that are resulting in the decommodification of social reproduction in the advanced economies. To compete in a more global commodity economy, Western nations have had to reduce social costs (see European Commission, 2001b) resulting in a growth of the non-market sphere to occupy spaces of production (and reproduction) previously covered by market relations and state subsidies.

Caution is required, however, before accepting this structural 'economic' explanation for the persistence of the non-commodified sphere. As Part II of this book revealed, non-commodified work is far more prolific among affluent than deprived populations; the notion that non-commodified work is conducted out of economic necessity does not appear to explain why this is the case. In consequence, the argument here has been that non-commodified work takes place not only due to economic constraints but also because of the prevalence of cultures of resistance to the edicts of commodification. Put another way, non-commodified work is sometimes used out of choice rather than constraint.

Although economic constraints and choice have often been viewed as alternative and competing explanations for participation in non-commodified work, the argument throughout this book is that one way of synthesizing such apparently contradictory

explanations is to distinguish between the motives of contrasting populations. Put another way, there is now clear evidence
that although economic constraints continue to be the principal
reason for lower-income populations engaging in non-commodified
work, such work tends to be conducted out of choice by more
affluent populations. In this view, there is a 'culture of resistance'
to commodification among affluent populations, who engage in
non-commodified economic practices out of preference in order to
forge identities, seek meaning and receive pleasure from productive
activity outside of their employment.

For economic essentialists, nevertheless, it might be argued that
these cultures of resistance to the edicts of commodification are
themselves the product of the structural economic transformations taking place in the advanced economies. As commodified
work has become more intense under a post-Fordist regime of
accumulation, rather than externalize their household services and
reduce their reciprocal obligations, people may be using the non-
commodified realm in order to get the pleasure that they cannot
find in their commodified work (see Gorz, 1999). Alternatively,
such non-commodified work may be viewed to result from capital
offloading the final stages of production onto non-commodified
labour, as in do-it-yourself activity, in order to rework how profit
is appropriated in ways more in keeping with a consumer society
(see Bauman, 1998; Narotsky, 1998). As such, this 'cultural' resistance to commodification or 'choice' could be seen as a product
of the economic transformations currently underway. In contrast,
however, since economic processes are always culturally inflected
or 'embedded' (see, e.g., Crang, 1996; Crewe and Gregson, 1998;
Lee, 1996, 1997, 2000a, 2000b), culture could also be seen as
the determinant. Depending upon one's viewpoint, therefore, this
evidence could be used to support either cultural or economic
essentialism (see Amin and Thrift, 2000; Martin and Sunley, 2001;
Rodriguez-Pose, 2001).

In a bid to transcend such dualistic either/or thinking, a pluralistic and spatially sensitive both/and approach has been adopted
here. This explains the persistence of the non-commodified sphere
and its uneven contours by examining *both* economic *and* cultural forces, but the weight given to each in explanations is seen

to vary significantly according to the locality and/or population under investigation. While cultures of resistance are far more influential than economic forces in sustaining a decommodified sphere in higher-income populations, more emphasis is required on the influence of economic forces in lower-income populations in maintaining a decommodified realm.

It is important, therefore, not to see these non-commodified economic spaces purely as a by-product of structural economic transformations arising from the highly contested concept of a post-Fordist transition. They also need to be read more positively as sites of resistance to the logic of commodification. Participation in many forms of self-provisioning such as do-it-yourself activity, as well as in caring work for example, is often conducted on a non-commodified basis out of choice rather than economic necessity. Viewed in this way, non-commodified sites are not purely 'spaces of despair'; instead, these chosen spaces can be also given symbolic value as 'spaces of hope' (Harvey, 2000) in that they can be read as development sites for the demonstrable construction and practice of alternative social relations and logics of work outside profit-motivated market-orientated exchange.

Among some affluent populations, for example, the de-commodified sphere can be interpreted at times as a 'chosen space'. However, this is not largely the case among deprived populations where they are much more accurately explained in structural economic terms as 'spaces of despair'. As Sayer (1997: 16) puts it, 'economic forces continue to dominate contemporary life, and thus, however unfashionable, economic analysis cannot be sidelined'. The same is true, however, of cultural issues, especially with regard to affluent populations. Here, it is primarily cultures of resistance, rather than economic logic, that hinder the advance of the commodity economy. To explain the shallow and uneven penetration of the commodity economy, in consequence, there is a need for a pluralistic and socio-spatially sensitive both/and approach.

Even if the economic or the cultural cannot be reduced to one another, nevertheless, this does not mean that these economic and cultural forces are entirely independent. Economic determinants and cultures of resistance mutually constitute each other in the sense that they are in a state of mutual simultaneous shaping. To see how they shape, and are shaped by, each other, one has only to consider, for example, how the 'cultures of resistance' that result in households engaging in self-service activities are themselves more often than not inescapably embedded in commodified practices. These cultures of resistance both feed, and are fed by, the advent of market-orientated do-it-yourself business and household appliance and product companies as well as the dissatisfaction that is resulting from the intensification of employment. For some, the result is that such 'cultures of resistance' to commodification are often recuperated into successive rounds of commodification (e.g. Jackson, 2002; Narotsky, 1998). Yet it takes only a little reflection to realize that this is not a one-way process. Indeed, it is the changes in commodified work practices themselves that are helping to instigate non-commodified practices.

What is certain, nevertheless, is that social-scientific inquiry, journalists, politicians and policymakers have been very slow to take seriously the non-commodified realm. Given that the non-commodified sphere now involves over half of total working time and is gaining an ever greater share, it is no longer possible to justify the focus upon the commodified sphere with claims that capitalism is totally hegemonic, victorious, penetrating, expansive and all-powerful (Gibson-Graham, 1996). Contrary to those who claim that the pervasive reach of the commodity economy makes it ever more difficult to imagine and legitimate non-market forms of organization and provision (e.g. Amin et al., 2002b), non-market forms of organization and provision not only have far from disappeared but are also witnessing a resurgence.

Conclusions

In sum, this chapter has revealed that adopting a 'do nothing' approach towards the non-commodified sphere will merely leave those excluded from the commodified sphere in their current position of also being the population least able to engage in the non-commodified realm. Currently, in other words, it is precisely those who are not included in the commodified realm, either as participants in the formal labour market or as major consumers of its products, who also find themselves unable to engage to the same extent as affluent populations in the non-commodified sphere and, when they do so, find themselves confined to participation in routine, unrewarding and repetitive non-commodified work that is conducted out of economic necessity rather than choice. The result is that they are less able to pursue means of livelihood in either the commodified or the non-commodified sphere than their more affluent counterparts. Thus the argument of this chapter is that 'doing nothing' is not an option. Such a non-decision will serve merely to leave the current disparities intact that result in marginalized populations being offloaded by the commodified sphere onto the non-commodified realm without the capacities to pursue means of livelihood.

12

Fostering Plural Economies

It has been shown that the first option of more fully commodify-ing work is both impractical and undesirable. It is impractical because non-commodified work is deeply embedded in everyday life and the evidence points towards a decommodification rather than a commodification of work. It is undesirable because non-commodified work is often the preferred means by which people conduct many activities. A laissez-faire approach, meanwhile, results in numerous negative consequences. The ever popular 'marginality thesis' assumes that non-commodified work is under-taken by marginalized populations as a survival strategy and is thus more prevalent in deprived than affluent communities. The empirical evidence, however, is that these populations conduct less non-commodified work than the relatively affluent. As such, a laissez-faire approach merely leaves the existing socio-spatial disparities intact and does little to help those excluded from the commodified sphere to develop means of livelihood.

In consequence, this chapter will evaluate the option of swim-ming with the tide and working with the economic plurality that prevails in advanced economies. To do this, first, some rationales for pursuing the cultivation of economic plurality are reviewed that are found in third-way, non-market social-democratic, radical ecological and post-development thought. Second, it is argued that if this is to be achieved, then there is a need to replace the currently all-pervasive goal of commodification with a new target, namely 'full-engagement', which refers to the provision of sufficient work (both commodified and non-commodified economic activity) and income so as to give citizens the ability to satisfy both their basic material needs and their creative potential. To start to discuss how to achieve a full-engagement society, the third and final section of this chapter then addresses the issue of the barriers to engagement in non-commodified work. This is focused upon here because although there is a vast amount of previous research on how to insert people into the commodified realm, identifying and tackling the barriers to engagement in non-commodified work have so far been little discussed. By identifying the obstacles to participation in non-commodified work, the scene will thus be set for the next chapter, which investigates strategies that can be used to develop economic plurality.

Discourses on Cultivating Economic Pluralism

Recent decades have witnessed the emergence of a range of discourses that both recognize economic plurality and argue the case for actively cultivating heterogeneous economic practices rather than seeking either to repress non-commodified work or to adopt a laissez-faire approach. Here, these various discourses are outlined along with their arguments so as to provide an understanding of the rationales that underpin the advocacy of such an approach. Four discourses are reviewed: third-way, non-market social democracy, radical ecology and post-development thought.

Third-way discourses

Until now there has been a good deal of confusion and debate over the approach that third-way thought, especially New Labour in the UK, adopts towards non-commodified work in particular and economic pluralism more generally (see, for example, Jordan, 1998; Jordan and Jordan, 2000; Levitas, 1998). In order to understand the approach of New Labour, it is suggested here that it is first of all necessary to recognize that a clear (if artificial) distinction is drawn between the role attached to non-commodified activity in the 'economic' sphere and its contribution in the realm of 'welfare' provision. In the 'economic' realm, New Labour views such work as something to be, at worst, repressed or, at best, used as a springboard for inserting people into the commodified realm (e.g. by improving employability). In the 'social' or 'welfare' sphere, however, New Labour recognizes non-commodified work in its own right as a form of activity that can complement the private and public formal spheres as an additional means of welfare provision.

It is in the welfare sphere and this sphere alone, in consequence, that third-way exponents believe that not only private- and public-sector provision but also a third prong of 'civil society' need to be harnessed to meet welfare needs. As Giddens (2000: 55–6) puts it,

> The 'design options' offered by the two rival political positions were ministic – they looked either to government or to the market as the means of co-ordinating the social realm. Others have turned to the community or civil society as the ultimate sources of social cohesion. However, social order, democracy and social justice cannot be developed where one of these sets of institutions is dominant. A balance between them is required for a pluralistic society to be sustained.

In third-way thought, therefore, it is a mixed economy of welfare delivery that is advocated. Transcending the public versus private provision debate, civil society is added into the equation as an additional means of welfare provision. As Giddens (2000: 81–2) continues,

> In the past, some on the left have viewed the 'third sector' (the voluntary sector) with suspicion. Government and other professional agencies should as far as possible take over from third-sector groups, which are often amateurish and dependent upon erratic charitable impulses. Developed in an effective manner, however, third-sector groups can offer choice and responsiveness in the delivery of public services. They can also help promote local civic culture and forms of community development.

Or, as the UK prime minister, Tony Blair (1998: 14), puts it,

> The Old Left sometimes claimed that the state should largely subsume civil society, the New Right believes that if the state retreats from social duties, civic activism will automatically fill the void. The Third Way recognizes the limits of government in the *social sphere*, but also the

need for government, within those limits, to forge new partnerships with the voluntary sector … 'enabling' government strengthens civil society rather than weakens it, and helps families and communities improve their own performance. (my emphasis)

If third-way thought recognizes the role of non-commodified work as a tool for delivering welfare provision, it is necessary to reiterate, however, that this is not the case when viewed through the lens of 'economic' policy. Here, the approach remains entrenched in an ideology of commodification, and a repressive attitude is adopted in which the only rationale for cultivating such work is to provide a trampoline into the commodified sphere by using it variously to develop and enhance skills, as a test-bed for self-employment and means of improving employability. This starkly contrasts with a second approach that seeks to facilitate heterogeneous economic practices, namely non-market social democracy.

Non-market social-democratic thought

Below the surface of mainstream European social-democratic discourse is a strong current of radical thought that advocates the development of non-commodified work as an alternative and/or complement to the commodified realm (e.g. Archibugi, 2000; Aznar, 1981; Beck, 2000; Delors, 1979; Gorz, 1999; Greffe, 1981; Lalonde and Simmonet, 1978; Laville, 1995, 1996; Mayo, 1996; Rifkin, 1996; Sachs, 1984). This has a long history (O'Neill, 2003). For non-market social democrats, there are at least three reasons for seeking to reduce the hegemony of the commodity economy in the lives of all citizens and to develop alternatives or complements to commodified work.

First, it is maintained that an increasing number of people find work grounded in profit-motivated monetized exchange stultifying and alienating (e.g. Amado and Stoffaes, 1980; Archibugi, 2000; Aznar, 1981; Gorz, 1985, 1999; Laville, 1995, 1996; Mayo, 1996). As Archibugi (2000: 9) puts it, employees 'are all deeply isolated and dissatisfied. The workplace and the activity no longer seem to be "places" of social integration.' Given this lack of opportunity for personal growth in the commodified realm as well as the fact that the only alternative to such a job is unemployment that cannot provide self-esteem, social respect, self-identity, companionship and time structure, the commodification of work is not perceived as at all positive. Aznar (1981: 39) assesses this situation in the following manner: 'any society which proposes that its citizens spend the whole of their time, energy and empathy engaged in an activity which cannot, by its very nature, soak up this energy, is fundamentally perverse.' The solution, as Beck (2000: 58) puts it, is that 'the idea that social identity and status depend only upon a person's occupation and career must be taken apart and abandoned, so that social esteem and security are really uncoupled from paid employment.' This is reinforced by Gorz (1999: 72):

> The imperative need for a sufficient, regular income is one thing. The need to act, to strive, to test oneself against others and be appreciated by them is quite another. Capitalism systematically links the two, conflates them, and upon that conflation establishes capital's power and its ideological hold on people's minds.

The second reason why the commodified realm should not remain centre stage flows from the observation of non-market social democrats that society, in pursuing corporate profit and economic growth for its own sake rather than as a means to an end, has lost its way (Douthwaite, 1996; Gorz, 1985; Mayo, 1996; Robertson, 1985). In consequence, an individual's work, as embodied in employment, no longer responds to the real needs of the consumer. The result, as Friedmann (1982) states, is that only 35–40 per cent of the economically active population engage in 'indispensable' production. The rest are obliged to produce essentially unnecessary goods in order to earn the income necessary for personal survival. Gorz (1985: 58) agrees, and suggests that 'for a section of the population, only the production of inessentials allows them access to necessities'. In this non-market social-democratic discourse, however, nobody should have to work at such production to earn the money necessary for survival: 'employment should be seen not as an end in itself, but as a means to achieving a better quality of life' (Mayo, 1996: 147).

Third and finally, these analysts argue that the relentless pursuit of commodification has led to a devaluation of non-commodified work. The prolonged structural crisis of unemployment, however, is considered to provide an opportunity to revalorize this work. As the OECD (1996) report produced by some advocates of this discourse suggests, there is a need to put the economy back into society rather than see it as an autonomous element. For them, and mirroring much of the recent academic interest shown in analysts such as Polanyi (1944) and Granovetter (1973), the desire is to develop a socially embedded view of economic activity (Lee, 1996; Verschave, 1996). The current structural crisis of unemployment provides just such an impetus for rethinking whether all social goals should be subjugated to the economic aim of continued profit and growth rather than viewing the 'economy' as serving the interests of society.

For non-market social democrats, the way forward is not to insert people more fully into precisely the profit-motivated exchange relations that they view as causing so many problems. Instead, they assign non-commodified work a crucial role in the future of work and welfare. However, they are not only, or indeed necessarily, concerned with such activity as it exists today, but in the possible emergence or reinforcement of a category of work which one could call 'autonomous' in the future. Although some radicals view the green shoots of this autonomous work in the present-day non-commodified sphere (e.g. Jordan, 1998; Rifkin, 1996), others view autonomous work as a conceptual, as opposed to concrete, phenomenon (e.g. Gorz, 1999; Sachs, 1984). For these latter analysts, autonomous work is not currently a tangible, empirically observable category of activity. Instead, it is a new form of socially useful work that should be created where the producer has control over the work and in which creativity and conviviality will be the driving forces. This form of work will have a purpose for the person performing it other than earning a wage (for a summary, see Windebank, 1991).

Uniting all of these non-market social democrats, nevertheless, is their wish to put an end to, or at least considerably reduce the domination of, 'heteronomous' work in people's lives. Heteronomous work is understood as those productive activities over which individuals have little or no control and is characterized by commodified work. Some radicals with leanings towards old-style socialism argue that this can be achieved by the state taking control of heteronomous production and designating the boundaries between the autonomous and heteronomous spheres of life. Increasingly, however, many non-market social democrats are instead seeking changes to work patterns through piecemeal initiatives to foster non-commodified work as an alternative to the market. In adopting this approach to change, these non-market social democrats overlap considerably with a separate but inter-related stream of thought that is also seeking to value and cultivate economic plurality.

Radical ecology

The desire to challenge the domination of the commodified realm and display the economic plurality that exists are not only present in third-way and non-market social-democratic thought. There is also a large body of green political thought that seeks to recognize and foster economic pluralism in order to achieve sustainable economic development (e.g. Dobson, 1993; Ekins and Max-Neef, 1992; Fodor, 1999; Goldsmith et al., 1995; Henderson, 1978, 1999; Hoogendijk, 1993; Mander and Goldsmith, 1996; McBurney, 1990; Robertson, 1991; Roseland, 1998; Trainer, 1996; Warburton, 1998; Wright, 1997).

Grounded in a green political ideology, these analysts view social-ism as a spent political force, as displayed by both the changes in the political economy of central and eastern Europe and the parallel shifts in the politics of first world 'advanced' economies. For them, this is not to be mourned. The old quarrels between neoliberals and socialists were simply over the best way of boosting productivism and realizing greater materialism for the majority of people. The advent of New Labour's third way grounded in employment-centred social integrationism is argued to continue in the same vein, merely introducing a further alternative to free-market capitalism now that socialism is dead. For these greens, the differences between all of these approaches are differences that make no difference. The pursuit of greater materialism and enhanced productivism displays how what were originally means to an end have become ends in themselves in these approaches (e.g. Capra and Spretnak, 1985; Dobson, 1993; Mander and Goldsmith,

1996; Robertson, 1991). For these radical ecologists, there is a need to recapture the ends. To do this, it is argued that there is a need to reconsider, first, the relationship between people and nature and, second, and flowing from this, the direction of society (see, e.g., Devall, 1990; Eckersley, 1992; Goodin, 1992).

Rather than protect natural ecosystems simply for the pleasure of people (i.e. anthropocentrism), these analysts adopt an ecocentric approach, viewing nature as having biotic rights that require no justification in human terms (e.g. Capra and Spretnak, 1985; Devall, 1990; Devall and Sessions, 1985; Naess, 1986, 1989; Skolimowski, 1981). Flowing from this ecocentrism, their argument is that ecologically sustainable development can only occur if a smaller-scale, decentralized way of life is pursued based upon greater self-reliance and the cultivation of non-commodified work practices (e.g. Douthwaite, 1996; Ekins and Max-Neef, 1992; Gass, 1996; Goldsmith et al., 1995; Henderson, 1999; Lipietz, 1995; Mander and Goldsmith, 1996; McBurney, 1990; Morehouse, 1997; Robertson, 1985; Roseland, 1998; Trainer, 1996). To achieve this, the now established concept of 'thinking globally and acting locally' is the key. The belief is that global problems such as the destruction of nature can be overcome only by acting in a local manner (e.g. Hines, 2000; Mander and Goldsmith, 1996). Rather than pursue the end of economic growth through outward-looking development policies, their objective is instead to nurture more 'inward-looking' approaches focused on meeting local basic needs through the pursuit of self-reliance (e.g. Ekins and Max-Neef, 1992; Robertson, 1985, 1991; Morehouse, 1997). The development of forms of non-commodified work thus resonates strongly with this overarching desire for more localized, self-reliant and sustainable economic development (e.g. Henderson, 1999; Mander and Goldsmith, 1996; Warburton, 1998).

Post-development discourse

In the final discourse of post-development theory, the starting point is that engagement in the mapping of an ever more commodified world creates what is then seen and that there is a need to recognize, value and create non-capitalist economic practices that are already here and emerging so as to shine a light on the demonstrable construction of alternative possibilities and futures (e.g. Byrne et al., 1998; Escobar, 1995; Community Economies Collective, 2001; Gibson-Graham, 1996; Gibson-Graham and Ruccio, 2001; Williams, 2002a, 2002b, 2003). For these analysts, a discursive analysis of the commodification thesis is required, coupled with the articulation of alternative regimes of representation and practice, in order to imagine and enact alternatives to a commodified world.

The first task of these analysts is to deconstruct commodification as a natural and inevitable future. On the one hand, and using discourse analysis (see Derrida, 1967), this is achieved by questioning, first, the Western idea that there are objects/identities that are stable, bounded and constituted via negation, and, second, the hierarchical nature of this binary mode of thinking whereby the first term is endowed with positivity at the expense of the other (e.g. firm and household, production and reproduction, reason and emotion, objectivity and subjectivity, man and woman, economic and non-economic). To do this, at least three approaches are available.

One approach is to revalue the subordinate term, namely non-commodified practices, as witnessed in attempts to attach a value to unpaid forms of work. The problem, however, as Derrida points out, is that revaluing the subordinate term in a binary hierarchy is difficult since it also tends to be closely associated with the subordinate terms in the other dualisms (e.g. non-commodified work is associated with reproduction, emotion, subjectivity, women and the non-economic, and commodification with production, reason, objectivity, men and the economic). Another strategy is thus to blur the boundaries between the terms, highlighting similarities on both sides of the dualism so as to undermine the solidity and fixity of identity/presence, showing how the excluded other is so embedded within the primary identity that its distinctiveness is ultimately unsustainable. For example, the household is represented as also a site of production – of various goods and services – and the factory also as a place of reproduction (see Gibson-Graham, 2003). A final approach, and the one primarily adopted throughout this book, is to recognize the interdependencies between the two sides of the dualism and how they shape and are shaped by each other in a process of mutual iteration. This is clearly shown by the fact that non-commodified work is larger and of a more creative, rewarding and non-routine character in relatively commodified households, and that the existence of such non-commodified work is not only a by-product of engagement in the commodified sphere but also how participation in the commodified sphere is in part also a by-product of such engagement in the non-commodified realm (e.g. where a model railway enthusiast sets up a self-employed business). Pursuing any of these three strategies can thus challenge the hierarchical binaries that pervade contemporary thought and have until now stifled recognition of the 'other' that is non-commodified work.

On the other hand, and alongside this Derridean challenge to the hierarchical dualism of commodified work/non-commodified work, post-development theorists have also followed in the path of Foucault (1981) and sought to deconstruct commodification through, first, a critical analysis of the violences and injustices perpetrated by a theory or system of meaning (what it excludes, prohibits and denies) and, second, a genealogical analysis of the processes, continuities and discontinuities by which a discourse comes to be formed.

Escobar (1995) exemplifies this approach when discussing com-modification/'development' in a third world context. His work traces the historical production of the 'third world' – that collection of countries whose populations came to be represented as poor, illiterate, malnourished, underemployed, requiring aid, and in need of Western models of development. The third world was the problem for which 'development' was the solution – through the establishment of a range of institutions, practices and experts that were empowered to exercise domination in the name of the scientifically justified development project. Escobar's close reading reveals how the practice of identifying barriers to growth and prescribing development pathways has in effect violently 'subjected' individuals, regions and entire countries to the powers and agencies of the development apparatus. The subjects produced within and by this discourse are ill-equipped to think outside this presumed order and truth of the economic development story and to reject a vision of the 'good society' emanating from the West. Escobar's

Foucauldian approach to development discourse has opened the way towards 'unmaking' the third world, by highlighting its constructedness and the possibility of alternative constructions. Importantly, his work points the way towards a repositioning of subjects outside a discourse that produces subservience, victimhood and economic impotence (Gibson-Graham and Ruccio, 2001).

Similar to Escobar, Gibson-Graham (1996) also attempt(s) to reread economic development. For her/them (they are two authors writing as one), and adopting a similar Foucauldian approach, the commodification thesis is seen to produce a regime of representation that constructs identities and that symbolizes, manages and creates the place of people and nations. To represent commodification cartographically is thus to locate and chart the configurations of power in the world. With Western commodification both the referent and the context, the plural economies of other nations have been deemed to have a problem of backwardness that needs to be resolved. Using commodification as a benchmark of 'development' and 'progress' and measuring countries against it, a linear and unidimensional trajectory of economic development is imposed that represents non-Western nations as backward, traditional and so forth, and positions those at the front with a closed future of ever greater commodification. This, for them, is a representation of reality and discursive construction that reflects the power, and serves the interests, of capital. By representing the future as a natural and inevitable shift towards commodification, one is engaged in the active constitution of economic possibility, shaping and constraining the actions of economic agents and policymakers. As Byrne et al. (1998: 3) put it,

> To re-read a landscape we have always read as capitalist, to read it as a landscape of difference, populated by various capitalist and non-capitalist economic practices and institutions – that is a difficult task. It requires us to contend not only with our colonized imaginations, but with our beliefs about politics, understandings of power, conceptions of economy, and structures of desire.

By re-visioning the economic landscape of the advanced economies as composed of a plurality of economic practices – both market and non-market – the implications are twofold. First, it suggests that out there in the world are other economic practices besides the market. Second, by locating non-market practices as existing in the here and now, one is engaged in the demonstrable construction and practice of alternatives to the market. Unlike some on the left who still seek a complete system that could overthrow capitalism and provide a replacement, what is being considered by these post-development theorists is the multiplicity of ways of leaving, abandoning the market or becoming and practising non-market activities. By representing non-market economic activities as existing and emerging, and as therefore possible, the act of making such activities visible enables the constitution of alternatives to the market. This rereading of the advanced economies is not simply about bringing minority practices to light. It is about opening up the Western economies to resignification.

For some, nevertheless, it might be asserted that pinpointing such alternative economic practices only reveals a series of disjointed and dispersed economic practices that represent no real challenge to the market. How, for example, can the presence of mundane and routine subsistence work possibly represent a challenge to the grandeur of the market? Byrne et al. (1998: 16), however, do not feel that this is the case:

> We can view the household as hopelessly local, atomized, a set of disarticulated and isolated units, entwined and ensnared in capitalism's global order, incapable of serving as a site of class politics and radical social transformation. Or we can avoid conflating the micro logical with the merely local and recognize that the household is everywhere; and while it is related in various ways to capitalist exploitation, it is not simply consumed or negated by it. Understanding the household as a site of economic activity, one in which people negotiate and change their relations of exploitation and distribution in response to a wide variety of influences, may help to free us from the gloom that descends when a vision of socialist innovation is consigned to the wholesale transformation of the 'capitalist' totality.

To view the market in this light is to decentre it from its position at the heart of the advanced economies and to bring to the fore the possibility of alternative economic practices and futures beyond its hegemony. The intention here, therefore, is to destabilize the market as a presumed or inherently hegemonic system, questioning its naturalized dominance by representing it as one of many forms of economic practice.

For many commentators in the earlier discussed perspectives that seek to foster economic plurality, recognizing non-capitalist economic practices was simply the first step in the process. Their view, perhaps somewhat naive, is that this is something that has already been achieved, not least by the feminist movement. Based on this, the emphasis has been on trying to move the discussion forward by constructing alternative means of livelihood through which these non-capitalist economic practices might be cultivated (rather than merely recognized). The importance of this post-development perspective is that it perhaps explains the reasons for their lack of success in gaining acceptance of a perspective of economic plurality and initiatives to foster non-commodified work. It reveals how revaluing non-commodified work and envisaging futures beyond commodification directly challenge not simply core beliefs about the contemporary mode of economic organization and the future of work but also capitalism itself.

From Commodification to Full Engagement

In all of these discourses, therefore, the common intention is to recognize and value non-commodified work and to develop it either in tandem with, or as an alternative to, the commodified sphere. For these perspectives, in consequence, the pursuit of an ever more commodified world is not the goal of economic development. Instead, the normative desire is to foster hetero-geneous economic practices. As such, a new goal of economic development needs to be named. In this section, I wish to argue that targeting 'full engagement' enables this to be achieved. By 'full engagement' is meant providing sufficient work (both com-modified and non-commodified economic activity) and income so as to give citizens the ability to satisfy both their basic material needs and creative potential.

In a full-engagement society, it is thus not an either/or choice between commodified and non-commodified work. Instead, a both/and approach is adopted. Given the evidence already presented of economic plurality, some may assert that this is already the case.

The problem at present, however, is twofold. First, those least able to participate in the commodified sphere are also least able to draw upon the non-commodified sphere for sustenance. Second, policymakers have prioritized the development of the commodified sphere over the non-commodified realm as the way forward, and even in some cases sought to eradicate the non-commodified realm in order to develop further the commodified sphere.

The first step required in order to make the transition from the goal of a commodified world to a society based on full engagement, therefore, is that non-commodified work needs to be recognized and valued. As Beck (2000: 58) puts it,

> In the transition from the work [commodified] society to the multi-activity society, a new answer is given to the question: what is work? The concept of an 'activity society' does, it is true, include a reference to paid work, but only as one form of activity alongside others such as family work, parental work, work for oneself, voluntary work or political activity. This reminds us that people's everyday lives and work are stretched on the procrustean bed of *plural activities* – a self-evident fact that is usually obscured in the perspective of a society centred upon paid employment.

Once non-commodified modes of production and delivery are recognized and valued, the next step is to work towards giving such work equal status to commodified work. At present, this has occurred nowhere. Although there is widespread recognition in the 'social' or welfare sphere that civil society is a third prong in the welfare equation that needs to be given equal status to the formal public and private spheres, the same reconceptualization has not occurred in the so-called 'economic' sphere. Here, com-modified work retains its status as the only form of work of any true worth and there is strong resistance to recognizing and valuing non-commodified modes of production as of equal value to com-modified work. The result is that people are currently helped in all manner of ways with 'carrots' and 'sticks' to enter the world of commodified work, but there is much less attention given to helping people to engage in non-commodified modes of production.

If full engagement is to be achieved, however, then there will be a need to rebalance the priority accorded to commodified work and to place as much emphasis on enabling people to engage in non-commodified work as is given to enticing them into the commodified world. If policymaking can achieve this, then as argued in Chapter 2, the desires of the population at large will be reflected. As Beck (2000: 106) once again puts it,

> more and more people are looking both for meaningful work and opportunities for commitment outside of [commodified] work. If society can upgrade and reward such commitment and put it on a level with gainful employment, it can create both individual identity and social cohesion.

For some, it might be believed that the way to do this is simply to develop the commodified sphere. After all, the commodified and non-commodified spheres are complementary, working in tandem. This argument that it is only necessary to develop commodified work, however, assumes a one-way cause-and-effect relationship. It is based on the view that it is the commodified sphere that determines the nature of the non-commodified sphere. Such a reductive view, nevertheless, is unproven. Indeed, all of the evidence seems to suggest that there is a complementary co-constitutive relationship whereby the two spheres mutually and iteratively shape, and are shaped by, each other. If correct, then it is not simply a case of cultivating the commodified sphere. It is also necessary to foster the non-commodified realm.

In order to move towards a full-engagement society where people can use a plurality of economic practices to meet their needs and desires, the barriers to participation in both commodified and non-commodified work will need to be tackled. Given the academic and policy effort that has already been put into identifying and tackling the barriers to participation in the commodified sphere, attention here turns to the barriers to participation in non-commodified work, which is an issue upon which there has been very little discussion. This will then allow policies to be formulated to tackle these barriers in order to cultivate non-commodified work.

Barriers to Engagement in Non-commodified Work

Evaluating the extent and character of non-commodified work is an important first step in challenging many of the myths that have grown up surrounding commodification. However, merely challenging myths cannot and should not be an end in itself. Given that non-commodified work is growing and that lower-income populations are unable to draw upon this sphere as a resource, these populations also need to be facilitated to engage in such work if a more fully engaged society is to be achieved in which populations are able to draw upon the resources of both the commodified and the non-commodified realms to meet their needs and desires.

A crucial question is thus whether non-commodified work can be harnessed in order to provide households and communities with additional means of meeting their needs and wants (see, for instance, Burns and Taylor, 1998; Donnison, 1998; Macfarlane, 1996). To formulate policy initiatives for enabling populations to develop their capacities to help themselves to a greater extent than at present, the first step is to understand the barriers to participation in non-commodified work. Here, the principal barriers are reviewed that have been identified in a host of studies conducted throughout the advanced economies (e.g. Home Office, 1999; Pahl, 1984; Renooy, 1990; Williams and Windebank, 2003a). Indeed, it is only once these barriers have been identified that strategies and initiatives can be discussed to foster non-commodified work since they have to be capable of tackling these barriers.

Social network capital

A first barrier to participation, especially so far as the giving and receiving of paid and unpaid support is concerned, is that people do not generally feel that they know others well enough either to ask or to be asked to do something. Hence, if lower-income populations in general and jobless households in particular are to engage in greater levels of non-commodified exchange, then there will be a need to widen their social networks and social support structures. This is increasingly recognized in the literature associated with the fuzzy concept of social capital (e.g. Coleman, 1988; Putnam, 1993, 1995a, 1995b, 2000). This argues that the 'strong' ties commonly but not always associated with kinship and close-knit communities may actually be less effective than a large and more diverse network of ties that are developed through other social networks. Thus, Granovetter (1973) writes of the 'strength of weak ties'. Weaker ties might have limits on the claims that can be made on them, but they also tend to provide indirect access to a greater diversity of resources than do stronger, more socially homogeneous, ties. As Granovetter (1973: 1371) points out, 'those to whom we are weakly tied are more likely to move in circles different from our own and will thus have access to information different from that which we receive'. Put another way, diversity represents strength because it provides access to a wider variety of opportunities and perspectives on issues and problems, an idea also developed by Perri 6 (1997).

The problem, however, as Burns and Taylor (1998) point out, is that the reality for many lower-income populations is that they have neither the dense overlapping networks of yesteryear nor the sparse overlapping networks required in today's world. The long-term unemployed in particular mix mostly with other long-term unemployed (see also Engbersen et al., 1993; Kempson, 1996; Morris, 1994; Renooy, 1990; Thomas, 1992). They also have relatively few friends or acquaintances in employment (Kempson, 1996; Morris, 1994) and the majority of their unpaid community exchange is between friends and acquaintances (Kempson, 1996; Van Eck and Kazemeier, 1985). They are also less likely to have kin living locally. The result is that jobless households have fewer people to call upon for aid than those with people in employment. In consequence, if non-commodified work is to be facilitated, then both these strong and weak ties will need to be further developed. How this can be achieved will be addressed in the next chapter. Tackling the barrier of social network capital, however, is a necessary but insufficient means of facilitating participation in non-commodified work. There is little use having large social networks, for example, if one has little to offer or lacks the time to maintain and use them.

Time capital

Lack of time is often a principal constraint on participation in non-commodified work. This applies both to the ability to engage in self-provisioning and to non-commodified exchange. Such a constraint is most acutely felt among those spending long hours in the commodified sphere and/or those who commute long distances in relation to their job. For example, some 76 per cent of all multiple-earner households defined time as a barrier to their participation in non-commodified work in contemporary England (Williams and Windebank, 2003a). Many of these households wanted to do jobs for themselves but were unable to do so due to their long hours in the employment place. When sufficiently paid to be able to afford to pay formal labour to do these tasks, this is not a problem so far as the coping capabilities of households are concerned. However, when multiple-earner households receive relatively lower incomes, then the impacts of long hours can be acutely felt in terms of their ability to get necessary work completed. As one multiple-earner household living in a lower-income English urban neighbourhood put it,

> We both work long hours just to keep our jobs and when we get home we are really knackered. You don't feel like doing anything. The problem though is that at least if you are unemployed, or one of you isn't working, you get the time to do things. We don't. And we definitely cannot afford to pay the prices builders and everyone charges. So loads of jobs that need doing get left undone. It's not just repairing the broken gutter. It's loads of things. We often wonder whether it's worth us working.

Another impact of long hours spent in employment is that many households complain that their social networks tend to be largely based on the employment place. This unravels yet another facet of the 'work/life balance' problem. It reveals that it is not simply the case that the time spent in employment is reducing the time available to spend with children and kin; it is also reducing the wider networks of social and material support beyond the employment place. The outcome is that their struggle to earn sufficient to make ends meet often results in a contraction of their wider support networks, spiralling them yet further down the path of needing more money in order to pay for formal services.

Some 89 per cent of multiple-earner households in deprived English urban neighbourhoods, as a result, asserted that they would engage in greater levels of non-commodified work if they had more time. Indeed, the complex problems confronted by these households provide many lessons for current policy. As pioneers of the 'commodification is the route out of poverty' model, these households provide a useful exemplar of its problems. Earning low pay yet working long hours, these households find themselves not only unable to maintain social networks outside of the employment place but also without the time or energy to engage in self-provisioning activity and non-commodified exchange. The result is that they have to rely even more heavily on formal labour, which they can ill afford, in order to get necessary tasks completed around the home due to their lack of time (Williams and Windebank, 2003a).

Human capital

Besides social network and time barriers to participation in non-commodified work, there are also human capital constraints (see Fortin et al., 1996; Howe, 1988; Renooy, 1990; Smith, 1986). These take two forms. First, people perceive themselves to lack the skills necessary to help out others. Indeed, 52 per cent of households in the English localities survey agreed that they would engage in more non-commodified work if they had more or different skills. Second, there is the issue of health. Some 28 per cent asserted that their health prevented them from doing more for others, and this rose to 40 per cent in a deprived ex-pit village.

This reveals therefore that skills and health are necessary for insertion not only into the commodified sphere but also into non-commodified modes of production. For example, many asserted that they would have liked to help out others with maintaining their home (e.g. decorating, mending broken windows, repairing guttering, gardening) but felt that they did not have the skills or competencies to do so. The human capital constraint, however, is not simply one of skills or competencies. It is also one of a lack of confidence. Many who are unemployed quite simply lack the confidence to offer to help out others.

More importantly, poor health prevents over a quarter of households from giving or receiving help to others in the English communities studied by Williams and Windebank (2003a). On the one hand, this means that they are unable to contribute to helping others. On the other hand, and perhaps more saliently, it means that they feel unable to ask others for help because they feel unable to reciprocate the favour. Indeed, it is in these households that help tends to be rewarded with gifts and/or money to a greater extent than other households. For them, such payments act as a substitute for reciprocity and prevent social relations turning sour when they are unable to repay favours.

This human capital barrier is relevant across the whole spectrum of non-commodified work. Take, for example, cash-in-hand work. Having a formal job often means that customers recognize a person as having a skill to offer and it is a legitimization of their skills in the eyes of the recipient. Those without formal jobs thus suffer in terms of gaining access to cash-in-hand work. There is no legitimization of their skills. It is not solely a perception of skills, however, that prevents the unemployed from gaining access to cash-in-hand work. If their skills are inappropriate for finding formal employment, there seems little reason to believe that they can sell or exchange them on the informal labour market. Indeed, perhaps this helps explain why multiple-earner households engage in more cash-in-hand work than no-earner households. Having a formal job means that the outside world recognizes a person as having a skill to offer and is a legitimization of these skills in the eyes of potential customers. It is also because these households quite simply have skills that are desired by customers.

Economic capital

Besides the hurdles of social networks, time and human capital, a further barrier to participation in non-commodified work, especially among lower-income populations, is that they often lack the money to acquire the goods and resources necessary to engage in such work. This barrier has been identified elsewhere (e.g. Pahl, 1984; Smith, 1986; Thomas, 1992). The result of having little or no disposable income is that a household's access to many of the ways in which it could help itself is curtailed. For example, if one cannot afford the paint, brushes and sandpaper, then one cannot paint exterior windows so as to prevent the degradation of the fabric of the house.

Overall, some 52 per cent of all households in the English localities survey asserted that they would engage in greater amounts of self-provisioning if they had more money. Such an explanation, however, was particularly prominent among jobless households. Some 70 per cent of no-earner households perceived money as a barrier to their participation in self-provisioning activity, compared with just 43 per cent of multiple-earner households. Interestingly, it was not the case that if households had more money, they would do less for themselves. Only 3 per cent of households asserted that they would engage in less self-provisioning if they had more money. The vast majority said that it would enable them to do more. As such, there is a popular perception among people that they want to engage in more non-exchanged work and non-monetized exchange. Money is a constraint that prevents this being achieved, and their perception was that if they had more money they would do more for themselves, not less.

A direct product of having insufficient money was that households could not access the equipment to engage in subsistence work and non-commodified exchange. As a result, many perceived a lack of equipment as a principal constraint on their ability to engage in such activity. Some 48 per cent of households asserted that they would do more self-provisioning and 43 per cent more cash-in-hand work if they had the right equipment. For example, when asked if there is any work that they have not done which they would like to complete, households often cited activities like redecorating, installing a shower, creating a workshop or even vacuuming. In nearly all cases, they could not do these activities due to their lack of money and/or their lack of tools.

For instance, without access to a car it is frequently more difficult to engage in self-provisioning. Take, for example, engagement in DIY activity. If there is bus access to DIY stores and one manages to overcome this hurdle, it is then necessary to carry home the ladder, pots of paint, wallpaper or other goods on the bus. This is not an easy task, as anybody will testify who has ever tried to do it. Moreover, without a car, it is also often more difficult to travel to engage in unpaid or paid informal exchange. The outcome is that without access to a car, one is unlikely to be able to engage easily in both self-provisioning and unpaid or paid informal exchange for others. This has a knock-on effect in the sense that others are then less likely to reciprocate favours. Indeed, examining the results from the survey of English affluent and deprived neighbourhoods, those no-earner households without access to a car received considerably less paid and unpaid informal exchange than those no-earner households with access to a car, displaying the extent to which ease of mobility matters.

It is not only a car that is vital to engage in self-provisioning and informal exchange. Those lacking economic capital also cannot gain access to many other vital pieces of equipment with much lower unit costs in order to engage in such activity. If households do not possess tools such as a ladder and workbenches, they cannot conduct many tasks that are essential to maintain or prevent the degradation of the fabric of their dwelling (e.g. cleaning gutters). In consequence, money matters. Without it, the opportunities to engage in non-commodified work are severely limited.

Institutional barriers

Another barrier to participation in non-commodified work, particularly for benefit claimants, is that they feel more inhibited for fear of being reported to the authorities and having their benefit curtailed. This was cited as a barrier to engagement in such work by 5 per cent of all respondents in the English localities study reported in this book. Superficially, therefore, it does not appear a major barrier to participation. However, the fact that 57 per cent of the registered unemployed cited this shows that for this group it is a major constraint. For example, an unemployed member of a no-earner household possessed the desire to set up a facility in their home to utilize their skills in glass painting and textile making commercially, but had not done so due to what they referred to as 'the social security trap'. That is, if they earned over the 'income disregard limit' their benefit allowances would be reduced pound for pound. Such households also feared that neighbours might report them to the authorities. Indeed, such fears are perhaps not without foundation given the way in which working informally whilst claiming social security is considered to be a more serious offence than engaging in tax fraud (Cook,

1997; Dean and Melrose, 1996; Jordan et al., 1992). Reflecting this, many respondents in the English localities survey expressed vehement opposition to people being paid cash in hand, especially the unemployed. Their fear is thus perhaps well founded. Some unemployed respondents even expressed a fear of engaging in unpaid community work in case they were mistakenly reported to the authorities.

Environmental barriers

A further barrier to participation in non-commodified work is the type of area in which people live. So far as non-monetized exchange is concerned, many adopted the attitude of 'keeping themselves to themselves' in lower-income areas due to a perceived lack of trust, community and sense of well-being around them. Respondents in the English lower-income neighbourhoods reported in this volume wished to engage in closer social relations with others but had taken on board the image constructed of their area by outsiders that it was a dangerous place. This negated their desires to get to know other local people. Indeed, many asserted that they would engage in more community exchange if they lived somewhere else.

The perception of the area resulted in a low level of unpaid and paid informal support. However, it was not only the perception of the locality that led to a low level of such exchange. The lack of money in such areas also results in diminished levels of exchange. Take, for example, the task of window cleaning. Most households in these deprived areas do this task themselves. There is little point, therefore, being a window-cleaner in this area if few employ people to have their windows cleaned. As such, there is simply less demand for exchange in these areas than in other more affluent localities. The important point here is that it is not only the lack of money in these localities that leads to a diminished level of non-commodified work. It is also the sense of community. Inhabitants often take on board the image of their own area that is depicted in media and local government narratives and this leads them to retreat further into themselves, resulting in even less sense of community and social support.

In sum, the widespread desire to engage in greater amounts of non-commodified work is curtailed by numerous barriers, including time, money, social networks, skills and physical ability as well as institutional and environmental barriers. If these barriers to participation in non-commodified work could be addressed, then there would be an opportunity for the growth of such activity.

Conclusions

Here, in Part III, it has been revealed that the first option of commodification is both impractical and undesirable. It is impractical because non-commodified work is deeply embedded in everyday life and the evidence points towards a decommodification rather than commodification of working lives. It is undesirable because this work is often the preferred means by which people conduct many activities and a key ingredient of the social cement that binds communities together. A laissez-faire approach, meanwhile, results in numerous negative consequences. The ever popular 'marginality thesis' assumes that informal work is undertaken by those marginalized from employment as a survival strategy for unadulterated economic reasons and is thus more prevalent in deprived than in affluent communities. The empirical evidence, however, is that non-commodified work is greater among affluent populations. As such, a laissez-faire approach merely intensifies the socio-spatial inequalities resulting from employment.

In consequence, this chapter has argued that swimming with the tide and fostering non-commodified alongside commodified work so as to cultivate plural economies are the only viable option. Reviewing the rationales for pursuing the cultivation of the non-market sphere in third-way, non-market social democracy, radical ecology and post-development thinking, this chapter has argued that if non-capitalist futures are to be imagined and enacted, then there is a need to replace the goal of commodification with full engagement, which requires the development of not only the commodified but also the non-commodified sphere. Given the lack of attention so far paid to the interventions required in order to foster the non-commodified sphere, this chapter has sought to lay the foundations by setting out the main barriers that currently prevent the populations of advanced economies from engaging in non-commodified work. This has revealed that such households are prevented from engaging in non-commodified work by their lack of human capital, social network capital, financial capital and time capital, as well as environmental and institutional constraints. These are the key hurdles that will thus need to be tackled if non-commodified work is to be cultivated so as to advance plural economies. The next chapter considers a range of initiatives that might be used in this regard.

13

Cultivating Work beyond the Commodity Economy

How is the goal of full engagement to be achieved? Until now, the focus in economic development has been almost entirely upon developing policies and initiatives to cultivate a commodified world. Little attention has been paid to how participation in the non-commodified sphere can be fostered. The intention in this chapter, therefore, is to begin to explore a range of strategies that can tackle the barriers to participation in non-commodified work outlined in the last chapter.

However, before commencing this identification of a range of grassroots and top-down initiatives that can tackle the barriers to participation in non-commodified work, especially for lower-income populations, it is first of all necessary to address a key issue. It is often stated that promoting the development of the non-commodified sphere may result in a bifurcated society in which the majority of the population will continue to achieve their well-being through the commodified sphere, while those marginalized from the commodified sphere will increasingly eke out a living in the non-commodified sphere (see, e.g., Eisenschitz, 1997).

Towards a Plural Economy, Not a Dual Society

As a precursor to discussing initiatives that can foster participation in the non-commodified realm, it is thus necessary to confront directly this important issue that developing a plural economy will lead to the creation of a dual society. Here, I wish to argue that a dual society (i.e. the polarization of society into those who find their work through the commodified sphere and those marginalized in the non-commodified realm) is not the inevitable outcome of seeking to develop plural economies (i.e. societies in which both commodified and non-commodified work are recognized and valued, and households are facilitated to engage in both forms of work in order to meet their needs and wants).

Whether this occurs depends on the objectives underpinning the pursuit of economic plurality. If the primary intention is to offload those populations surplus to the requirements of capital onto the non-commodified sphere, then the pursuit of economic pluralism will inevitably result in a dual society. To avoid the advent of a dual society, therefore, it is necessary to promote economic pluralism among the *whole* population, whereby all households and/or individuals are encouraged to engage in both commodified and non-commodified work in order to meet their needs and desires.

Indeed, wherever a plural economy has been advocated, this argument that it should be applied to all households is strongly upheld. Beck (2000) indicates that this is the case in Germany among the various liberal, green and communitarian groups pursuing a 'multi-activity' or 'dual-activity' society. It is similarly the case in France, where there is a long tradition of advocating such a future for work in a way that avoids the creation of a dual society (e.g. Aznar, 1981; Delors, 1979; Gorz, 1999; Windebank, 1991). So, too, is such an argument prevalent in the UK (e.g. Boyle, 1999; Douthwaite, 1996; Jordan, 1998; Mayo, 1996) and in the USA (e.g. Cahn, 2000).

Conscious of the fact that both the mainstream left and right in politics might seize upon the idea of a plural economy so as to reduce formal welfare costs, therefore, plural economy advocates regard multi-activity to apply to the population as a whole rather than solely the marginalized. As Beck (2000: 60) explicitly puts it, 'Only when every man and woman has one foot in paid employment, and perhaps the other in civil labour, will it be possible to avoid a situation where the "third sector" ... becomes a ghetto of the poor.' This is the central and essential requirement if a plural economy is to avoid the creation of a dual society.

The problem, nevertheless, is that it is precisely among the marginalized that policy interventions are required in order to develop their capacities to engage in non-commodified work. Indeed, unless this is the focus of policy interventions, then the non-commodified realm will continue to consolidate, rather than reduce, socio-spatial inequalities. However, as soon as policy focuses upon the development of non-commodified work among these populations (e.g. deprived neighbourhoods, the unemployed), accusations will start to be raised that a dual society is being forged. There thus seems little that can be done to calm such fears in the short run.

It is not only those who fear for the plight of the jobless and lower-income populations, however, that are concerned about the creation of a plural economy. Another source of opposition is what I here call 'old-style feminists'. When seeking emancipation for women, much feminist literature retains a deeply ingrained belief that 'employment is the route to liberation' (see Gregory and Windebank, 2000). Viewing non-commodified work, whether in the form of housework or caring labour, as a 'burden' that unevenly falls on women's shoulders, the argument has been that insertion into commodified work is the royal road to emancipation. However, and as Hochschild (1989) has pointed out, this has been a 'stalled revolution'. Women, although entering the formal labour market in their masses, have remained responsible for non-commodified work in all its many guises. Indeed, even when some women escape this work, it is only at the expense of other women, who are employed on low wages to free them. It is not men who have taken over this work. For many 'new style' feminists, in consequence, the route to women's liberation is being reconceptualized. It is not so much that women need to adopt work patterns more like men, but that men need to adopt work patterns more akin to those conventionally associated with women. Only if this occurs will a dual society, in which women remain responsible for the non-commodified sphere, be tackled (see Gregory and Windebank, 2000). For these analysts, the route to liberation for women is not through insertion into employment but through men adopting dual-activity lifestyles. Until this is accepted, one can expect a good deal of opposition from 'old-style feminists' who continue to cling to the commodified sphere as the route to women's liberation.

In this chapter, in consequence, the vision of a full-engagement society is one that adopts ways of working that are more akin to those which women have known for the past few decades than to those with which men are now familiar. Working lives will not involve careers but rather combinations of part-time employment, casual contracts, unpaid work and volunteer activity for the public good.

The rest of this chapter primarily focuses upon policies to harness participation in non-commodified modes of production so as to develop the capacities of people to meet their needs and desires. This is the focus, to repeat, simply because there is so little literature on how this might be achieved. It is not meant to display a lack of interest in the crucial question of how to insert people into commodified work or even to suggest that this is unimportant. Indeed, unless alterations to participation in the non-commodified sphere are accompanied by radical changes in how people participate in the commodified sphere, then the outcome will be a dual society. For example, leaving the distribution of commodified work concentrated among multiple-earner households with a large minority of households excluded from employment, and at the same time harnessing the ability of these latter households to engage in non-commodified work, will inevitably create a dual society. For full engagement to be achieved in a way that does not produce such a society, harnessing the non-commodified sphere must march hand in hand with a redistribution of commodified work. Possible policies to redistribute commodified work time include reducing the hours spent in employment so as to create a larger number of jobs, introducing a lifetime 'cap' on the number of hours spent in employment, and sharing out some forms of employment (see, e.g., Beck, 2000; Gorz, 1999; Windebank, 1991). Although the focus here is primarily upon how to cultivate the non-commodified sphere, these are issues that cannot be ignored. The non-commodified side of the coin is the focus here, to reiterate, merely because this is the realm that has so far received the least attention.

Many arguments might be mounted against this focus upon developing the non-commodified sphere. One is that harnessing non-market activity is impossible in a complex society such as our own where one cannot function without money and/or the profit motive. However, this is not the argument here. It is not being suggested that we should rid the economy of either money or the profit motive, merely that a better balance should be struck between profit-motivated monetary transactions, not-for profit monetized exchange, non-monetized exchange and subsistence work. At present, the whole thrust of economic policy is upon developing the commodity economy and pursuing active intervention so as to ensure its continuing growth. The call here, however, is for greater emphasis to be put on harnessing the abilities of people to engage also in forms of non-commodified work. The argument is not one of eradicating commodified work but of developing the complementary means of livelihood to be found in the non-commodified realm. It is one of advocating non-commodified work not as an alternative, but as a complement, to the commodified sphere.

Here, therefore, ways are sought not to deepen our subordination to the commodity economy, but to achieve our release or at least to develop complementary alternative means of livelihood. It is to create *not-for-profit zones* of economic practice. To do this, first, bottom-up initiatives are reviewed and, second, top-down initiatives are considered that can cultivate economic plurality by developing non-commodified work, in a way that enables those currently unable to use such work to do so.

Grassroots Initiatives to Foster Non-commodified Work

Can bottom-up or grassroots initiatives be used to develop non-commodified work? If so, what types of initiative need to be developed and for what purpose? For exponents of commodification, bottom-up initiatives, mostly in the form of third-sector organizations or social enterprises, are often seen as additional means of creating commodified work and/or improving employability by helping people to maintain and acquire skills, to develop self-confidence and self-esteem (e.g. Archibugi, 2000; Blair, 1998; Community Development Foundation, 1995; ECOTEC,

1998; European Commission, 1996, 1997, 1998b; Fordham, 1995; Giddens, 1998; Leadbeater, 1999; OECD, 1996). However, a rather different approach is adopted here in terms of, first, the types of association focused upon and, second, the rationales for developing them. Rather than develop the third sector (organized community-based associations) as a means of filling the jobs gap left by the state and market sectors so as to achieve a more commodified world, the approach towards cultivating bottom-up initiatives here seeks to develop what is called the 'fourth sector' (i.e. subsistence work, informal non-monetized exchange and one-to-one not-for-profit monetized exchange) in order to develop alternative means of livelihood so as to achieve 'full-engagement' (see, e.g., Chanan, 1999; Mayo, 1996; Jordan et al., 2000; Macfarlane, 1996; OECD, 1996; Williams and Windebank, 2003a).

The objective, therefore, is to improve what Sen (1998) refers to as the 'capabilities' of people to help themselves by facilitating participation in non-commodified work. To do this, bottom-up initiatives are sought that tackle the major barriers to participation in non-commodified work identified in the last chapter. These include the fact that people lack, first, the money to acquire the goods and resources necessary to participate in reciprocal exchange (economic capital). Second, they know few people well enough either to ask or to be asked to do something (social network capital). Third, they lack the appropriate skills, confidence and/or physical ability to engage in self-help (human capital). Fourth and finally, they fear being reported to the tax and/or benefit authorities if they engage in such work (an institutional barrier).

To achieve this, moreover, grassroots initiatives are sought that develop alternative means of livelihood that are in keeping with the contemporary attitudes towards reciprocal exchange identified in Chapter 6. As shown, in deprived populations the culture of community engagement is not only orientated towards engaging in one-to-one aid for the purpose of providing and receiving material aid, rather than participation in groups for purely sociability purposes; it is also grounded in a culture of participation where some form of tally system or payment is used whenever favours are given or received. Any proposed initiative to harness the capacity of such populations to help each other out, therefore, needs to work with the grain of these desires for help to be provided on a one-to-one basis, for help to be in the form of material aid, and for tallies to be kept whenever help is provided or received. Taking this into account, four bottom-up initiatives are documented below that resonate strongly with this participatory culture. These are local exchange and trading schemes (LETS), time banks, employee mutuals and mutual aid contracts. Each is outlined here in turn. Until now, as will be shown, where these initiatives have been considered by governments, they have been evaluated primarily as 'third sector' initiatives that provide additional means of creating commodified work and/or improving employability by helping people to maintain and acquire skills, and to develop self-confidence and self-esteem. In every case, such initiatives have been found to be relatively ineffective. Here, however, they are evaluated against a different objective. The intention is to evaluate these initiatives in terms of their ability to facilitate engagement in non-commodified work, especially for those currently unable to partake in such activity.

Local exchange and trading Schemes (LETS)

Local currency experiments have a long history, and those advocating them in the contemporary era have learned much from past experiences. In earlier times, local currencies were often advocated as 'alternative' currencies. History has shown, however, that such an approach results in them being banned, as witnessed in the 1930s in Worgl, Austria, as well as in the USA with 'scrip' money (Greco, 1994; Offe and Heinze, 1992; Pacione, 1997). Today, therefore, advocates promote local currencies as 'complementary' rather than 'alternative' currencies (e.g. Dauncey, 1988; Dobson, 1993; Seyfang, 1998).

By far the most popular form of contemporary local currency system is Local Exchange and Trading Schemes (LETS). How do LETS operate? LETS are created when a group of people form an association and create a local unit of exchange. Members then list their offers of, and requests for, goods and services in a directory that they exchange priced in a local unit of currency. Individuals decide what they want to trade, who they want to trade with, and how much trade they wish to engage in. The price is agreed between the buyer and the seller. The association keeps a record of the transactions by means of a system of cheques written in the local LETS units. Every time a transaction is made, these cheques are sent to the treasurer, who works in a similar manner to a bank sending out regular statements of account to the members. No actual cash is issued since all transactions are by cheque and no interest is charged or paid. The level of LETS units exchanged is thus entirely dependent upon the extent of trading undertaken. Neither does money need to be earned before it is spent. Credit is freely available and interest-free.

What makes LETS so interesting as an initiative is that there are many people who have needs and wants, and many people who would like to work, but what prevents this supply and demand coming together is a lack of money. For advocates of LETS, however, the solution is simple. If there is insufficient money, then why not create your own? In the contemporary period, it was Michael Linton who first raised this simple but radical idea in response to widespread unemployment in his hometown near Vancouver in Canada. Having established a local currency system, he then ran a workshop at The Other Economic Summit (TOES) in 1986, an 'alternative summit' that ran alongside the G7 economic summit. Those attending this workshop then took the idea back to their own communities and began to implement it. The first LETS in the UK was thus formed in Norwich in that year, and most of the early LETS in both Australia and New Zealand were established by those attending this TOES workshop (Williams, 1996c). It was not until the 1990s, however, that LETS really began to take off. Indeed, from the mid-1990s until the turn of the century, there was an exponential growth curve so far as LETS creation was concerned. Although today the number of new LETS being created is not quite at the same level as during the mid- to late 1990s, LETS is an initiative in which there remains great interest in terms of its potential, especially for those seeking to develop economic plurality.

One principal reason for this interest in LETS is because of its potential ability to tackle every one of the barriers that prevent engagement in non-commodified work. Starting with the extent to which LETS tackle the barrier of economic capital, a recent nationwide survey in the UK of LETS members conducted by Williams et al. (2001a) reveals that some 40 per cent assert that LETS provided them with access to interest-free credit (but 62 per cent of the registered unemployed and 51 per cent of low-income households). LETS, therefore, provide people with access to money. For two-thirds (65 per cent) of the registered unemployed, this had helped them cope with unemployment, with some 3 per cent of their total income coming from their LETS activity.

This survey also reveals that LETS enable the barrier of social network capital that prevents engagement in non-commodified work to be overcome. Some 76 per cent of respondents asserted that the LETS had helped them to develop a network of people upon whom they could call for help, whilst 56 per cent asserted that it had helped them develop a wider network of friends and 31 per cent deeper friendships. LETS, therefore, develop 'bridges' (i.e. bringing people together who did not know each other before) more than 'bonds' (i.e. bringing people who already know each other closer together). Given that most members lacked kinship networks in the localities they inhabited and that kinship networks are the principal source of mutual aid in contemporary society (Williams and Windebank, 2000b), LETS thus provide those without such a local network with a substitute. Some 95 per cent of LETS members, that is, had no grandparents living in the area, 79 per cent had no parents, 84 per cent had no brothers or sisters, 58 per cent had no children, 93 per cent had no uncles or aunts, and 91 per cent had no cousins.

Besides tackling the barriers of economic and social network capital, there is also evidence that LETS overcome the human capital obstacle that can constrain participation in non-commodified work. LETS provide an opportunity for people both to maintain and to develop their skills, as well as to rebuild their self-confidence and self-esteem by engaging in meaningful and productive activity that is valued and recognized by others who display a willingness to pay for such endeavour (see Williams et al., 2001a).

Finally, there is an institutional barrier to engaging in alternative means of livelihood. Many who are unemployed are fearful of being reported to the authorities, even if they engage in unpaid mutual aid. Unfortunately, this is not currently being overcome by LETS. Although only 13 per cent of members feel worried about tax liabilities, 65 per cent of registered unemployed members are concerned about their situation. Moreover, all of the registered unemployed not currently involved in LETS interviewed by Williams et al. (2001) were put off joining by worries about its impact on their benefit payments. Ironically, therefore, those who would most benefit from LETS are discouraged from joining and trading due to the uncertainty over their legal position vis-à-vis the benefits disregard. The current 'laissez-faire' approach of government, in consequence, is insufficient to appease both members and non-members who are registered unemployed.

One of the principal reasons for such inactivity by government vis-à-vis LETS is because until now these schemes have been evaluated only in terms of their ability to facilitate commodified work and/or improve people's employability. The notion that the non-commodified work facilitated by LETS may be important in itself, especially in terms of helping those marginalized from the commodified world to develop alternative means of livelihood, has not been considered important enough to warrant changes in tax and social security regulations. Those in government who have conventionally pursued a commodified world, however, have much to learn from LETS and their participants. Rather than rely on commodified work in order to meet needs and desires, the members of these pioneering initiatives are adopting a 'work ethic' rather than an 'employment ethic' in order to alleviate their situation. They are using not-for-profit monetized exchanges to create alternative means of livelihood. Government perhaps needs to follow suit. By harnessing these grassroots initiatives as a tool for encouraging non-commodified work (rather than job creation), the full potential of such initiatives could start to be realized.

Time banks

Another initiative that has the potential to tackle the barriers to participation in non-commodified work in a way that resonates with contemporary attitudes is the time banks scheme. Here, participants are paid one 'hour' for each hour that they work, which they can at any time 'cash in' by requesting an hour's work in return from the time bank (see Boyle, 1999; Cahn, 1994, 2000; Cahn and Rowe, 1992; Seyfang and Smith, 2002).

This 'sweat equity' local currency initiative has its contemporary origins in the mid-1980s in the USA, when Edgar Cahn, a Washington DC-based lawyer, developed the idea of rewarding people for every hour of their community service in time dollars. The objective in creating time banks was thus to develop a means of recording, storing and rewarding transactions where neighbours help neighbours. People earn time currency by helping others (e.g. by providing child- or eldercare, transportation, cooking, home improvement). They then spend time currency to get help themselves or for their families, or to join a club that gives them discounts on food or health care.

As such, time banks allow those endeavours in people's lives for which the market economy assigns no value to become valued contributions, and it gives society a way to recompense activities that the market economy does not. Time currency thus empowers people to convert personal time into purchasing power, so as to enable them to stretch their limited cash further. It also reinforces reciprocity and trust, and rewards civic engagement and acts of decency in a way that generates social capital, one hour at a time. The result of valuing such work is that it can help: harness under-utilized human resources, give value and recognition to activities that are currently unvalued and unrecognized, and generate social capital in communities by rebuilding the non-market economy of family, neighbourhood and community.

At present, governments can only resort to calls for greater 'civic engagement' and 'community involvement'. They have no way of rewarding such activity on the part of participants. Time banks, however, provide a means by which people can be recompensed for such activity; they reward reciprocity and convert that contribution into a form of currency that can be used to acquire goods and services that one needs and/or desires. Most importantly, they strongly resonate with the participatory culture so prevalent in deprived populations and beyond, which seeks to engage in one-to-one acts of material aid and for a tally system and/or some form of payment to be involved. It is thus little surprise that since time banks were first advocated, they have rapidly grown and spread, not only within the USA but also to other Western nations.

Indeed, by 1998 over 200 time banks and service credit programmes were operating in thirty states in the USA and these schemes frequently have thousands of members. To understand both the size and the nature of time dollar schemes in the USA, some brief sketches of just a few of the schemes in existence are provided:

- In New York, a time dollar scheme called Elderplan focuses on the provision of health care for senior citizens. In 1999, 97,623 time dollars were earned, serving 4,316 members through 41,985 care-giving episodes.
- In Chicago, a time dollar scheme centred on the school system enables Chicago to be able to boast that it possesses the nation's largest after-school cross-age peer tutoring programme. In its fourth year of operation in 2000, it had spread to 25 schools. Older students tutor younger ones and earn time dollars for doing so. In the academic year 1999–2000, 1,500 students participated in this scheme.
- In Baltimore's Hope VI project, the rent for accommodation includes the payment of 8 time dollars per month. This has encouraged 150 households to provide help to each other, to the local school and to their community. Families use additional time dollars earned to buy their bus pass, obtain discounts at shops, purchase furniture, clothing and membership at the Boys and Girls Club.
- The St Louis Grace Hill Neighbourhood Services programme uses time dollars; in the first ten months of 1999, there were 12,378 exchanges involving 42,519 time dollars.

On the basis of such examples of their potential cited in Cahn (2000), recent years have seen these schemes receive considerable attention elsewhere. One of the first countries to try to replicate these schemes has been the UK. In an evaluation of time banks in the UK, Seyfang and Smith (2002) have shown not only that these schemes tackle all of the major barriers to participation in non-commodified work but also that the membership of time banks is heavily skewed towards those who are marginalized from the commodified realm.

Unlike LETS, moreover, the institutional barrier to participation has been overcome. The Benefits Agency in the UK has decided that the 'credits' earned on time banks should not be treated as earnings for income-related benefit purposes. Participation in time banks is not seen as remunerative work, and entitlement to benefits is not affected. Similarly, these credits are ignored for income tax purposes. Support by the Home Office's Active Community Unit for the development of time banks, furthermore, means that the next few years should see the rapid expansion of time banks in the UK. It appears, therefore, that this grassroots initiative represents a key tool that can be used for developing alternative means of livelihood.

Mutual aid contracts

In September 1998, Manningham Housing Association in a deprived neighbourhood of Bradford in the UK introduced a pilot scheme to encourage mutual aid among its new tenants. Applicants for social housing were requested to fill in a 'social needs audit' of their present neighbourly interactions, the tasks that they could offer their potential neighbours, and the work that they would like to have undertaken for them. Having returned these audits, the Housing Association chose twenty-two tenants whose offers and requests closely matched and asked them to sign a voluntary 'mutual aid' contract before handing them the tenancy. The activities involved included car maintenance and repair, computer training, babysitting and a DIY club. So far as is known, this is the first such pilot scheme in the country.

Viewed as a tool for creating commodified work, this initiative offers little to policymakers. At best, it develops self-esteem and confidence and improves the employability prospects of the residents by enabling them to develop, maintain or enhance skills that may be useful when seeking formal employment. Analysed as a tool for generating alternative means of livelihood, however, they are more important. By contracting people to engage in mutual aid with others, these schemes kick-start non-commodified exchange in situations where it might not take place. These initiatives thus have a place in specific contexts. They are 'contractual' tools for facilitating non-monetized exchange in contexts where it is perceived that such exchange would be lacking. It is a *Gesellschaft*-like approach to the creation of communitarian relations. Obviously, this would not always be applicable. In this sense, they are useful in facilitating mutual aid in situations where 'environmental' barriers to participation predominate. If such environmental barriers do not exist, they seem limited in their usefulness. Although they also tackle the social network barriers, it appears that their utility is more in situations where environmental barriers predominate.

This scheme could be replicated in the context of many social housing projects. From the experience of similar initiatives such as LETS, however, issues that will require consideration are: whether and how to keep accounts of this mutual aid; the nature of the quality control mechanisms to be used; and ensuring that the momentum is maintained beyond the initial phase. Moreover, how to incorporate those who perceive themselves to lack human capital will need to be more fully considered. Such an initiative seems to do little to help people to tackle the human capital barriers and may even reinforce such barriers to participation by only choosing households to participate where pre-existing skills prevail or are recognized by household members to prevail. Until now, nevertheless, this project has not been evaluated. If it has proven to be successful, such an initiative could be implemented in many other localities where environmental barriers are prominent. It is a relatively simple way of developing mutual aid through a 'contractual' approach.

Employee mutuals

Another idea still on the drawing board, but receiving some attention lately from the UK government, is the employee mutual. This is advocated as a new social institution that might act as a bridge into work for the socially excluded and provide greater security in an age of increased flexibility (Bentley and Mulgan, 1996; Leadbeater and Martin, 1997). These are localized bodies that the unemployed, employed and firms can voluntarily join through the payment of a weekly subscription fee. Building on the concept of LETS, members would earn points on a smart card from their work for the mutual that would enable them to 'buy' goods and services from it. As such, employee mutuals are envisioned as 'new institutions for collective self-help' that match local demand for work with local supply. Their intention is to allow people to undertake the many one-off jobs that need doing but that they are unable to afford to do formally. Unlike present-day LETS, however, the intention is also to help employers fill vacancies and to bring together workers and businesses to meet shared needs for training.

Learning lessons from the problems of LETS in relation to social security benefit rules, the proponents of employee mutuals have argued from the outset for special benefit rules to be applied to members of the mutual. These would make it easier for members to combine income from part-time or temporary work on the mutual with benefits so as to reduce the insecurity that deters people from engaging in such organizations and making the transition from welfare to work. In return for such preferential treatment regarding the income disregard, jobless members of a mutual would make a token contribution of 50 pence per week but would contribute at least 15 hours per week of services in kind. In return, the mutual would provide not only work but also training where necessary and childcare facilities, job searches and a job placement service, as well as job accreditation and a social life. Although the idea is still on the drawing board, the minister for employment in the UK has advocated the development of these new institutions. It seems likely, therefore, that pilot employee mutuals will be set up in the near future.

The current proposal is that central government should set up a National Council for Employee Mutuals to establish a legal and regulatory framework for the new movement. Having done this, benefit rules would need to be modified for the employee mutual members, to allow easier transfer from welfare into work via part-time or temporary jobs; and tax incentives should be given to encourage individuals and organizations to join such mutuals. A series of pilot schemes would then be set up to test how different variations on the employee mutual model would work under different circumstances, and the aim would be to create a national movement of at least 250 employee mutuals with half a million members by 2007. If this is to go ahead, then the suggestion proposed here is that serious consideration needs to be given at the pilot stage to evaluating two specific types of employee mutual: those seeking to create jobs and improve employability and those seeking to promote alternative means of livelihood.

There is little doubt that the concept of the employee mutual is an attempt to transfer the ideas from local currency schemes into a new vehicle that is more oriented towards job creation and improving employability than current local currency experiments. As such, the employee mutual has been designed to shift the use of local currency towards the goal of commodification. It attempts to create a third-sector local currency initiative that is more in keeping with the goal of commodification than the schemes already discussed above. At present, they are perhaps envisaged more in terms of being vehicles for helping employers fill vacancies and for bringing together workers and businesses to meet shared needs for training.

The employee mutual can also be used, however, as a vehicle for facilitating alternative means of livelihood. By approaching the mutual whenever one has a task that needs conducting and returning the favour later by fulfilling a task for somebody else, the organization would be akin to a LETS. In consequence, rather than view them as a new 'labour exchange' for businesses and employees to be put together, they can also just as validly be perceived as tools for bringing together individuals to engage in reciprocal exchange with each other. Given that Tessa Jowell, the UK minister for employment, gave a talk in mid-2001 on these new institutions, it seems likely that they may be moving off the drawing board and that pilot schemes might be set up. If this is the case, then there will be a need to consider their value not only as vehicles to facilitate a commodified world but also as facilitators of non-commodified work.

Top-down Initiatives to Cultivate Non-commodified Work

If full engagement is to be achieved, it is insufficient to rely on bottom-up initiatives. As shown above, even the most prominent of such initiatives are presently small-scale piecemeal projects that are incapable alone of harnessing non-commodified work on a broad scale, especially for lower-income groups, which do not always widely participate in such initiatives. Just as the creation of commodified work requires top-down initiatives to be effective, so non-commodified work needs top-down initiatives. Today, few people question the need for tax breaks, subsidies, incentives and high levels of state intervention in the market in order to generate commodified work. Until now, however, the same has not applied to the non-commodified sphere. Instead, it has been viewed perhaps as some organic or natural economy. If so, and just as is the case with the commodified realm, this is incorrect.

Without intervention, the socio-spatial disparities that exist in the ability of households to engage in non-commodified economic practices will persist. Here, in consequence, a number of top-down initiatives are presented that could be implemented to help people to engage in non-commodified work to help themselves and others. The first considered is a basic income scheme. The second is the development of 'active community service', through either a civilizing New Deal or the creation of an active citizens' credits (ACC) scheme.

Basic income scheme

Is the commodified sphere the most appropriate means of distributing income? Given that less than three-quarters of the population of working age in most advanced economies have a job and that society is heavily polarized into multiple- and no-earner households, it appears that there is a need to reconsider whether this is the case. One outcome of rethinking how to distribute income is the idea of a 'basic income scheme'. Alternatively known as a citizen's income, social wage, social dividend, social credit, guaranteed income, citizen's wage, citizenship income, existence income or universal grant, this would provide every citizen with a basic 'wage' as a social entitlement without means test or work requirement (see, e.g., Fitzpatrick, 1999; Jordan et al., 2000; Van Parijs, 1995, 1996a, 1996b, 2000a, 2000b). Eligibility is automatic for all citizens and unconditional. There would be no tests of willingness to work.

With this minimum income guarantee in hand, individuals could choose to improve their well-being by engaging in employment so as to earn additional money in order to purchase goods and services, or they could instead choose to invest their time in self-provisioning those goods and services or helping others. The aim is to give individuals and groups increased resources for taking charge of their own lives, further power over their way of life and living conditions. If implemented, it would no longer be solely the labour market that integrated people into society but also this scheme that would offer limited material security, esteem and identity.

The origins of the idea of citizen's income have been traced to Tom Paine, Saint-Simon, Bertrand and Dora Russell, and Major C.H. Douglas among others (Van Trier, 1995). Currently, it is advocated by economists (e.g. Atkinson, 1995, 1998; Desai, 1998), political philosophers (Van Parijs, 1995, 2000a, 2000b) and social policy commentators (Jordan, 1998). Among leading UK politicians, only Paddy Ashdown has given it support, and his party went into the 1992 general election with basic income in its manifesto. Recent research, however, shows that it is supported by many backbench MPs in all parties at Westminster and is on the mainstream policy agenda in Ireland (Jordan et al. 2000). Among the main advantages claimed for such a basic income scheme are:

- It is neutral between paid and unpaid work, giving better incentives for low-paid employment than tax credits, but allowing choice over how to combine the two.
- It treats men and women as equals, allowing them to negotiate how to share unpaid work in households (see McKay and Vanavery, 2000).
- It combats exploitation, by allowing individuals to survive without relying on dangerous or demeaning work.
- It promotes economic efficiency, by ensuring that low-paid work is not given a special subsidy (as in tax credits) and hence labour power is not wastefully deployed.
- It promotes social justice, by treating all individuals alike, and giving extra income only to those with special care needs.

Even among advocates of a basic income, however, it is now accepted that a fully individualized and unconditional basic income could not be introduced in one operation, if only because of the way in which it would upset the current distribution of incomes and labour supply. Instead, and particularly for the working-age population, the growing consensus is that one should not proceed by cohorts or by categories, but start with a very modest (partial) basic income that would not be a full substitute for existing guaranteed minimum income provisions (Desai, 1998; Jordan et al., 2000; Parker and Sutherland, 1998).

Whatever the costs of a basic income scheme, the contention here is that such a top-down solution, although necessary, is by itself insufficient if the desire is to cultivate engagement in non-commodified economic practices. To achieve this, such a scheme needs to be coupled with initiatives to facilitate participation in non-commodified work. As Gough (2000: 27) argues,

> It is not enough to pay citizens a minimum income without enabling them to participate in socially significant activities, including paid and unpaid work. Similarly, the divorce of rights from duties ... contradicts ... the strong link between the two.... All persons who can, should have the right – and the duty – to contribute in some way to the common wealth.

Lipietz (1992: 99) similarly argues that a universal basic allowance 'would be acceptable only if it meant that those who received it were prepared to show their solidarity with society, which is paying them'. The crucial issue confronting basic income, to borrow a phrase, is that 'there are no rights without responsibilities'. Elson (1988: 29) puts this well:

> Alongside the right to a grant should be the duty, on the part of able-bodied adults, of undertaking some unpaid household work of caring and providing for those who are unable to take care of themselves. Persons already undertaking care of a young or sick or handicapped person would be exempt.

There is thus a groundswell of opinion that a basic income needs to be tied to some form of active citizenship. Atkinson (1998), for example, argues for a 'participation income' and Lipietz (1995) for a new sector engaged in socially useful activity and composed of 10 per cent of the labour force (the unemployment rate at the time he was writing). The idea, therefore, is to tie a basic income scheme to some form of participation in society. Advocates of an unconditional basic income, however, have argued against such an approach (e.g. Gorz, 1999; Jordan, 1998; Jordan and Jordan, 2000). For them, the result will be new forms of compulsion akin to workfare, such as compulsory work in the third sector (e.g. Offe, 1995; Rifkin, 1996; Elson, 1988).

This, however, does not necessarily follow. It is argued here that it is wholly possible to create what have been variously called 'passports to participation', 'participation incomes' or forms of 'community service employment' (see Williams and Windebank, 2003a) that provide basic incomes for active citizenship in a way that avoids compulsion.

Active community service

At the core of most models for security, esteem and identity is the notion of the 'working citizen'. Here, the intention is not to challenge this model. The only concern is to broaden out what is meant by 'work' to incorporate the non-commodified sphere. At present, the promotion of security, esteem and identity is through a model that views the 'working citizen' as somebody participating in formal employment. In this view, everything is linked to a paid job, including citizenship itself as manifested by the lack of distinction drawn between citizens' rights and workers' rights.

Here, however, and based upon a broader definition of work that encompasses non-commodified economic practices, the desire is to promote an alternative model for security, esteem and identity. In this view, the 'working citizen' is integrated not only through commodified but also through non-commodified work. To see how this new model of the 'working citizen' might operate, two policy options are here considered. The first seeks to extend the 'voluntary and community sector' of the New Deal programme, which has been adopted in many Western nations, so as to promote integration through active citizenship (rather than formal employment alone) and the second seeks to introduce an active citizens' credits scheme that again broadens the routes to integration. Each is considered in turn. Other similar proposals are being launched by the National

Centre for Volunteering, which is exploring the idea of 'citizenship credits' whereby national insurance contributions could be awarded for active citizenship; and the idea of piloting a 'participation income' in Brighton and Birmingham has been mooted by the Scarman Trust (see MacGillivray et al., 2001: 39).

Civilizing New Deal

Following the lead of the USA, many advanced economies have implemented workfare-type regimes as part of a general reorientation of labour market intervention towards active policies (see Lodemel and Trickey, 2001; OECD, 2000; Peck, 2001). These workfare programmes represent a significant departure from traditional welfare systems. People are required to work in return for social assistance payments. In contrast to previous welfare and unemployment benefit programmes in which state support was passive, unconditional and entitlement based, these new workfare regimes are conditional, work-focused and oblige participants to be active in order to receive social payments (Campbell, 2000; Robinson, 1998). The principal critique of them is that there is a compulsion element, whereby people are forced to do work that they would not otherwise wish to conduct (e.g. Peck, 2001).

The intention here is to consider a modification to the New Deal that would reduce the compulsion critiques that currently blight it and at the same time unleash the unemployed from the shackles that prevent them from engaging in non-commodified economic practices that they might wish to undertake but are currently prevented from carrying out. The proposal is that the 'voluntary and community' sector of the New Deal programme could be extended to allowing the unemployed to define the 'social contribution' that they wish to make. This would not only negate the workfare critiques aimed at this programme but also release the unemployed to take greater responsibility for the nature of their integration into the world of work.

Indeed, precedents already exist. In June 1998, it was announced that musicians were to be funded under the New Deal. They received a training allowance equivalent to their normal job-seekers allowance (JSA), plus a grant of £15.38 per week. The outcome was that they were paid not because they are 'available for work' but in recognition of their individual talent and contribution to society. This is a precedent to extend. Individuals could be empowered to stake a claim under the 'voluntary and community sector' of New Deal concerning their contribution to society. The precise scope of work that might be acceptable and the problems involved in deciding on the breadth of such activity are dealt with below but would certainly include caring activities and organizing community groups. Hence, somebody who was principal carer of a young pre-school child or an elderly dependent person would have this essential work recognized under the 'community and voluntary sector' of the New Deal and they would be paid an activity benefit for doing this work. Similarly, those organizing and running community groups such as LETS, time banks and credit unions would again receive an activity benefit paid at a higher rate than the zero-activity benefit level in recognition of their contribution.

An example of a similar initiative is to be found in Australia. Here, there has been some recognition that various activities are socially legitimate for those who are claiming out-of-work benefits. It has been understood, for example, that care work should be accredited. Both lone parents and one parent in a couple can claim a 'parenting allowance'. This is income-tested on one's own and one's partner's income, and is payable to parents with children aged up to 16 years old (Hirsch, 1999).

Although this policy proposal would start to counter the work-fare critiques associated with active labour market policies such as the New Deal, a key problem that this proposal fails to modify is the meaning of a 'working citizen' among those who are not eligible for the New Deal. The likely outcome is that it would introduce a 'dual society'. Those eligible to choose the contribution that they wish to make to their communities are only those who are unemployed. The likelihood, therefore, is that the new forms of work undertaken would be seen as a second-rate and second-class 'economy' for those excluded from the formal labour market. Below, therefore, a more comprehensive top-down strategy for facilitating a full-engagement society is explored that is more inclusive in terms of the groups that could be mobilized to renegotiate their contribution to society.

Active citizens' credits (ACC)

The conventional contract between the state and out-of-work households offers income in exchange for a duty to search for employment if one is able. Only those considered inactive because, for example, they are sick and disabled, rather than those engaged in non-commodified economic practices, are exempted from this obligation. The biggest exception to this rule in the UK (but no longer in the USA) has been lone parents, who have been effectively allowed to opt for parenting as an alternative to employment.

Here, however, a scheme is proposed that could not only recognize the contributions of non-commodified work but also reward those individuals who engage in such endeavour, and thus promote a full-engagement society. This scheme is based on the notion of accrediting active citizenship. Drawing upon the ideas for citizens' service (Briscoe, 1995; Hirsch, 1999; McCormick, 1994) and a participation income (Atkinson, 1998), the intention of 'active citizens' credits' (ACC) is to record, store and reward participation in caring and other work conducted for the good of their community. Under this non-compulsory scheme, individuals would engage in a self-designed portfolio of work of their choosing for which they would be reimbursed.

This would be non-compulsory in that individuals could freely choose whether or not to participate. It would also allow the individuals participating in this scheme to decide themselves the portfolio of economic practices that they wish to undertake. The goals behind such a proposal are: to recompense and value work which currently goes unrecognized and unvalued; to encourage active citizenship without recourse to compulsion; to harness non-commodified work; to create a 'full-engagement' society by enabling people who wish to make a particular 'social contribution' to do so; to incorporate the multi-dimensionality of social inclusion and exclusion into policymaking, and to tackle poverty through means other than merely insertion into the commodified realm.

The idea that such a scheme should be developed to encourage individuals to engage in freely chosen work to benefit their community is perhaps uncontroversial. The major controversy is over how to reward people. One option is to embed this proposal within the tax credit approach that is emerging in many

Table 13.1 A comprehensive tax credit framework for the UK

Tax credits	Qualifying condition
Employment tax credit	Working as a full-time employee or self-employed
Pensioner tax credit	Reaching pension age
Disability and sickness tax credit	Absence from work on grounds of sickness, injury or disability
Training tax credit	Engaging in approved forms of full-time education or training
Active citizens' tax credits, comprising:	Participating in caring activities and other work for the good of the community
Parents' tax credit	Principal full-time carer of a pre-school child
Carers' tax credit	Principal full-time carer of a dependent adult
Community worker tax credit	Engaging in full-time work for the good of the community

advanced economies (e.g. Liebman, 1998; Meadows, 1997; Millar and Hole, 1998). To see how this might occur, the case of the UK, which introduced tax credits in October 1999, is considered here (Bennett and Hirsch, 2001; HM Treasury, 1998). In the UK, tax credits were first applied to working families with children in that a parent working over 16 hours per week was effectively guaranteed a minimum income (HM Treasury, 1998). Therefore, families without children, single people, part-timers working less than 16 hours per week and the unemployed were excluded from Working Family Tax Credits (WFTC), despite such groups facing the same 'poverty' and 'unemployment' traps as working families with children.

This was to change in the April 2002 Budget statement of the UK chancellor of the exchequer when the tax credit system was extended to incorporate single people, couples aged over 25 years old without children, lone parents and pensioners. The intention behind this rolling out of the WFTC to a 'working' tax credit, or what is perhaps more accurately called a 'labour market participation' tax credit, is to move towards a fully integrated tax/benefit system using this tax credit approach. How, therefore, must the tax credit approach be extended in the future in order to create this integrated tax/benefit system?

Presently, the unemployed and part-time employed are not included. If paid a guaranteed minimum income, then they would receive this for engaging in employment for fewer hours or not at all. Although exponents of an unconditional citizen's income might support such a move (e.g. Jordan, 1998; Jordan and Jordan, 2000), tax credits should not be paid for doing nothing or doing less than others. Those able to do so should be required to make a 'full' contribution to society to warrant their tax credit/guaranteed minimum income. How could this be achieved?

To give everybody who wishes to receive the guaranteed minimum income the opportunity to do so, an extension of tax credit in the manner outlined in Table 13.1 is required. In the UK, both employment and pensioner tax credits have already been implemented. To incorporate the rest of society into such a tax credit system, therefore, a number of additional tax credits are required.

First, a disability and/or sickness tax credit for those absent from work on the grounds of sickness, injury or disability is needed, which might be implemented in a very similar manner to the current Disability Living Allowance. This has received some attention in recent years but has so far made little progress, not least due to opposition from disability pressure groups. Second, and to incorporate those engaged in post-compulsory training and education, a training tax credit could be introduced for those engaged in full-time education or training.

Even if both of these tax credits were introduced, however, some would still not meet any of the qualifying conditions. This is because they are unemployed and cannot find a job, or because they are engaged in employment or training only on a part-time basis. A final tax credit is thus required. This is here referred to as active citizens' credits.

What type of work would be undertaken under active citizens' credits? Although this is very much a matter for political debate, and as Table 13.1 displays, it is here argued that at a minimum it should include not only caring activity for young, elderly or disabled dependants but also any service activity that is undertaken by individuals for the benefit of their communities, such as organizing community groups. Indeed, this is the reason why active citizens' credits have been subdivided here into three further types of tax credit: parents' tax credits, carers' tax credits and community worker tax credits (for a more detailed discussion, see Williams and Windebank, 2003a).

If adopted, full engagement would be engendered by recording, storing and rewarding engagement in non-commodified work. As shown earlier, most people are unwilling to engage in reciprocal exchanges beyond kin unless there is some form of tally system through which their contributions can be recorded, stored and rewarded. This proposal works with the grain of these current desires by rewarding active citizens in the form of tax credits. The result would be the creation of a society founded upon the principle of full engagement without a radical policy overhaul.

Conclusions

In sum, this chapter has outlined that if strategies to develop plural economies are to avoid the creation of a dual society, it will be necessary to pursue an approach that seeks to encourage heterogeneous economic practices across the whole population rather than solely among marginalized populations. Presently, commodified work as well as non-commodified work is distributed in a highly uneven manner. If the plight of marginalized populations is to be resolved, therefore, then what is required are not only policies to redistribute commodified work (e.g. lifetime hours caps, part-time contracts, maximum working hours) but also policies to facilitate engagement in non-commodified work among those currently unable to participate in this sphere. In this chapter, and given the lack of attention so far paid to developing participation in non-commodified work, a range of initiatives have been outlined that seek to harness the ability of people to engage in such work. This has reviewed a range of both grassroots initiatives (LETS, time banks, mutual aid contracts, employee mutuals) and top-down policies (a basic income scheme, a 'civilization' of New Deal and active citizens' credits) that could be used to tackle the current barriers to participation in non-commodified work so as to facilitate engagement in such activity. This has shown that grassroots initiatives alone are likely to prove insufficient to enable any significant change and that what is required are top-down initiatives that more fully integrate the notion of full-engagement into existing policies such as tax credits in order to pave the way for a society based on economic plurality.

14

Conclusions

The overarching objective of this book has been to deconstruct the metanarrative of a natural and inevitable ongoing penetration of the market. In this concluding chapter, the threads of the preceding chapters that together form a critique of the commodification thesis and its closed vision of the future are thus synthesized so as to review the overall argument of the book. To do this, the organization of this final chapter is based on the overall structure of the book. First, the discourse of market penetration is evaluated critically by reviewing the extent to which advanced economies can be described as permeated by the commodity economy; second, the uneven contours of commodification are analysed; third, the options for the future of work available to Western nations and their implications are considered; and, finally, practical initiatives to move beyond the pursuit of commodification and towards a 'full-engagement' society are outlined.

A Critical Evaluation of the Commodification Thesis

Part I of the book addressed the widely accepted notion that late capitalism involves an inevitable and natural shift of daily life towards ever more commodified economic relations under the market-driven search for corporate profit. In this linear and unidimensional view of the trajectory of economic development, 'non-capitalist' activities have been often caricatured as a weak, primitive, traditional, stagnant, marginal and residual sphere that is dwindling and disappearing as the commodified realm becomes more powerful, pervasive, victorious, expansive, hegemonic and totalizing.

In Part I, therefore, the extent, pace and depth of the penetration of commodification were analysed so far as working life is concerned in the advanced economies. Chapter 2 set out the tenets of the commodification thesis and displayed how, although such a thesis is widely held, albeit often implicitly, in social inquiry, there is a very disturbing lack of evidence in support of it. Given the paucity of evidence for this accepted canon of wisdom, Chapters 3–5 then analysed the degree to which the advanced 'market' economies can be read as commodified. Recognizing that commodification refers to the advent of profit-motivated monetized exchange, first analysed was the persistence of non-exchanged (or subsistence) work, in Chapter 3; second was the prevalence of non-monetized exchange, in Chapter 4; and finally the existence of not-for-profit monetized transactions was analysed in Chapter 5. This revealed that for all the talk of a hegemonic, enveloping, dynamic, pervasive and totalizing commodified realm, there exists in the heartlands of commodification – the advanced 'market' economies – a non-commodified sphere that is not only as large as the commodified sphere but also growing relative to it.

Chapter 3 revealed that despite the oft-told tale that the subsistence economy has disappeared with the advent of a commodified world, such subsistence or non-exchanged work represents around a half of the total time that people spend working in the advanced economies and is valued at between 50 and 120 per cent of the existing GDP. Chapter 4, meanwhile, found that despite the assertions that monetized exchange has penetrated every nook and cranny of contemporary economic life, non-monetized exchanges are the equivalent of another 10–12 per cent of current GDP. Unpaid work alone, therefore, has been identified here as representing the equivalent of 60–132 per cent of GDP in these so-called advanced 'market' economies. Even when solely the vast amount of unpaid work taking place in the advanced economies is recognized, therefore, some serious questions need to be raised with regard to the picture painted by adherents to the commodification thesis of a hegemonic, enveloping, pervasive and totalizing commodified sphere.

When attention turns to the sphere of paid work, the doubts grow even stronger. Chapter 5 set out to deconstruct the view that widely prevails in economistic discourse that monetized exchange is universally profit-motivated. Previous research has shown how monetized transactions can be conducted under relations other than market-like profit-motivated exchange by highlighting the existence of alternative economic spaces such as local currency systems and car boot sales where the characters and logics of monetary transactions are non-market-like and conducted for not-for-profit rationales. The problem, however, is that this has had little impact on how 'mainstream' monetary transactions have been viewed. Such spaces are simply explained away as the study of small trivial sites, superfluous to an understanding of the mainstream. Here, therefore, some much larger realms of monetized exchange were examined so as to show that the profit motive can be absent from monetized exchange and economic relations are not always market-like. Analysing the public sector, social economy, cash-in-hand work and the private sector, this chapter revealed that even if one excludes the significant proportion of paid work that takes place in the public sphere from the calculations, as well as those private-sector enterprises where the search for corporate profit is not to the fore, and measures only the proportion of GDP provided by not-for-profit businesses (some 4.6 per cent of GDP) and 'cash-in-hand' work where it is conducted for motives other than money (about 5–12 per cent of GDP), there is a large segment of paid work conducted under economic relations where the search for corporate profit is absent.

Drawing together these threads, Part I thus concluded by providing an overall estimate of the degree to which work in the advanced economies has been commodified. Estimating the maximum and minimum sizes of the spheres of non-exchanged work, non-monetized exchange, not-for-profit exchange and the commodified sphere in the advanced economies, this uncovered that anywhere between 28 and 51 per cent of total GDP derives from non-exchanged work, 4–7 per cent from non-monetized exchange, 4–10 per cent from not-for-profit monetized exchange, and between 39 and 57 per cent from profit-motivated monetized exchange. Over time, moreover, there was found to be scant evidence that non-commodified work is diminishing in importance and of the commodified sphere capturing greater 'market share'. Indeed, if any process can be discerned in the advanced economies, it is that over the past forty years or so, many advanced economies have been undergoing a process of decommodification. Not only is the commodity economy far from hegemonic, enveloping, totalizing or dominant, therefore, but even to name the so-called advanced economies as 'capitalist', 'market' or 'commodified' societies appears to be an act of myopia at best, and desecration and defilement at worst, obliterating from view vast swathes of working life.

The Uneven Penetration of Commodification

Having revealed in Part I that, despite the hyperbole about a hegemonic and all-pervasive commodified realm, Western economies are characterized by a heterogeneity of economic practices and there is little evidence of commodification, Part II turned its attention towards charting the uneven contours of commodification within Western nations in Chapters 6–8, as well as how the pace and extent of commodification differ between the advanced economies and the other major regions of the world in Chapter 9.

Starting with the socio-economic disparities, Chapter 6 contested the widely held view that as populations become more affluent, they adopt more commodified lifestyles and, conversely, that non-commodified work where it persists is concentrated in deprived populations. The finding of this chapter was that this is an over-simplification. Participation in non-commodified work practices is not concentrated in deprived socio-economic groups. Instead, relatively affluent populations, despite leading more commodified lifestyles overall, still conduct a wider array of non-commodified work than their deprived counterparts. Although affluent groups tend to commodify routine tasks, they then use some of the free time created to engage in more creative, rewarding and non-routine forms of non-commodified work that they conduct out of choice rather than economic necessity.

The argument of this chapter was thus that, although the persistence and even growth of non-commodified work among lower-income groups can be read as a product of structural economic constraints and a new phase of capitalism where the costs and activities of social reproduction of those surplus to capitalism's requirements are being offloaded into the non-commodified sphere, the engagement of relatively affluent social groups cannot be explained in such a manner. Displaying how relatively affluent populations often make an active choice to engage in non-commodified work, it has been revealed that 'cultures of resistance' to commodification prevail among these socio-economic groups and that unless this anti-commodification ethic is recognized and incorporated into explanations for the growth of non-commodified work, then the uneven socio-economic contours of commodification cannot be fully understood. Here, in consequence, rather than adopt either a structural economic reading of non-commodified work or an agency-oriented reading, a both/and approach has been adopted sensitive to the different meanings of such spaces among different socio-economic groups.

This was similarly found to be necessary to explain the uneven geographies of commodification in Chapter 7. Again, although the populations of affluent areas were found to adopt more commodified lifestyles, this did not mean that they conducted less non-commodified work. Instead, quite the opposite was found to be the case. They not only conducted a wider array of non-commodified work but much of this was shown to be of the non-routine, creative and rewarding variety and conducted out of choice rather than economic necessity. As such, it was again argued that to understand the persistence of non-commodified work a spatially sensitive both/and approach is required that reads non-commodified work to be primarily a result of structural economic processes in deprived areas, but much more a result of choice in affluent areas where identity, meaning and self-esteem are sought not solely through commodified work but also through non-commodified economic practices that reflect the prevalence of a 'culture of resistance' to total commodification.

Chapter 8 then turned its attention to the gender disparities and revealed that although women are leading more commodified lifestyles, the working lives of men are decommodifying. Chapter 9, broadening the focus, turned its gaze beyond the advanced economies to the situation in both the so-called 'transition' economies of central and eastern Europe and the 'third world'. Contrary to the linear and hierarchical view that all regions of the world are at different stages on the same unidimensional trajectory of economic development towards a commodified world, this revealed through a detailed analysis of both the transition economies and different parts of the third world that heterogeneous development paths are being pursued. Contesting the notion that a hierarchical depiction of 'progress' and 'moving backwards' can be overlaid onto these heterogeneous trajectories, this chapter called for greater appreciation of the diversity of development paths and that working life might be other than commodified.

Policy Options and Their Implications

In Part III, the recognition that commodification was not an inevitable and natural future was addressed. Here, three major policy options towards the non-commodified realm were thus considered, namely commodification, doing nothing and harnessing this sphere. In Chapter 10, the first option of further commodifying work was considered. The argument of this chapter was that, at least in the advanced economies, there appears to be surfacing a commodified/non-commodified balance beyond the limits of which populations do not seek to pass and capitalism seems incapable of transcending. This chapter argued that there exist 'blockages' that capitalism cannot overcome. Drawing upon examples from across the advanced economies of the existence of blocked exchanges, work/life balance debates, changing attitudes towards commodified work and the emergence of resistance practices, this chapter thus called into question both the feasibility and the desirability of further commodification.

If an ongoing process of commodification does not appear achievable, Chapter 11 reflected, what are the implications of doing nothing with regard to the balance between the commodified/decommodified spheres? Pointing to the ways in which those cast adrift from the commodified realm throughout the advanced economies are also the least able to eke out an existence in the non-commodified sphere, the argument of this chapter was that such a strategy of 'doing nothing' is not an option. Such a non-decision will serve merely to leave those marginalized from the commodified realm bereft of the means of survival.

Chapter 12 thus considered the option of fostering non-commodified work alongside commodified work so as to cultivate plural economies. Reviewing the rationales for pursuing the cultivation of the non-market sphere in third-way, non-market social democracy, radical ecology and post-development thinking, this chapter argued that if non-capitalist futures are to be imagined and enacted, then there is a need to replace the goal of commodification with full engagement, which requires the development of not only the commodified but also the non-commodified sphere. Given the lack of attention so far paid to the interventions required in order to foster the non-commodified sphere, the main barriers that currently prevent the populations of advanced economies from engaging in non-commodified work were identified.

Beyond a Commodified World

If strategies to develop plural economies are to avoid the creation of a dual society, Chapter 13, argued, it is necessary to pursue an approach that seeks to encourage heterogeneous economic practices across the whole population rather than solely among marginalized populations. Given how commodified work as well as non-commodified work is currently distributed in a highly uneven manner, it argued that what is required are not only policies to redistribute commodified work (e.g. lifetime hours caps, part-time contracts, maximum working hours) but also policies to facilitate engagement in non-commodified work among those currently unable to participate in this sphere. Recognizing the lack of attention so far paid to developing participation in non-commodified work, this chapter outlined a range of initiatives to harness this sphere in the form of both grassroots initiatives (LETS, time banks, mutual aid contracts, employee mutuals) and top-down policies (a basic income scheme, a 'civilization' of New Deal and active citizens' credits) that could be used to tackle the current barriers to participation in non-commodified work so as to facilitate engagement in such activity. This revealed that grassroots initiatives alone are unlikely to prove sufficient to enable any significant change, and that what is required are top-down initiatives that more fully integrate the goal of full engagement into existing policies such as tax credits in order to pave the way for a society based on economic plurality.

The overarching message of this book, in sum, is that it is now time to reimagine the future of work. Here, the view of a hegemonic, all-encompassing, totalizing and victorious capitalism has been uncovered as an *illusion*. The result is that alternative futures no longer seem so implausible as when commodification was viewed as a natural and inevitable phenomenon.

This does not mean, however, and as has been emphasized throughout this book, that there should be any headlong rush towards developing the non-commodified sphere so as to create post-capitalist futures. It has been revealed that the current growth of the non-commodified sphere is not solely a product of the populations of the advanced economies expressing their discontentment with a commodified world by voting with their minds and hands to engage in acts of resistance. The growth of the non-commodified sphere is also, in equal part, a product of capitalism itself seeking to offload the social reproduction of those no longer of any use to it. In other words, the non-commodified sphere is as much a 'space of despair' as a 'space of hope' and, as such, great care is required when advocating its development. Indeed, unless caution is exercised, then those seeking to develop alternatives to capitalism may well find themselves merely aiding and abetting this very order by creating depositories into which those excluded from the market can be abandoned.

Nevertheless, even though such cautionary pleas litter the pages of this book, this should not mask the broader positive message. For those who have believed that there is only one future and it is one in which there is an inevitable and natural shift towards an ever more commodified world under the market-driven search for corporate profit, this book provides a source of renewed optimism. A commodified world has been widely held to be the one and only future available, not least by those with a powerful vested interest in the further encroachment of the market. This book, however, has revealed that 'buying into' this future is not the only option available. It is wholly feasible to imagine and enact alternatives to a commodified world.

References

Albert, M. (1993) *Capitalism against Capitalism*, New York: Four Walls Eight Windows.

Amado, J., and Stoffaes, C. (1980) 'Vers une socio-economie duale', in A. Danzin, A. Boublil and J. Lagarde (eds) *La Société française et la technologie*, Paris: Documentation Française.

Amin, A., and Thrift, N. (2000) 'What kind of economic theory for what kind of economic geography?', *Antipode* 32(1): 4–9.

Amin, A., Cameron, A., and Hudson, R. (2002a) *Placing the Social Economy*, London: Routledge.

Amin, A., Cameron, A., and Hudson, R. (2002b) 'The UK social economy: panacea or problem?', in I. Bartle and D. Castiglione (eds) *Social Capital in the Economy*, Colchester: Russell Papers Civic Series 2002/4, University of Essex.

Anderson, B. (2001a) 'Why madam has so many bathrobes: demand for migrant domestic workers in the EU', *Tijdschrift voor Economische en Sociale Geografie* 92(1): 18–26.

Anderson, B. (2001b) 'Different roots in common ground: trans-nationalism and migrant domestic workers in London', *Journal of Ethnic and Migration Studies* 27(4): 673–83.

Anheier, H.K. (1992) 'Economic environments and differentiation: a comparative study of informal sector economies in Nigeria', *World Development* 20(11): 1573–85.

Archibugi, F. (2000) *The Associative Economy: Insights beyond the Welfare State and into Post-capitalism*, London: Macmillan.

Atkinson, A.B. (1995) *Public Economics in Action: The Basic Income/flat Tax Proposal*, Oxford: Oxford University Press.

Atkinson, A.B. (1998) *Poverty in Europe*, Oxford: Blackwell.

Aznar, G. (1981) *Tous a Mi-temps, ou le scenario bleu*, Paris: Seuil.

Bauman, Z. (1998) *Work, Consumerism and the New Poor*, Milton Keynes: Open University Press.

Beck, U. (2000) *The Brave New World of Work*, Cambridge: Polity Press.

Beneria, L. (1999) 'The enduring debate over unpaid labour', *International Labour Review* 138: 287–309.

Bennett, F., and Hirsch, D. (2001) 'Balancing support and opportunity', in F. Bennett and D. Hirsch (eds) *The Employment Tax Credit and Issues for the Future of In-Work Support*, York: York Publishing Services.

Bennholdt-Thomsen, V. (2001) 'What really keeps our cities alive, money or subsistence?', in V. Bennholdt-Thomsen, N. Faraclas and C. von Werlhof (eds) *There is an Alternative: Subsistence and Worldwide Resistance to Corporate Globalization*, London: Zed Books.

Bennholdt-Thomsen, V., and Mies. M. (1999) *The Subsistence Perspective: Beyond the Globalized Economy*, London: Zed Books.

Bennholdt-Thomsen, V., Faraclas, N., and von Werlhof, C. (eds) (2001) *There is an Alternative: Subsistence and Worldwide Resistance to Corporate Globalization*, London: Zed Books.

Bentley, T., and Mulgan, G. (1996) *Employee Mutuals: The 21st Century Trade Union?*, London: Demos.

Berger, S., and Dore, R. (eds) (1996) *National Diversity and Global Capitalism*, Ithaca, NY: Cornell University Press.

Berking, H. (1999) *Sociology of Giving*, London: Sage.

Beveridge, W. (1944) *Full-Employment in a Free Society*, London: George Allen & Unwin.

Beveridge, W. (1948) *Voluntary Action: A Report of Methods of Social Advance*, London: George Allen & Unwin.

Birchall, J. (ed.) (2001) *The New Mutualism in Public Policy*, London: Routledge.

Blair, J.P., and Endres, C.R. (1994) 'Hidden economic development assets', *Economic Development Quarterly* 8(3): 286–91.

Blair, T. (1998) *The Third Way: New Politics for the New Century*, London: Fabian Society.

Bloch, M., and Parry, J. (1989) 'Introduction', in J. Parry and M. Bloch (eds) *Money and the Morality of Exchange*, Cambridge: Cambridge University Press.

Block, F. (1990) *Postindustrial Possibilities: A Critique of Economic Discourse*, Berkeley, CA: University of California Press.

Block, F. (1994) 'The roles of the state in the economy', in N.J. Smelser and R. Swedbert (eds) *The Handbook of Economic Sociology*, Princeton, NJ: Princeton University Press.

Block, F. (2002) 'Rethinking capitalism', in N.W. Biggart (ed.) *Readings in Economic Sociology*, Oxford: Blackwell.

Boren, T. (2003) 'What are friends for? Rationales of informal exchange in Russian everyday life', in K. Arnstberg and T. Boren (eds) *Everyday Economy in Russia, Poland and Latvia*, Stockholm: Almqvist & Wiksell.

Boswell, J. (1990) *Community and the Economy*, London: Routledge.

Boulding, E. (1968) *Toward a Global Civic Culture: Education for an Interdependent World*, New York: Columbia University Press.

Bourdieu, P. (2001) 'The forms of capital', in N.W. Biggart (ed.) *Readings in Economic Sociology*, Oxford: Blackwell.

Bourdieu, P. (2003) *Firing Back: Against the Tyranny of the Market 2*, London: Verso.

Boyle, D. (1999) *Funny Money: In Search of Alternative Cash*, London: Harper Collins.

Bradley, A. (1987) 'Poverty and dependency in village England', in P. Lowe, A. Bradley and A. Wright (eds) *Disadvantage and Welfare in Rural Areas*, Norwich: GeoBooks.

Braverman, H. (1971) *Labour and Monopoly Capital*, New York: Monthly Review Press.

Briscoe, I. (1995) *In Whose Service? Making Community Service Work for the Unemployed*, London: Demos.

Bromley, R., and Gerry, C. (1979) *Casual Work and Poverty in Third World Cities*, Chichester: Wiley.

Burns, D., and Taylor, M. (1998) *Mutual Aid and Self-Help: Coping Strategies for Excluded Communities*, Bristol: The Policy Press.

Burns, D., Williams, C.C., and Windebank, J. (2004) *Community Self-Help*, London: Palgrave Macmillan.

Button, K. (1984) 'Regional variations in the irregular economy: a study of possible trends', *Regional Studies* 18: 385–92.

Byrne, K., Forest, R., Gibson-Graham, J.K., Healy, S., and Horvath, G. (1998) *Imagining and Enacting Non-capitalist Futures*, Rethinking Economy Project Working Paper no.1, www.arts.monash.edu.au/projects/cep/knowledges/byrne.html.

Cahn, E. (1994) 'Reinventing poverty law', *Yale Law Journal* 103(8): 2133–55.

Cahn, E. (2000) *No More Throw-away People: the Co-production Imperative*, Washington DC: Essential Books.

Cahn, E., and Rowe, J. (1992) *Time Dollars: The New Currency that Enables Americans to Turn Their Hidden Resource – Time – into Personal Security and Community Renewal*, Chicago: Family Resource Coalition of America.

Campbell, M. (2000) 'Reconnecting the long-term unemployed to labour market opportunity: the case for a local active labour market policy', *Regional Studies* 34(7): 655–68.

Cannon, D. (1994) *Generation X and the New Work Ethic*, London: Demos.

Caplow, T. (1982) 'Christian gifts and kin networks', *American Sociological Review* 47: 383–92.

Capra, F., and Spretnak, C. (1985) *Green Politics*, London: Hutchinson.

Carrier, J.G. (1990) 'Gifts in a world of commodities', *Social Analysis* 29: 19–37.

Carrier, J.G. (1998) 'Introduction', in J.G. Carrier and D. Miller (eds) *Virtualism: A New Political Economy*, Oxford: Berg.

Carrier, J.G. (ed.) (1997) *Meanings of the Market: The Free Market in Western Culture*, Oxford: Berg.

Carruthers, B.G., and Babb, S.L. (2000) *Economy/Society: Markets, Meanings and Social Structure*, Thousand Oaks, CA: Pine Oaks.

Carruthers, B.G., and Espeland, W.N. (2001), 'Money, meaning and morality', in N.W. Biggart (ed.) *Readings in Economic Sociology*, Oxford: Blackwell.

Castells, M., and Portes, A. (1989) 'World underneath: the origins, dynamics and effects of the informal economy', in A. Portes, M. Castells and L.A. Benton (eds) *The Informal Economy: Studies in Advanced and Less Developing Countries*, Baltimore: Johns Hopkins University Press.

Cattell, V., and Evans, M. (1999) *Neighbourhood Images in East London: Social Capital and Social Networks on Two East London Estates*, York: York Publishing Services.

Chabaud-Richter, D., and Fougeyrollas-Schwebel, D. (1985) *Espace et temps du travail domestique*, Paris: Méridiens.

Chadeau, A., and Fouquet, A.-M. (1981) 'Peut-on mesurer le travail domestique?', *Economie et Statistique* 136: 29–42.

Chanan, G. (1999) 'Employment and the third sector: promise and misconceptions', *Local Economy* 13(4): 361–8.

Chapman, P., Phiminster, E., Shucksmith, M., Upward, R., and Vera-Toscano, E. (1998) *Poverty and Exclusion in Rural Britain: The Dynamics of Low Income and Employment*, York: York Publishing Services.

Cheal, D. (1988) *The Gift Economy*, London: Verso.

Cheng, L.L., and Gereffi, G. (1994) 'The informal economy in East Asian development', *International Journal of Urban and Regional Research* 18(2): 194–219.

Ciscel, D.H., and Heath, J.A. (2001) 'To market, to market: imperial capitalism's destruction of social capital and the family', *Review of Radical Political Economics* 33(4): 401–14

Clark, G.L., and Root, A. (1999) 'Infrastructure shortfall in the UK: the private finance initiative and government policy', *Political Geography* 18: 341–65.

Clarke, A. (1998) 'Window shopping at home: classified catalogues and new consumer skills', in D. Miller (ed.) *Material Cultures*, London: UCL Press.

Clarke, A. (2000) '"Mother swapping": the trafficking of nearly new children's wear', in P. Jackson (ed.) *Commercial Cultures: Economies, Practices, Spaces*, Oxford: Berg.

Cloke, P., Milbourne, P., and Thomas, C. (1994) *Lifestyles in Rural England*, London: Rural Research Report 18, Rural Development Commission.

Coates, D. (ed.) (2002a) *Capitalist Models: Divergence and Convergence*, Aldershot: Edward Elgar.

Coates, D. (ed.) (2002b) *Capitalist Models under Challenge*, Aldershot: Edward Elgar.

Coates, D. (ed.) (2002c) *The Ascendancy of Liberal Capitalism*, Aldershot: Edward Elgar.

Coleman, J. (1988) 'Social capital in the creation of human capital', *American Journal of Sociology* (Supp.) 94: 95–120.

Comeliau, C. (2002) *The Impasse of Modernity*, London: Zed Books.

Community Development Foundation (1995) *Added Value and Changing Values: Community Involvement in Urban Regeneration: A 12 Country Study for the European Union*, Brussels: CEC DG XVI.

Community Economies Collective (2001) 'Imagining and enacting noncapitalist futures', *Socialist Review* 28: 93–135.

Connolly, P. (1985) 'The politics of the informal sector: a critique', in N. Redclift and E. Mingione (eds) *Beyond Employment: Household, Gender and Subsistence*, Oxford: Blackwell.

Cook, D. (1997) *Poverty, Crime and Punishment*, London: Child Poverty Action Group.

Coulthard, M., Walker, A., and Morgan, A. (2002) *People's Perceptions of Their Neighbourhood and Community Involvement: Results from the Social Capital Module of the General Household Survey 2000*, London: Home Office.

Countryside Agency (2000) *The State of the Countryside 2000*, London: Countryside Agency.

Coupland, D. (1991) *Generation X: Tales for an Accelerated Culture*, New York: St Martin's Press.

Crang, P. (1996) 'Displacement, consumption and identity', *Environment and Planning A* 28: 47–67.

Crang, P. (1997) 'Cultural turns and the (re)constitution of economic geography', in R. Lee and J. Wills (eds) *Geographies of Economies*, London: Arnold.

Crewe, L., and Gregson, N. (1998) 'Tales of the unexpected: exploring car boot sales as marginal spaces of contemporary consumption', *Transactions of the Institute of British Geographers* 23(1): 39–54.

Crouch, C., and Streek, W. (eds) (1997) *Political Economy of Modern Capitalism: Mapping Convergence and Diversity*, Thousand Oaks, CA: Sage.

Dasgupta, N. (1992) *Petty Trading in the Third World: The Case of Calcutta*, Aldershot: Avebury.

Dauncey, G. (1988) *After the Crash: The Emergence of the Rainbow Economy*, London: Green Print.

Davis Smith, J. (1998) *The 1997 National Survey of Volunteering*, London: Institute for Volunteering Research.

Davis, J. (1992) *Exchange*, Milton Keynes: Open University Press.

De Pardo, M.L., Castano, G.M., and Soto, A.T. (1989) 'The articulation of formal and informal sectors in the economy of Bogota, Colombia', in A. Portes, M. Castells and L. Benton (eds) *The Informal Economy: Studies in Advanced and Less Developed Countries*, Baltimore: Johns Hopkins University Press.

De Soto, H. (1989) *The Other Path*, London: Harper & Row.

Dean, H., and Melrose, M. (1996) 'Unravelling citizenship: the significance of social security benefit fraud', *Critical Social Policy* 16: 3–31.

Dekker, P., and Van den Broek, A. (1998) 'Civil society in comparative perspective: involvement in voluntary associations in North America and Western Europe', *Voluntas* 9(1): 11–38.

Delors, J. (1979) 'Le troisième secteur: le travail au-delà de l'emploi', *Autrement* 20: 147–52.

Delphy, C. (1984) *Close to Home*, London: Hutchinson.

Department of Local Government, Transport and the Regions (2000) *Index of Multiple Deprivation*, London: Department of Local Government, Transport and the Regions.

Derrida, J. (1967) *Of Grammatology*, Baltimore: Johns Hopkins University Press.

Desai, M. (1998) *A Basic Income Proposal*, London: Social Market Foundation.

DETR (1998) *Community-based Regeneration Initiatives: A Working Paper*, London: DETR.

Devall, B. (1990) *Simple in Means, Rich in Ends: Practising Deep Ecology*, London: Green Print.

Devall, B., and Sessions, G. (1985) *Deep Ecology: Living as if Nature Mattered*, Salt Lake City: Peregrine Smith Books.

Dickens, R., Gregg, P., and Wadsworth, J. (2000) 'New Labour and the labour market', *Oxford Review of Economic Policy* 16(1): 95–113.

Dobson, R.V.G. (1993) *Bringing the Economy Home from the Market*, New York: Black Rose Books.

Donnison, D. (1998) *Policies for a Just Society*, London: Macmillan.

Dorsett, R. (2001) *Workless Couples: Characteristics and Labour Market Transitions*, London: Employment Service.

Douthwaite, R. (1996) *Short Circuit: Strengthening Local Economies for Security in an Unstable World*, Dartington: Green Books.

DSS (1998) *A New Contract for Welfare*, London: HMSO.

Dumontier, F., and Pan Ke Shon, J.-L. (1999) *En 13 ans, moins de temps contraints et plus de loisirs*, Paris: INSEE Première 675, INSEE.

Eckersley, R. (1992) *Environmentalism and Political Theory: Towards an Ecocentric Approach*, London: UCL Press.

ECOTEC (1998) *Third System and Employment: Evaluation Inception Report*, Birmingham: ECOTEC.

Eisenschitz, A. (1997) 'The view from the grassroots', in M. Pacione (ed.) *Britain's Cities: Geographies of Division in Urban Britain*, London: Routledge.

Ekins, P., and Max-Neef, M. (1992) *Real-Life Economics: Understanding Wealth Creation*, London: Routledge.

Elkin, T., and McLaren, D. (1991) *Reviving the City: Towards Sustainable Urban Development*, London: Friends of the Earth.

Elson, D. (1988) 'Market socialism or socialization of the market?', *New Left Review* 172: 11–29.

Engbersen, G., Schuyt, K., Timmer, J., and van Waarden, F. (1993) *Cultures of Unemployment: A Comparative Look at Long-term Unemployment and Urban Poverty*, San Francisco: Westview Press.

Escobar, A. (1995) *Encountering Development: The Making and Unmaking of the Third World*, Princeton, NJ: Princeton University Press.

Esteva, G. (2001) 'Mexico: creating your own path at the grassroots', in V.

Bennholdt-Thomsen, N. Faraclas and C. von Werlhof (eds) *There is an Alternative: Subsistence and Worldwide Resistance to Corporate Globalization*, London: Zed Books.

European Commission (1990) *Underground Economy and Irregular Forms of Employment*, Luxembourg: Office for Official Publications of the European Communities.

European Commission (1996a) *Employment in Europe 1996*, Luxembourg: European Commission DG for Employment, Industrial Relations and Social Affairs.

European Commission (1996b) *For a Europe of Civic and Social Rights: Report by the Comité des Sages*, Luxembourg: European Commission DG for Employment, Industrial Relations and Social Affairs.

European Commission (1997) *Towards an Urban Agenda in the European Union*, COM (1997) 197, Brussels: Communication from the European Commission.

European Commission (1998) *On Undeclared Work*, COM (1998) 219, Brussels: Commission of the European Communities.

European Commission (2000a) *The Social Situation in the European Union 2000*, Brussels: European Commission.

European Commission (2000b) *Employment in Europe 2000*, Brussels: European Commission.

European Commission (2001a) *EU Employment and Social Policy, 1999–2001: Job, Cohesion, Productivity*, Luxembourg: Office for Official Publications of the European Communities.

European Commission (2001b) *The Social Situation in the European Union 2001*, Brussels: Commission of the European Communities.

Faraclas, N.G. (2001) 'Melanesia, the banks, and the BINGOs: real alternatives are everywhere (except in the consultants' briefcases)', in V. Bennholdt-Thomsen, N. Faraclas and C. von Werlhof (eds) *There is An Alternative: Subsistence and Worldwide Resistance to Corporate Globalization*, London: Zed Books.

Fashoyin, T. (1993) 'Nigeria: consequences for employment', in A. Adepoju (ed.) *The Impact of Structural Adjustment on the Population of Africa*, London: James Currey.

Feige, E.L. (1990) 'Defining and estimating underground and informal economies', *World Development* 18(7): 989–1002.

Felt, L.F., and Sinclair, P.R. (1992) '"Everyone does it": unpaid work in a rural peripheral region', *Work Employment and Society* 6(1): 43–64.

Field, J., and Hedges, B. (1984) *A National Survey of Volunteering*, London: SCPR.

Findlay, A., Short, D., Stockdale, A. (1999) *Migration Impacts in Rural England*, Cheltenham: CAX 19, Countryside Agency.

Fitzpatrick, T. (1999) *Freedom and Security: An Introduction to the Basic Income Debate*, London: Macmillan.

Fodor, E. (1999) *Better Not Bigger: How to Take Control of Urban Growth and Improve Your Community*, Stony Creek, NJ: New Society.

Ford, J., Quilgars, D., Burrows, R., and Pleace, N. (1997) *Young People and Housing*, London: Rural Research Report 31, Rural Development Commission.

Fordham, G. (1995) *Made to Last: Creating Sustainable Neighbourhood and Estate Regeneration*, York: Joseph Rowntree Foundation.

Forrest, R., and Kearns, A. (1999) *Joined-up Places? Social Cohesion and Neighbourhood Regeneration*, York: York Publishing Services.

Fortin, B., Garneau, G., Lacroix, G., Lemieux, T., and Montmarquette, C. (1996) *L'Economie souterraine au Quebec: mythes et réalités*, Laval: Presses de l'Université Laval.

Foster, V. (1997) 'What value should be placed on volunteering?', in C. Pharaoh (ed.) *Dimensions of the Voluntary Sector*, London: Charities Aid Foundation.

Foucault, M. (1981) 'The order of discourse: Inaugural lecture at the Collège de France, given 2 December 1970', in R. Young (ed.) *Untying the Text: A Poststructuralist Reader*, London: Routledge & Kegan Paul.

Frank, A.G. (1996) 'The underdevelopment of development', in S.C. Chew and R.A. Denemark (eds) *The Underdevelopment of Development*, London: Sage.

Franks, S. (2000) *Having None of It: Women, Men and the Future of Work*, London: Granta.

Friedmann, Y. (1982) 'L'art de la survie', *Autogestions* 8/9: 89–95.

Furlong, A., and Cartnel, F. (2000) *Youth Unemployment in Rural Areas*, York: Joseph Rowntree Foundation.

Gardiner, J. (1997) *Gender, Care and Economics*, London: Macmillan.

Gaskin, K. (1999) 'Valuing volunteers in Europe: a comparative study of the Volunteer Investment and Value Audit', *Journal of the Institute of Volunteering Research* 2(1): 1–18.

Gass, R. (1996) 'The next stage of structural change: towards a decentralised economy and an active society', in OECD (ed.) *Reconciling Economy and Society: Towards a Plural Economy*, Paris: OECD.

Gershuny, J. (2000) *Changing Times: Work and Leisure in Post-industrial Society*, Oxford: Oxford University Press.

Gershuny, J., and Jones, S. (1987) 'The changing work/leisure balance in Britain 1961–84', *Sociological Review Monograph* 33: 9–50.

Gershuny, J., and Miles, I. (1983) *The New Service Economy: The Transformation of Employment in Industrial Societies*, London: Frances Pinter.

Gershuny, J., and Pahl, R.E. (1979) 'Work outside employment: some preliminary speculations', *New Universities Quarterly* 34: 120–35.

Gershuny, J., Godwin, M., and Jones, S. (1994) 'The domestic labour revolution: a process of lagged adaptation', in M. Anderson, F. Bechhofer and S. Kendrick (eds) *The Social and Political Economy of the Household*, Oxford: Oxford University Press.

Gibson-Graham, J.K. (1996) *The End of Capitalism as We Knew It?: A Feminist Critique of Political Economy*, Oxford: Blackwell.

Gibson-Graham, J.K. (2003) 'Poststructural interventions', in E. Sheppard and T.J. Barnes (eds) *A Companion to Economic Geography*, Blackwell, Oxford.

Gibson-Graham, J.K., and Ruccio, D. (2001) '"After" development: re-imagining economy and class', in J.K. Gibson-Graham, S. Resnick and R. Wolff (eds) *Re/presenting Class: Essays in Post-modern Marxism*, Durham, NC: Duke University Press.

Giddens, A. (1998) *The Third Way: The Renewal of Social Democracy*, Cambridge: Polity Press.

Giddens, A. (2000), *The Third Way and its Critics*, Cambridge: Polity Press.

Giddens, A. (2002) *Where Now for New Labour?*, Cambridge: Polity Press.

Gilbert, A. (1994) 'Third World Cities: poverty, unemployment, gender roles and the environment during a time of restructuring', *Urban Studies* 31(4/5): 605–33.

Gittell, R., and Vidal, A. (1998) *Community Organizing: Building Social Capital as a Development Strategy*, London: Sage.

Goldschmidt-Clermont, L. (1982) *Unpaid Work in the Household: A Review of Economic Evaluation Methods*, Geneva: ILO.

Goldschmidt-Clermont, L. (1993) *Monetary Valuation of Unpaid Work: Arguing for an Output Measurement*, Geneva: Bulletin of Labour Statistics no. 3, ILO.

Goldschmidt-Clermont, L. (1998) *Measuring and Valuing non-SNA activities, Handbook of National Accounting, Household Accounting: Experiences in the Use of Concepts and their Compilation – Household Satellite Extensions*, New York: United Nations.

Goldschmidt-Clermont, L. (2000) *Household Production and Income: Some Preliminary Issues*, Geneva: Bureau of Statistics, ILO.

Goldsmith, E., Khor, M., Norberg-Hodge, H., and Shiva, V. (eds) (1995) *The Future of Progress: Reflections on Environment and Development*, Dartington: Green Books.

Goodin, R. (1992) *Green Political Theory*, Cambridge: Polity Press.

Gorz, A. (1985) *Paths to Paradise*, London: Pluto.

Gorz, A. (1999) *Reclaiming Work: beyond the Wage-based Society*, Cambridge: Polity Press.

Gough, I. (2000) *Global Capital, Human Needs and Social Policies*, London: Palgrave Macmillan.

Grabiner, Lord (2000) *The Informal Economy*, London: HM Treasury.

Granovetter, M. (1973) 'The strength of weak ties', *American Journal of Sociology* 78(6): 1360–80.

Greco, T.H. (1994) *New Money for Healthy Communities*, Tucson, AZ: Thomas H. Greco Jr.

Greffe, X. (1981) 'L'économie non-officielle', *Consommation* 3: 5–16.

Gregg, P., and Wadsworth, J. (1996) *It Takes Two: Employment Polarisation in the OECD*, Discussion Paper no. 304, London: Centre for Economic Performance, London School of Economics.

Gregory, A., and Windebank, J. (2000) *Women and Work in France and Britain: Theory, Practice and Policy*, London: Macmillan.

Gregory, C.A. (1982) *Gifts and Commodities*, London: Academic Press.

Gudeman, S. (2001) *The Anthropology of Economy*, Oxford: Blackwell.

Guisinger, S., and Irfan, M. (1980) 'Pakistan's informal sector', *Journal of Development Studies* 16(4): 412–26.

Gutmann, P.M. (1977) 'The subterranean economy', *Financial Analysts Journal* 34(11): 26–7.

Gutmann, P.M. (1978) 'Are the unemployed, unemployed?', *Financial Analysts Journal* 35: 26–7.

Habermas, J. (1993) *The Structural Transformation of the Public Sphere*, Cambridge, MA: MIT Press

Haicault, M. (1984) 'La gestion ordinaire de la vie en deux', *Sociologie du Travail* 3: 268–77.

Hakim, C. (2000) *Work–Lifestyle Choices in the 21st century*, Oxford: Oxford University Press.

Hall, P. (1996) 'The global city', *International Social Science Journal* 147: 15–24.

Harkness, S. (1994) 'Female employment and changes in the share of women's earnings in total family income in Great Britain', in S. Hardy, G. Lloyd and I. Cundell (eds) *Tackling Unemployment and Social Exclusion: Problems for Regions, Solutions for People*, London: Regional Studies Association.

Hart, K. (1973) 'Informal income opportunities and urban employment in Ghana', *Journal of Modern African Studies* 11: 61–89.

Hart, K. (1990) 'The idea of economy: six modern dissenters', in R. Friedland and A.F. Robertson (eds) *Beyond the Marketplace: Rethinking Economy and Society*, New York: Aldine de Gruyter.

Harvey, D. (1982) *The Limits to Capital*, Oxford: Blackwell.

Harvey, D. (1989) *The Condition of Post-Modernity: An Enquiry into the Origins of Cultural Change*. Oxford: Blackwell.

Harvey, D. (2000) *Spaces of Hope*, Edinburgh: Edinburgh University Press.

Haughton, G. (1998) 'Principles and practice of community economic development', *Regional Studies* 32(9): 872–8.

Hedges, A. (1999) *Living in the Countryside: The Needs and Aspirations of Rural Populations*, London: Countryside Agency.

Hellberger, C., and Schwarze, J. (1986) *Umfang und Struktur der Nebenerwerbstatigkeit in der Bundesrepublik Deutschland*, Berlin: Mitteilungen aus der Arbeits-market- und Berufsforschung.

Hellberger, C., and Schwarze, J. (1987) 'Nebenerwerbstatigkeit: ein Indikator für Arbeitsmarkt-flexibilitat oder Schattenwirtschaft', *Wirtschaftsdienst* 2: 83–90.

Henderson, H. (1978) *Creating Alternative Futures*, New York: Putnam and Sons

Henderson, H. (1999) *Beyond Globalisation: Shaping a Sustainable Global Economy*, London: Kumarian Press.

Himmelweit, S. (ed.) (2000) *Inside the Household: From Labour to Care*, London: Macmillan.

Hines, C. (2000) *Localization: A Global Manifesto*, London: Earthscan.

Hirsch, D. (1999) *Welfare beyond Work: Active Participation in a New Welfare State*, York: York Publishing Services.

HM Treasury (1998) *The Modernisation of Britain's Tax and Benefit System: the Working Families Tax Credit and Work Incentives*, London: HM Treasury.

Hochschild, A. (1989) *The Second Shift: Working Parents and the Revolution at Home*, New York: Viking.

Hollingsworth, J., and Bayer, R. (eds) (1997) *Contemporary Capitalism: The Embeddedness of Institutions*, Cambridge: Cambridge University Press.

Home Office (1999) *Community Self-Help – Policy Action Team no. 9*, London: Home Office.

Hoogendijk, W. (1993) *The Economic Revolution: Towards a Sustainable Future by Freeing the Economy From Money-making*, Utrecht: International Books.

Horton Smith, D. (1994) 'Determinants of voluntary association participation and volunteering: a literature review', *Nonprofit and Voluntary Sector Quarterly* 23: 243–63

Howe, L. (1988) 'Unemployment, doing the double and local labour markets in Belfast', in C. Cartin and T. Wilson (eds) *Ireland from Below: Social Change and Local Communities in Modern Ireland*, Dublin: Gill & Macmillan.

Howe, L. (1990) *Being Unemployed in Northern Ireland: An Ethnographic Study*, Cambridge: Cambridge University Press.

ILO (International Labour Organization) (1972) *Employment, Incomes and Equality: A Strategy for Increasing Productive Employment in Kenya*, Geneva: ILO.

ILO (International Labour Organization) (1996) *World Employment 1996/97: National Policies in a Global Context*, Geneva: ILO.

ILO (International Labour Organization) (1997) *World Employment 1997–98*, Geneva: ILO.

ILO (International Labour Organization) (2002) *Decent Work and the Informal Economy*, Geneva: ILO.

Ironmonger, D. (2000) 'Measuring volunteering in economic terms', in J. Warburton and M. Oppenheimer (eds) *Volunteers and Volunteering*, Sydney: Federation Press.

Ironmonger, D. (2002) *Valuing Volunteering: The Economic Value of Volunteering in South Australia*, Melbourne: Government of South Australia.

Ironmonger, D., and Soupromas, F. (2002) *Calculating Australia's Gross Household Product: Measuring the Economic Value of the Household Economy 1970–2000*, Melbourne: Research Paper Number 833, Department of Economics, University of Melbourne.

Jackson, P. (2002) 'Commercial Cultures: Transcending the Cultural and the Economic', *Progress in Human Geography* 26(1): 3–18.

Jacob, J. (2003) 'Alternative lifestyle spaces', in A. Leyshon, R. Lee and C.C. Williams (eds) *Alternative Economic Spaces*, London: Sage.

James, S. (1994) 'Women's unwaged work: the heart of the informal sector', in M. Evans (ed.) *The Woman Question*, London: Sage.

Jensen, L., Cornwell, G.T., and Findeis, J.L. (1995) 'Informal work in nonmetropolitan Pennsylvania', *Rural Sociology* 60(1): 91–107.

Jessop, B. (2002) *The Future of the Capitalist State*, Cambridge: Polity Press.

Jordan, B. (1998) *The New Politics of Welfare: Social Justice in a Global Context*, London: Sage.

Jordan, B., and Jordan, C. (2000) *Social Work and the Third Way: Tough Love as Social Policy*, London: Sage.

Jordan, B., Agulnik, P., Burbridge, D., and Duffin, S. (2000) *Stumbling towards Basic Income: The Prospects for Tax-Benefit Integration*, London: Citizen's Income Study Centre.

Jordan, B., James, S., Kay, H., and Redley, M. (1992) *Trapped in Poverty? Labour-market Decision in Low-income Households*, London: Routledge.

Juster, T.F., and Stafford, F.P. (1991) 'The allocation of time: empirical findings, behavioural models and problems of measurement', *Journal of Economic Literature* 29(2): 471–522.

Kempson, E. (1996) *Life on a Low Income*, York: York Publishing Services.

Kerr, D. (1998) 'The private finance initiative and the changing governance of the built environment', *Urban Studies* 35: 277–301.

Kershaw, C., Budd, T., Kinshott, G., Mattinson, J., Mayhew, P., and Myhill, A. (2000) *The 2000 British Crime Survey: England and Wales*, Home Office Statistical Bulletin 18/00, London: Home Office.

Kesteloot, C., and Meert, H. (1999) 'Informal spaces: the geography of informal economic activities in Brussels', *International Journal of Urban and Regional Research* 23: 232–51.

Korte, C., and Kerr, N. (1975) 'Responses to altruistic opportunities in urban and nonurban settings', *Journal of Social Psychology* 95: 183–4.

Kovel, J. (2002) *The Enemy of Nature: The End of Capitalism or the End of the World?*, London: Zed Books.

Krishnamurthy, A., Prime, D., and Zimmeck, M. (2001) *Voluntary and Community Activities: Findings from the 2000 British Crime Survey*, London: Home Office.

La Valle, I., and Blake, M. (2001) *National Adult learning Survey (NALS) 2001*, Brief no. 321, London: Department for Education and Skills, www.dfes.gov.uk/research/data/uploadfiles/RR321.pdf, accessed 9 July 2002.

Lagos, R.A. (1995) 'Formalising the informal sector: barriers and costs', *Development and Change* 26: 110–31.

Lalonde, B., and Simmonet, D. (1978) *Quand vous voudrez*, Paris: Pauvert.

Lautier, B. (1994) *L'économie informelle dans le tiers monde*, Paris: La Découverte.

Laville, J.-L. (1995) 'La crise de la condition salariale: emploi, activité et nouvelle question sociale', *Esprit* 12: 32–54.

Laville, J.-L. (1996) 'Economy and solidarity: exploring the issues', in OECD (ed.) *Reconciling Economy and Society: Towards a Plural Economy*, Paris: OECD.

Leadbeater, C. (1999) *Living on Thin Air: The New Economy*, Harmondsworth: Penguin.

Leadbeater, C., and Martin, S. (1997) *The Employee Mutual: Combining Flexibility with Security in the New World of Work*, London: Demos.

Lee, R. (1996) 'Moral money? LETS and the social construction of economic geographies in southeast England', *Environment and Planning A* 28: 1377–94.

Lee, R. (1997) 'Economic geographies: representations and interpretations', in R. Lee and J. Wills (eds.) *Geographies of Economies*, London: Edward Arnold.

Lee, R. (1999) 'Production', in P. Cloke, P. Crang and M. Goodwin (eds) *Introducing Human Geographies*, London: Arnold.

Lee, R. (2000a) 'Informal sector', in R.J. Johnston, D. Gregory, G. Pratt and M. Watts (eds) *The Dictionary of Human Geography*, Oxford: Blackwell.

Lee, R. (2000b) 'Shelter from the storm? Geographies of regard in the worlds of horticultural consumption and production', *Geoforum* 31: 137–57.

Lemieux, T., Fortin, B., and Frechette, P. (1994) 'The effect of taxes on labor supply in the underground economy', *American Economic Review* 84(1): 231–54.

Leonard, M. (1994) *Informal Economic Activity in Belfast*, Aldershot: Avebury.

Leonard, M. (1998a) 'The long-term unemployed, informal economic activity and the underclass in Belfast: rejecting or reinstating the work ethic', *International Journal of Urban and Regional Research* 22(1): 42–59.

Leonard, M. (1998b) *Invisible Work, Invisible Workers: The Informal Economy in Europe and the US*, London: Macmillan.

Levitas, R. (1998) *The Inclusive Society? Social Exclusion and New Labour*, London: Macmillan.

Leyshon, A., Lee, R., and Williams, C.C. (eds) (2003) *Alternative Economic Spaces*, London: Sage.

Liebman, J. (1998) *Lessons about Tax-Benefit Integration from the US Earned Income Tax Credit Experience*, York: York Publishing Services.

Lipietz, A. (1992) *Towards a New Economic Order: Post-fordism, Ecology and Democracy*, Cambridge: Polity Press.

Lipietz, A. (1995) *Green Hopes: The Future of Political Ecology*, Cambridge: Polity Press.

Lister, R. (2000) 'Strategies for social inclusion: promoting social cohesion or social justice?', in P. Askonas and A. Stewart (eds) *Social Inclusion: Possibilities and Tensions*, London: Macmillan.

Lodemel, I., and Trickey, H. (2001) *An Offer You Can't Refuse: Workfare in International Perspective*, Bristol: Policy Press.

Lubell, H. (1991) *The Informal Sector in the 1980s and 1990s*, Paris: Organization for Economic Co-operation and Development.

Lutz, M. (1999) *Economics for the Common Good: Two Centuries of Social Economic Thought in the Humanistic Tradition*, London: Routledge.

Luxton, M. (1997) 'The UN, women and household labour: measuring and valuing unpaid work', *Women's Studies International Forum* 20: 431–9.

Lynn, P., and Davis Smith, J. (1992) *The 1991 National Survey of Voluntary Activity in the UK*, Berkhamsted: Volunteer Centre UK.

McBurney, S. (1990) *Ecology into Economics Won't Go: Or Life is Not a Concept*, Dartington: Green Books.

McCormick, J. (1994) *Citizens' Service*, London: Institute for Public Policy Research.

MacDonald, R. (1994) 'Fiddly jobs, undeclared working and the something for nothing society', *Work, Employment and Society* 8(4): 507–30.

McDowell, L. (1991) 'Life without father and Ford: the new gender order of post-Fordism', *Transactions of the Institute of British Geographers* 16: 400–19.

McDowell, L. (2001) 'Father and Ford revisited: gender, class and employment change in the new millennium', *Transactions of the Institute of British Geographers*, NS 26(4): 448–64.

MacGillivray, A., Conaty, P., and Wadhams, C. (2001) *Low Flying Heroes: Micro-social Enterprise below the Radar Screen*, London: New Economics Foundation.

McInnis-Dittrich, K. (1995) 'Women of the shadows: Appalachian women's participation in the informal economy', *Affilia: Journal of Women and Social Work* 10(4): 398–412.

McKay, A., and Vanavery, J. (2000) 'Gender, family and income maintenance: a feminist case for citizen's basic income', *Social Politics* 7(2): 266–84.

Macfarlane, R. (1996) *Unshackling the Poor: A Complementary Approach to Local Economic Development*, York: Joseph Rowntree Foundation.

Maffesoli, M. (1996) *The Time of the Tribes: The Decline of Individualism in Mass Society*, London: Sage.

Maldonado, C. (1995) 'The informal sector: legalization or laissez-faire?', *International Labour Review* 134(6): 705–28.

Mander, J., and Goldsmith, E. (eds) (1996) *The Case against the Global Economy, and for a Turn toward the Local*, San Francisco: Sierra Club.

Marcelli, E.A., Pastor, M., and Joassart, P.M. (1999) 'Estimating the effects of informal economic activity: evidence from Los Angeles County', *Journal of Economic Issues* 33: 579–607.

Martin, C.J. (1996) 'Economic strategies and moral principles in the survival of poor households in Mexico', *Bulletin of Latin American Research* 15(2): 193–210.

Martin, R., and Sunley, P. (2001) 'Rethinking the "economic" in economic geography: broadening our vision or losing our focus?', *Antipode* 33: 148–61.

Matthews, K. (1983) 'National income and the black economy', *Journal of Economic Affairs* 3(4): 261–7.

Mauss, M. (1966) *The Gift*, London: Cohen & West.

Mauthner, N., McKee, L., and Strell, M. (2001) *Work and Family Life in Rural Communities*, York: York Publishing Services.

Mayo, E. (1996) 'Dreaming of work', in P. Meadows (ed.) *Work Out or Work In? Contributions to the Debate on the Future of Work*, York: Joseph Rowntree Foundation.

Meadows, P. (1997) *The Integration of Taxes and Benefits for Working Families with Children: Issues Raised to Date*, York: York Publishing Services.

Meagher, K. (1995) 'Crises, informalization and the urban informal sector in sub-Saharan Africa', *Development and Change* 26(2): 259–84.

Millar, J., and Hole, D. (1998) *Integrated Family Benefits in Australia and Options for the UK Tax Return System*, York: York Publishing Services.

Miller, D. (ed.) (2001) *Home Possessions: Material Culture behind Closed Doors*, Oxford: Berg.

Mingione, E. (1991) *Fragmented Societies: A Sociology of Economic Life beyond the Market Paradigm*, Oxford: Basil Blackwell.

Mingione, E. (1994) 'Life strategies and social economies in the postfordist age', *International Journal of Urban and Regional Research* 181: 24–45.

Moller, I., and van Berkel, R. (eds) (2002) *Active Social Policies in the EU: Inclusion through Participation*, Bristol: Policy Press.

Morehouse, W. (ed.) (1997) *Building Sustainable Communities: Tools and Concepts for Self-reliant Economic Change*, Charlbury: Jon Carpenter.

Morel, C. (2003) 'Corporate support of the arts in France', Ph.D. thesis, Department of French Studies, University of Sheffield.

Morris, L. (1987) 'Constraints on gender: the family wage, social security and the labour market; reflections on research in Hartlepool', *Work, Employment and Society* 1(1): 85–106.

Morris, L. (1994) 'Informal aspects of social divisions', *International Journal of Urban and Regional Research* 18: 112–26.

Morris, L. (1995) *Social Divisions: Economic Decline and Social Structural Change*, London: UCL Press.

Murgatroyd, L., and Neuburger, H. (1997) 'A household satellite account for the UK', *Economic Trends* 527: 63–71.

Naess, A. (1986) 'The deep ecology movement: some philosophical aspects', *Philosophical Inquiry* III(1/2): 10–31.

Naess, A. (1989) *Ecology, Community and Lifestyle: Outline of an Ecosophy*, Cambridge: Cambridge University Press.

Narotsky, S. (1998) *New Directions in Economic Anthropology*, London: Pluto.

Neef, R. (2002) 'Observations of the concept and forms of the informal economy in eastern Europe', in R. Neef and M. Stanculescu (eds) *The Social Impact of Informal Economies in Eastern Europe*, Aldershot: Ashgate.

Nelson, M.K., and Smith, J. (1999) *Working Hard and Making Do: Surviving in Small Town America*, Los Angeles: University of California Press.

Nicaise, I. (1996) *Which Partnerships for Employment? Social Partners, NGOs and Public Authorities*, Brussels: European Social Policy Forum Working paper II, DG V, European Commission.

Norberg-Hodge, H. (2001) 'Local lifeline: rejecting globalization – embracing localization', in V. Bennholdt-Thomsen, N. Faraclas and C. von Werlhof (eds) *There is an Alternative: Subsistence and Worldwide Resistance to Corporate Globalization*, London: Zed Books.

North, P. (1996) 'LETS: a tool for empowerment in the inner city?', *Local Economy*, 11(3): 284–93.

North, P. (1999) 'Explorations in heterotopia: local exchange trading schemes (LETS) and the micropolitics of money and livelihood', *Environment and Planning D* 17: 69–86.

O'Connor, J. (1973) *The Fiscal Crisis of the State*, London: St Martin's Press.

O'Neill, J. (2003) 'Socialism, associations and the market', *Economy and Society* 32(2): 184–206.

O'Neill, P., and Gibson-Graham, J.K. (1999) 'Enterprise discourse and executive talk: stories that destabilize the company', *Transactions of the Institute of British Geographers* 24: 11–22.

O'Neill, P.M. (1997) 'Bringing the qualitative state into economic geography', in R. Lee and J. Wills (eds) *Geographies of Economies*, London: Edward Arnold.

Oakley, A. (1974) *The Sociology of Housework*, Oxford: Blackwell

Oberhauser, A.M. (1995) 'Towards a gendered regional geography: women and work in rural Appalachia', *Growth and Change* 26: 217–44.

OECD (1994) *Jobs Study: Part 2*, Paris: OECD.

OECD (ed.) (1996) *Reconciling Economy and Society: Towards a Plural Economy*, Paris: OECD.

OECD (1997) *Framework for the Measurement of Unrecorded Economic Activities in Transition Economies*, Paris: OECD.

OECD (2000) *Tax Avoidance and Evasion*, Paris: OECD.

OECD (2002) *Measuring the Non-Observed Economy*, Paris: OECD.

Offe, C. (1995) 'Freiwillig auf die Anteilnahme am Arbeitmarkt verzichten', *Frankfurter Rundschau*, 19 July

Offe, C., and Heinze, R.G. (1992) *Beyond Employment: Time, Work and the Informal Economy*, Cambridge: Polity Press.

Offer, A. (1997) 'Between the gift and the market: the economy of regard', *Economic History Review* 50(2): 450–76.

ODPM (Office of the Deputy Prime Minister) (2003) *Employment and Enterprise Project*, London: Office of the Deputy Prime Minister.

ONS (2003) *2000 UK Time Use Survey*, London: Office of National Statistics.

Orru, M., Biggart, N.W., and Hamilton, G.G. (1997) *The Economic Organisation of East Asian Capitalism*, Thousand Oaks, CA: Sage

Oxley, H. (1999) 'Income dynamics: inter-generational evidence', in Centre for Analysis of Social Exclusion (ed.) *Persistent Poverty and Lifetime Inequality: The Evidence*, London: CASE Report 5, London School of Economics.

Pacione, M. (1997) 'Local Exchange Trading Systems as a response to the globalization of capitalism', *Urban Studies* 34: 1179–99.

Pahl, R.E. (1984) *Divisions of Labour*, Oxford: Blackwell.

Pahl, R.E. (1995) 'Finding time to live', *Demos* 5: 12–3.

Painter, J. (2003) 'State and governance', in E. Sheppard and T.J. Barnes (eds) *A Companion to Economic Geography*, Oxford: Blackwell.

Paredes Cruzatt, P. (1987) *Condiciones de trabajo de los trabajadores del sector informal urbano de Lima Metropolitana*, Lima: Planificación del Mercado Labral, Projecto Per/85/007, Cuaderno del Informaciones 4.

Parker, H., and Sutherland, H. (1998) 'How to get rid of the poverty trap: basic income plus national wage', *Citizens Income Bulletin* 25: 11–4

Paugam, S., and Russell, P. (2000) 'The effects of employment precarity and unemployment on social isolation', in D. Gallie and S. Paugam (eds) *Welfare Regimes and the Experience of Unemployment in Europe*, Oxford: Oxford University Press.

Pavis, S., Platt, S., and Hubbard, S. (2000) *Young People in Rural Scotland: Pathways to Social Inclusion and Exclusion*, York: York Publishing Services.

Peattie, L.R. (1980) 'Anthropological perspectives on the concepts of dualism, the informal sector and marginality in developing urban economies', *International Regional Science Review* 5(1): 1–31.

Peck, J. (1996) *Work-Place: The Social Regulation of Labour Markets*, New York: Guilford Press.

Peck, J. (1999) 'New Labourers? Making a New Deal for the "Workless Class"', *Environment and Planning C* 17: 345–72.

Peck, J. (2001) *Workfare States*, New York: Guilford Press.

Perri 6 (1997) *Escaping Poverty: From Safety Nets to Networks of Opportunity*, London: Demos.

Piirainen, T. (1997) *Towards a New Social Order in Russia: Transforming Structures and Everyday Life*, Aldershot: Dartmouth.

Piliavin, J.A. (1990) 'Why do they give the gift of life? A review of research in blood donors since 1977', *Transfusion* 30: 444–59.

Polanyi, K. (1944) *The Great Transformation*, Boston, MA: Beacon Press.

Portes, A. (1994) 'The informal economy and its paradoxes', in N.J. Smelser and R. Swedberg (eds) *The Handbook of Economic Sociology*, Princeton: Princeton University Press.

Portes, A. (1998) 'Social capital: its origins and applications in modern sociology', *Annual Review of Sociology* 24(1): 1–24.

Portes, A., Blitzer, S., and Curtis, J. (1986) 'The urban informal sector in Uruguay: its internal structure, characteristics and effects', *World Development* 14(6): 727–41.

Powell, J. (2002) 'Petty capitalism, perfecting capitalism or post-capitalism? Lessons from the Argentinean barter network', *Review of International Political Economy* 9(4): 224–36.

Powell, W. (1990) 'Neither market nor hierarchy: network forms of organization', in G. Thompson, J. Frances, R. Lavacic and J. Mitchell (eds) *Markets, Hierarchies and Networks*, London: Sage.

Prime, D., Zimmeck, M., and Zurawan, A. (2002) *Active Communities: Initial Findings from the 2001 Home Office Citizenship Survey*, London: Home Office.

Putnam, R. (1993) *Making Democracy Work: Civic Traditions in Modern Italy*, Princeton University Press.

Putnam, R. (1995a) 'Tuning in, Tuning out: the strange disappearance of social capital in America', *Political Science and Politics* 28: 664–83.

Putnam, R. (1995b) 'Bowling alone: America's declining social capital', *Journal of Democracy* 6(1): 65–78.

Putnam, R. (2000) *Bowling Alone: The Collapse and Revival of American Community*, London: Simon & Schuster.

Putterman, L. (1990) *Division of Labor and Welfare: An Introduction to Economic Systems*, Oxford: Oxford University Press.

Quijano, A. (2001) 'The growing significance of reciprocity from below: marginality and informality under debate', in F. Tabak and M.A. Crichlow (eds) *Informalization: Process and Structure*, Baltimore: Johns Hopkins University Press.

Rakowski, C.A. (1994) 'Convergence and divergence in the informal sector debate: a focus on Latin America, 1984–92', *World Development* 22(4): 501–16.

Reid, M. (1934) *Economics of Household Production*, New York: John Wiley.

Renooy, P. (1990) *The Informal Economy: Meaning, Measurement and Social Significance*, Amsterdam: Netherlands Geographical Studies Association.

Richardson, H.W. (1984) 'The role of the informal sector in developing countries: an overview', *Regional Development Dialogue* 5(2): 3–55.

Rifkin, J. (1990) *The Myth of the Market: Promises and Illusions*, Dartington: Green Books.

Rifkin, J. (1996) *The End of Work: The Decline of the Global Labor Force and the Dawn of a Post-market Era*, New York: G.P. Putnam's Sons.

Rifkin, J. (2000) *The Age of Access*, Harmondsworth: Penguin.

Roberts, B. (1989) 'Employment structure, life cycle and life chances: formal and informal sectors in Guadalajara', in A. Portes, M. Castells and L. Benton (eds) *The Informal Economy: Comparative Studies in Advanced and Third World Countries*, Baltimore: Johns Hopkins University Press.

Roberts, B. (1990) 'The informal sector in comparative perspective', in M. Estellie Smith (ed.) *Perspectives on the Informal Economy*, New York: University Press of America.

Roberts, B. (1991) 'Household coping strategies and urban poverty in a comparative perspective', in M. Gottdiener and C.G. Pickvance (eds) *Urban Life in Transition*, London: Sage.

Robertson, J. (1985) *Future Work: Jobs, Self-employment and Leisure after the Industrial Age*, Aldershot: Gower/Temple Smith.

Robertson, J. (1991) *Future Wealth: A New Economics for the 21st Century*, London: Cassell.

Robinson, J., and Godbey, G. (1997) *Time for Life: The Surprising Ways Americans Use Their Time*, Pennsylvania: Pennsylvania State University Press.

Robinson, P. (1998) 'Employment and social inclusion', in C. Oppenheim (ed.) *An Inclusive Society: Strategies for Tackling Poverty*, London: Institute for Public Policy Research.

Rodriguez-Pose, A. (2001) 'Killing economic geography with a "cultural turn" overdose', *Antipode* 33: 176–83.

Rosanvallon, P. (1980) 'Le développement de l'économie souterraine et l'avenir des sociétés industrielles', *Le Debat* 2: 8–23.

Rose, R., and Haerpfer, C.W. (1992) *Between State and Market*, Strathclyde: Centre for the Study of Public Policy, University of Strathclyde.

Roseland, M. (ed.) (1998) *Towards Sustainable Communities: Resources for Citizens and Their Governments*, Stony Creek, CT: New Society Publishers.

Rostow, W.J. (1960) *The Stages of Economic Growth: A Non-communist Manifesto*, Cambridge: Cambridge University Press.

Rowlingson, K., Whyley, C., Newburn, T., and Berthoud, R. (1997) *Social Security Fraud*, DSS Research Report no. 64, London: HMSO.

Roy, C. (1991) 'Les emplois du temps dans quelques pays occidentaux', *Donnés Sociales* 2: 223–5.

Rugg, J., and Jones, A. (1999) *Getting a Job, Finding a Home: Rural Youth Transitions*, Bristol: Policy Press.

Ruston, D. (2003) *Volunteers, Helpers and Socialisers: Social Capital and Time Use*, London: Office of National Statistics.

Sachs, I. (1984) *Development and Planning*, Cambridge: Cambridge University Press.

Salamon, L.M., and Anheier, H.K. (1998) 'Social origins of civil society: explaining the non-profit sector cross-nationally', *Voluntas* 9(3): 213–48.

Salamon, L.M., and Anheier, H.K. (1999) *The Emerging Sector Revisited: A Summary, Revised Estimates*, Baltimore, MD: Center for Civil Society Studies.

Salamon, L.M., Anheier, H.K., List, R., Toepler, S., and Wojcieck Sokolowoski, S. (1999) *Global Civil Society: Dimensions of the Nonprofit Sector*, Baltimore: Center for Civil Society Studies.

Sanyal, B. (1991) 'Organising the self-employed: the politics of the urban informal sector', *International Labour Review* 130(1): 39–56.

Sassen, S. (1989) 'New York city's informal economy', in A. Portes, M. Castells and L.A. Benton (eds) *The Informal Economy: Studies in Advanced and Less Developing Countries*, Baltimore: Johns Hopkins University Press.

Sassen, S. (1991) *The Global City: New York, London, Tokyo*, Princeton: Princeton University Press.

Sassen, S. (1997) *Informalisation in Advanced Market Economies*, Issues in Development Discussion Paper 20, Geneva: ILO.

Sauvy, A. (1984) *Le travail noir et l'économie de demain*, Paris: Calmann-Lévy.

Sayer, A. (1997) 'The dialectic of culture and economy', in R. Lee and J. Wills (eds) *Geographies of Economies*, London: Arnold.

Schoenberger, E. (1998) 'Discourse and practice in human geography', *Progress in Human Geography* 22: 1–14.

Schor, J. (1991) *The Overworked American: The Unexpected Decline of Leisure*, New York: Basic Books.

Scott, A.J. (2001) 'Capitalism, cities and the production of symbolic forms', *Transactions of the Institute of British Geographers*, NS 26: 11–23.

Sen, A. (1998), *Inequality Re-examined*, Oxford: Clarendon Press.

SEU (Social Exclusion Unit) (1998) *Bringing Britain Together: A National Strategy for Neighbourhood Renewal*, Cm4045, London: HMSO.

SEU (Social Exclusion Unit) (2000) *National Strategy for Neighbourhood Renewal: A Framework for Consultation*, London: HMSO.

Seyfang, G. (1998) 'Green money from the grassroots: local exchange trading schemes and sustainable development', Ph.D. thesis, Leeds Metropolitan University, Leeds.

Seyfang, G., and Smith, K. (2002) *The Time of Our Lives: Using Time Banking for Neighbourhood Renewal and Community Capacity Building*, London: New Economics Foundation.

Sharpe, B. (1988) 'Informal work and development in the west', *Progress in Human Geography* 12(3): 315–36.

Shaw, A., and Pandit, K. (2001) 'The geography of segmentation of informal labor markets: the case of motor vehicle repair in Calcutta', *Economic Geography* 77(2): 180–96.

Shiva, V. (2001) 'Globalization and poverty', in V. Bennholdt-Thomsen, N. Faraclas and C. von Werlhof (eds) *There is an Alternative: Subsistence and Worldwide Resistance to Corporate Globalization*, London: Zed Books.

Shucksmith, M. (2000) *Exclusive Countryside? Social Inclusion and Regeneration in Rural Areas*, York: Joseph Rowntree Foundation.

Shucksmith, M., Chapman, P., Clark, G., with Black, S., and Conway, E. (1996) *Rural Scotland Today: The Best of Both Worlds*, Aldershot: Avebury.

Sik, E. (1993) 'From the second economy to the informal economy', *Journal of Public Policy* 12(2): 153–75.

Sik, E. (1994) 'From the multicoloured to the black and white economy: the Hungarian second economy and the transformation', *Urban Studies* 31(1): 47–70.

Silburn, R., Lucas, D., Page, R., and Hanna, L. (1999) *Neighbourhood Images in Nottingham: Social Cohesion and Neighbourhood Change*, York: York Publishing Services.

Simon, P.B. (1997) *Crises of Urban Employment: An Investigation into the Structure and Relevance of Small-scale Informal Retailing in Kaduna, Nigeria*, mimeo.

Skolimowski, H. (1981) *Eco-Philosophy: Designing New Tactics for Living*, London: Marion Boyars.

Slater, D., and Tonkiss, F. (2001) *Market Society: Markets and Modern Social Theory*, Cambridge: Polity Press.

Smith, A. (2002) 'Culture/economy and spaces of economic practice: positioning households in post-communism', *Transactions of the Institute of British Geographers* 27(2): 232–50.

Smith, D.M. (2000) 'Marxian economics', in R.J. Johnston, D. Gregory, G. Pratt and M. Watts (eds) *The Dictionary of Human Geography*, Oxford: Blackwell.

Smith, S. (1986) *Britain's Shadow Economy*, Oxford: Clarendon Press.

Smuts, R. (1971) *Women and Work in America*, New York: Schocken.

Soiffer, S.S., and Herrmann, G.M. (1987) 'Visions of power: ideology and practice in the American garage sale', *Sociological Review* 35(1): 48–83.

Steblay, N.M. (1987) 'Helping behavior in rural and urban environments: a meta-analysis', *Psychological Bulletin* 102: 346–56.

Storey, P., and Brannen, J. (2000) *Young People and Transport in Rural Areas*, Leicester: Youth Work Press.

Stratford, N., and Christie, I. (2000) 'Town and country life', in R. Jowell, J. Curtice, A. Park, K. Thomsen, L. Jarvis, C. Bromley and N. Stratford (eds) *British Social Attitudes, The 17th Report: Focusing on Diversity*, London: Sage.

Sue, R. (1995) *Temps et ordre social*, Paris: PUF.

Sundbo, J. (1997) 'The creation of service markets: the Danish Home Service', *The Service Industries Journal* 17(4): 580–602.

Tabak, F. (2000) 'Introduction: informalization and the long term', in F. Tabak and M.A. Crichlow (eds) *Informalization: Process and Structure*, Baltimore: Johns Hopkins University Press.

Thomas, J.J. (1992) *Informal Economic Activity*, Hemel Hempstead: Harvester Wheatsheaf.

Thomas, K., and Smith, K. (1995) 'Results of the 1993 Census of Employment', *Employment Gazette* 103: 369–84.

Thompson, G., Frances, J., Lavacic, R., and Mitchell, J. (eds) (1991) *Markets, Hierarchies and Networks*, London: Sage.

Thrift, N.J. (2000) 'Commodities', in R.J. Johnston, D. Gregory, G. Pratt and M. Watts (eds) *The Dictionary of Human Geography*, Oxford: Blackwell.

Thrift, N.J., and Olds, K. (1996) 'Refiguring the economic in economic geography', *Progress in Human Geography* 20(2): 311–37.

Tickell, A. (2001) 'Progress in the geography of services II: services, the state and the rearticulation of capitalism', *Progress in Human Geography* 25(2): 283–92.

Tokman, V.E. (1978) 'An exploration into the nature of informal–formal sector relationships: the case of Santiago', *World Development* 6 (September–October): 1065–75.

Townsend, A.R. (1997) *Making a Living in Europe: Human Geographies of Economic Change*, London: Routledge.

Trainer, T. (1996) *Towards a Sustainable Economy: The Need for Fundamental Change*, Oxford: Jon Carpenter.

United Nations (1995) *The Copenhagen Declaration and Programme of Action: World Summit for social development 6–12 March 1995*. Geneva: United Nations Department of Publications.

Urry, J. (2000) *Sociology beyond Societies: Mobilities for the Twenty-first Century*, London: Routledge.

Van Eck, R., and Kazemeier, B. (1985) *Swarte Inkomsten uit Arbeid: resultaten van in 1983 gehouden experimentele*, The Hague: CBS-Statistische Katernen nr 3, Central Bureau of Statistics.

Van Geuns, R., Mevissen, J., and Renooy, P.H. (1987) 'The spatial and sectoral diversity of the informal economy', *Tijdschrift voor Economische en Sociale Geografie* 78(5): 389–98.

Van Parijs, P. (1995) *Real Freedom for All: What (If Anything) is Wrong with Capitalism?*, Oxford: Oxford University Press.

Van Parijs, P. (1996a) 'Basic income and the two dilemmas of the welfare state', *Political Quarterly* 67(1): 57–8.

Van Parijs, P. (1996b) 'L'allocation universelle contre le chomage: de la trappe au sociale', *Revue Française des Affaires Sociales* 50(1): 111–25.

Van Parijs, P. (2000a) *Basic Income: Guaranteed Income for the XXIst Century?*, Barcelona: Fundació Rafael Campalans.

Van Parijs, P. (2000b) 'Basic income and the two dilemmas of the welfare state', in C. Pierson and F.G. Castles (eds) *The Welfare State: A Reader*, Cambridge: Polity Press.

Van Trier, W. (1995) 'Every one a king', Ph.D. thesis, Department of Sociology, University of Leuven.

Verschave, F.-X. (1996) 'The House that Braudel built: rethinking the architecture of society', in OECD (ed.) *Reconciling Economy and Society: Towards a Plural Economy*, Paris: OECD.

Wallace, C. (2002) 'Household strategies: their conceptual relevance and analytical scope in social research', *Sociology* 36: 275–92.

Wallace, C., and Haerpfer, C. (2002) 'Patterns of participation in the informal economy in East-Central Europe', in R. Neef and M. Stanculescu (eds) *The Social Impact of Informal Economies in Eastern Europe*, Aldershot: Ashgate.

Walzer, M. (1983) *Spheres of Justice*, New York: Basic Books.

Warburton, D. (1998) *Community and Sustainable Development: Participation in the Future*, London: Earthscan.

Watts, M. (1999) 'Commodities', in P. Cloke, P. Crang and M. Goodwin (eds) *Introducing Human Geographies*, London: Arnold.

Westerdahl, S., and Westlund, H. (1998) 'Third sector and new jobs: a summary of twenty case studies in European regions', *Annals of Public and Co-operative Economics* 69: 193–218.

Whitley, R. (ed.) (2002) *Competing Capitalisms: Institutions and Economies*, Aldershot: Edward Elgar.

Williams, C.C. (1996a) 'An appraisal of Local Exchange and Trading Systems (LETS) in the United Kingdom', *Local Economy* 11(3): 275–82.

Williams, C.C. (1996b) 'Informal sector responses to unemployment: an evaluation of the potential of Local Exchange and Trading Systems (LETS)', *Work, Employment and Society* 10(2): 341–59.

Williams, C.C. (1996c) 'Local currencies and community development: an evaluation of green dollar exchanges in New Zealand', *Community Development Journal* 31(4): 319–29.

Williams, C.C. (1996d) 'Local Exchange and Trading Systems (LETS): a new source of work and credit for the poor and unemployed?', *Environment and Planning A* 28(8): 1395–415.

Williams, C.C. (1996e) 'Local purchasing and rural development: an evaluation of Local Exchange and Trading Systems (LETS)', *Journal of Rural Studies* 12(3): 231–44.

Williams, C.C. (1996f) 'The new barter economy: an appraisal of Local Exchange and Trading Systems (LETS)', *Journal of Public Policy* 16(1): 55–71.

Williams, C.C. (1997) *Consumer Services and Economic Development*, London: Routledge.

Williams, C.C. (2002a) 'A critical evaluation of the commodification thesis', *Sociological Review* 50(4): 525–42.

Williams, C.C. (2002b) 'Beyond the commodity economy: the persistence of informal economic activity in rural England', *Geografiska Annaler B* 83(4): 221–33.

Williams, C.C. (2003) 'Evaluating the penetration of the commodity economy', *Futures* 35: 857–68.

Williams, C.C., and Paddock, C. (2003) 'Reconciling economic and cultural explanations for participation in alternative consumption spaces', *Geografiska Annaler B* 84(3): 137–48.

Williams, C.C., and Windebank, J. (1998) *Informal Employment in the Advanced Economies: Implications for Work and Welfare*, London: Routledge.

Williams, C.C., and Windebank, J. (2000a) 'Self-help and mutual aid in deprived urban neighbourhoods: some lessons from Southampton', *Urban Studies* 37: 127–147.

Williams, C.C., and Windebank, J. (2000b) 'Paid informal work in deprived neighborhoods', *Cities* 17(4): 285–91.

Williams, C.C., and Windebank, J. (2000c) 'Helping each other out? Community exchange in deprived neighbourhoods', *Community Development Journal* 35(2): 146–56.

Williams, C.C., and Windebank, J. (2000d) 'Helping people to help themselves: some policy lessons from deprived urban neighbourhoods in Southampton', *Journal of Social Policy* 29(3): 355–73.

Williams, C.C., and Windebank, J. (2001a) *Revitalising Deprived Urban Neighbourhoods: An Assisted Self-help Approach*, Aldershot: Ashgate.

Williams, C.C., and Windebank, J. (2001b) 'A critical evaluation of the formalization of work thesis: some evidence from France', *SAIS Review* 221(1): 117–22.

Williams, C.C., and Windebank, J. (2001c) 'Beyond profit-motivated exchange: some lessons from the study of paid informal work', *European Urban and Regional Studies* 8(1): 49–61.

Williams, C.C., and Windebank, J. (2001d) 'Beyond social inclusion through employment: harnessing mutual aid as a complementary social inclusion policy', *Policy and Politics* 29(1): 15–28.

Williams, C.C., and Windebank, J. (2001e) 'Paid informal work in deprived urban neighbourhoods: exploitative employment or co-operative self-help?', *Growth and Change* 32(4): 562–71.

Williams, C.C., and Windebank, J. (2001f) 'Paid informal work: a barrier to social inclusion?', *Transfer: Journal of the European Trade Union Institute* 7(1): 25–40.

Williams, C.C., and Windebank, J. (2001g) 'Reconceptualising paid informal exchange: some lessons from English cities', *Environment and Planning A* 33(1): 121–40.

Williams, C.C., and Windebank, J. (2001h) 'Acquiring goods and services in lower-income populations: an evaluation of consumer behaviour and preferences', *International Journal of Retail and Distribution Management* 29(1): 16–24.

Williams, C.C., and Windebank, J. (2003a) *Poverty and the Third Way*, London: Routledge.

Williams, C.C., and Windebank, J. (2003b) 'The slow advance and uneven penetration of commodification', *International Journal of Urban and Regional Research* 27(2): 250–64.

Williams, C.C., and Windebank, J. (2003c) 'Reconceptualizing women's paid informal work: some lessons from lower-income urban neighbourhoods', *Gender, Work and Organisation* 10(3): 281–300.

Williams, C.C., Aldridge, T., Lee, R., Leyshon, A., Thrift, N., and Tooke, J. (2001a) *Bridges into Work? An Evaluation of Local Exchange and Trading Schemes (LETS)*, Bristol: Policy Press.

Williams, C.C., Aldridge, T. Lee, R., Leyshon, A., Thrift, N., and Tooke, J. (2001b) 'Local Exchange and Trading Schemes (LETS): a tool for community renewal?', *Community, Work and Family* 4(3): 355–61.

Wilson, T.C. (1985) 'Settlement type and interpersonal estrangement: a test of the theories of Wirth and Gans', *Social Forces* 64: 139–50.

Windebank, J. (1991) *The Informal Economy in France*, Aldershot: Avebury.

Windebank, J. (1999) 'Political motherhood and the everyday experiences of mothering: a comparison of the child-care strategies of French and British working mothers', *Journal of Social Policy* 28(1): 1–25.

Wolff, A., (1989) *Whose Keeper?*, Berkeley: University of California Press.

Wolpert, J. (1993) *Patterns of Generosity in America: Who's Holding the Safety Net*, New York: Twentieth Century Fund Press.

Wood, M., and Vamplew, C. (1999) *Neighbourhood Images in Teeside: Regeneration or Decline?*, York: York Publishing Services.

Wright, C. (1997) *The Sufficient Community: Putting People First*, Dartington: Green Books.

Wuthnow, R. (1992) *Acts of Compassion: Caring for Others and Helping Ourselves*. Princeton, NJ: Princeton University Press.

Yankelovich, D. (1995) *Young Adult Europe*, Paris: Yankelovich Monitor.

Young, M., and P. Wilmott (1975) *The Symmetrical Family: A Study of Work and Leisure in the London Region*, Harmondsworth: Penguin.

Zafirovski, M. (1999) 'Probing into the social layers of entrepreneurship: outlines of the sociology of enterprise', *Entrepreneurship and Regional Development* 11: 351–71.

Zelizer, V.A. (1994) *The Social Meaning of Money*, New York: Basic Books.

Zoll, R. (1989) *Nicht So Wie Unsere Eltern*, Oplandan: Westdeutscher Verlag.

Index